KU-603-953

WELCOME,

MY TRIUMPH OVER SCHIZOPHRENIA

SILENCE

CAROL S. NORTH, M.D.

ARROW BOOKS

Arrow Books Limited
20 Vauxhall Bridge Road, London SW1V 2SA

An imprint of Random Century Group

London Melbourne Sydney Auckland
Johannesburg and agencies throughout
the world

First published in Great Britain by Simon & Schuster Limited 1988
Arrow edition 1990

© Carol S. North, 1987

This book is sold subject to the condition that it shall
not, by way of trade or otherwise, be lent, resold, hired
out, or otherwise circulated without the publisher's prior
consent in any form of binding or cover other than that
in which it is published and without a similar condition
including this condition being imposed on the
subsequent purchaser

Printed and bound in Great Britain by
Courier International Ltd, Tiptree, Essex

ISBN 0 09 965370 2

To Remi,

who made it all possible

CONTENTS

ACKNOWLEDGMENTS 9

PREFACE 11

1. YOU JUST CAN'T UNDERSTAND 13

2. A PERFECTLY NORMAL CHILD 27

3. "BABY" NO MORE 47

4. COLLEGE 74

5. "PSYCHO" 88

6. COLLEGE: NEW GOALS 130

7. MED SCHOOL 166

8. DR. HEMINGWAY 194

9. FINALS 211

10. SUMMER EXTERNSHIP 230

11. SOPHOMORE MEDICAL YEAR 246

12. HOSPITALIZED AGAIN 265

13. THE CHANGE 287

14. THE SILENCE IS DEAFENING 307

AFTERWORD 313

ACKNOWLEDGMENTS

This book is additionally dedicated to my family, especially my parents, who provided unfaltering love, patience, and support, even when things seemed bleak. They never lost hope, not even in the face of hopelessness expressed by myself and others. I can never thank them enough.

I also wish to thank Dr. Remi Cadoret, who provided support far beyond the call of duty, and who also made medical information accessible to me. I am deeply indebted to those who helped keep me alive until I was cured, including Dr. Gary Robins, Dr. Carl Davis, Dr. Peter Whitis, and Dr. Jerome Beckman. I wish to extend a special thanks to all my professors who were especially helpful to me during my college and medical years, including Dr. Kenneth Sando, Dr. Rubin Widmer, and Dr. Lucas Van Orden. I am very grateful to those who took the risk to believe in me and provide assistance in picking up the pieces afterward: Dr. Samuel Guze, Dr. John Herweg, Dr. John Schultz, Dr. Mary Parker, Dr. Robert Cloninger, Dr. Reed Simpson, and Ms. Donna

9

Chandler. Additional thanks to Mr. William Meardon for his expert legal advice.

I also wish to thank those who assisted me in preparing this book for publication: Dr. William Murray, Dr. William Clements, Mr. Barry Morrow, Dr. Gene Krupa, Dr. Sharon Farber, Ms. Judith Terrill-Breuer, Mr. Jack Bodnar, Ms. Karen Rile-Smith, who offered her very helpful writing talents, and especially to my two special editors at Simon and Schuster: Mr. Robert Eckhardt, who believed in me enough to take a risk, and Mr. Bob Bender, a truly delightful and dedicated editor who helped educate me and provide much-appreciated inspiration.

Finally, I wish to dedicate this book to my patients. I want them to know that there is reason for hope. I commend schizophrenics and psychiatric patients everywhere for bearing up under their suffering and for giving this book meaning and purpose. God bless them.

PREFACE

The book you are about to read is my personal story. Through it, you may better understand the experience of mental illness, at least through the mind of one person diagnosed as schizophrenic.

The events described in this book took place a few years ago, and the material has been recalled partly from a diary kept during the time of the original events. Other memories have been aided by the kind assistance of others who have helpfully added their own recollections and perspectives of the events as they recalled them. With the help of my physicians I have obtained my medical records, without which I could not have written this book. In places, dialogue has been recreated to represent as closely as possible the substance of what people actually said, although their exact words have been lost in the fog of time. Additionally, most names (other than my immediate family) and locations have been disguised to protect individual privacy.

Although this book includes considerable medical information, it is not intended as a psychiatric text nor as a book of advice for schizophrenics and their families. Psychiatric patients who are interested in any therapy or procedure they may learn about in this book are advised to consult with their doctors and to discuss their treatment with them.

R.T.C. LIBRARY, LETTE...

CHAPTER ONE

YOU JUST
CAN'T UNDERSTAND

I reached for the doorknob. It wouldn't turn. Waves of a strangely familiar nausea swelled in my stomach, squeezing up into my throat. So we've been assigned to the locked ward, I realized. Where they hold the sickest, craziest patients.

Keeping these thoughts to myself, I fumbled in my pocket for my newly issued ward key. I didn't want to alarm Linda, the other medical student.

She already seemed apprehensive enough. "Wait—did you hear that?" she whispered, tugging at my white coat sleeve.

"No," I said. "Hear what?"

"It echoes in here," Linda said. "No wonder the patients think they hear voices." She was right. Her words bounced around between the crumbling walls, collided with one another, and jumbled together.

I wasn't nervous. "The Municipal Psychiatric Institute is an old, old hospital, Linda. Haven't you ever been inside a mental institution before?"

She shook her head. The bare institutional ceiling lights

had drained her face of color. "I wish this wasn't a required rotation for third-year medical students," she said.

I struggled to straighten my nametag:

CAROL S. NORTH
MEDICAL STUDENT

"Come on, Linda," I said, turning my key in the lock. "You're in for an experience." The heavy metal door swung open. I stepped through, with Linda following closely behind. The door slammed decisively after us.

Before I had a chance to step away, a dumpy, middle-aged man shoved his unshaven face right up under my nose. Slurring his words and fighting against eyes that wanted to close, he mumbled, "Will ya gimme a cigarette, gimme a cigarette, gimme a cigarette . . ."

Recoiling from the gust of his foul breath in my face, I backed into Linda, accidentally bouncing my black bag off her knee.

The man ran his nicotine-stained fingers through the greasy strands of blond hair that clumped around his head. A dirty hospital gown hung backward over his shoulders, like a Superman cape. Beltless, his food-stained trousers had settled down around his potbelly. I tried not to stare, but his fly was open.

A heavyset woman in worn-out hospital slippers shuffled up to Linda. Tugging at Linda's white coat lapel, she said, "Doctor, are you a doctor? I wanna go home."

Linda stood helplessly as the patient continued tugging at her coat. "I don't want to go into psychiatry," Linda whispered in my ear. "I want to be an *ophthalmologist*. I don't want to have to deal with these crazy people."

A tall black orderly in hospital whites rounded the corner, and the patient shrank away. "Hi," the orderly greeted us. "You must be the new doctors."

"Medical students," I volunteered.

He smiled. "Yeah, well, it's all the same here—you're doctors to us. There's plenty of work to be done. Come on into the nursing station and meet your supervising psychiatrist, Dr. Hajara."

We dutifully followed the orderly down the hallway, parting the thick cloud of cigarette smoke suspended in the air. Almost every patient had a cigarette hanging out the side of his or her mouth, or burning long-forgotten between charred fingertips.

Inside the nursing station we found Dr. Hajara, who wore a conservative suit and tie and a turban. Seated next to a heavy plate-glass window that overlooked the ward lounge, he was writing on a stack of patient charts. Approximately thirty more charts stood upright on a nearby chart rack, patiently awaiting his attention. Across the room, the ward clerk was simultaneously balancing a telephone receiver on her shoulder, a cigarette in her mouth, and a pen in her hand, while she argued over the phone with a patient's family, explaining why they could not talk to him yet. Three nurses sat elbow to elbow at a counter, busily filling out pages and pages of forms and requisitions. Everywhere I looked, I saw more papers to be filled out. The whole scene was observed by an audience of patients who stood outside the big window, staring in at us with a bored, glazed look in their eyes.

When Dr. Hajara saw us, he smiled and said in a thick, barely understandable Indian accent, "Oh, good, medical students. You're just in time. We have two new admissions for you."

Admissions meant work. Linda turned her face toward me and wrinkled up her nose.

Dr. Hajara couldn't see Linda's face. "I know both these patients already," he said. "They are both chronic schizophrenics who have been here many times. Here are their charts—look these over and then do an admission history and physical." He handed us each a chart as thick as a phone book. "When you're done we can discuss the cases, okay?"

Linda stared wide-eyed at the chart in her hands. "Schizophrenic? Do you get many of those here?"

"Common as cockroaches," he said. "One percent of the population is afflicted—that makes over two million schizophrenics living in the United States. Each year a hundred thousand new cases are diagnosed."

"Can the disease be cured?" Linda wanted to know.

Dr. Hajara furrowed his eyebrows in thought. "No. Our drugs do not cure schizophrenia. To date it's an incurable disease with unknown causes."

Linda frowned. "I thought it was hereditary. Didn't they teach us that in our psychiatry lectures last year, Carol?"

I shrugged, not wanting to get involved in trying to explain schizophrenia to Linda. Even though there was quite a lot I could have told her—and Dr. Hajara. I let Dr. Hajara continue.

"Heredity is only one factor," he explained to Linda. "There are probably other predisposing factors. Research has a long way to go before it can provide us with answers. My guess is that schizophrenia is a clinical manifestation of a variety of biochemical or immunological errors."

"You mean, like diabetes or certain forms of arthritis?" Linda asked.

"Yes," he said, "but far more complicated. Until science can come up with a cure, we as psychiatrists can do very little for our schizophrenic patients. All we can do is help them learn to live with their disability and offer medications to keep their symptoms to a minimum."

Linda set her black bag and chart down on the desk and folded her arms across her chest. "But—can't you talk to them or something?"

Dr. Hajara smiled. "Of course we talk to them. They need help coping with the problems their illness causes in their lives. But just talking with them doesn't cure their schizophrenia. It's a chronic disease, and these people spend an appreciable portion of their lives locked away in institutions."

I wanted to say something without indicating how much I really knew. "Sad," I said, shaking my head. Unlike Dr. Hajara, I felt there was plenty that could be done to help schizophrenic patients in spite of the fact that their disease is largely incurable. The situation wasn't hopeless. From experience, I knew that schizophrenics could be helped to lead more productive and satisfying lives, with a little personal attention to their special needs.

"Yes," Dr. Hajara reflected, "it's sad. And expensive. Half of all psychiatric hospital beds in the country are occupied by schizophrenics."

"Is that true of Municipal?" I asked.

"Here at Municipal the percentage of schizophrenics is even higher. Because it's a state institution, psychiatric patients with no money or insurance end up here—and schizophrenics, often chronically debilitated and indigent, form a large part of this group."

I shuddered. Municipal Psychiatric Institute looked like a horrible place to be.

By this time the patient who had approached me in the hall was pounding on the window of the nursing station, demanding a smoke.

The psychiatrist turned and gestured. "Like Mr. Sanders here. You have to be very sick to get into Municipal. Our goal for most is to get them functioning well enough to live outside the hospital for as long as possible."

Linda sighed. "That's pretty pathetic."

"Yes," Dr. Hajara agreed, "and for the most part hopeless. Just remember that, when you find yourself yearning to produce that miracle cure for your schizophrenic patient."

The orderly appeared and dragged the protesting patient away from the window. The glass was left polka-dotted with greasy fingerprints and noseprints.

Dr. Hajara thought for a moment and added, "But it's not as pathetic as it was in the past, before Thorazine and the other antipsychotics. Back then, schizophrenics vegetated forever on back wards of large institutions. Now, with medications, they can get out and enjoy at least part of their lives on the outside."

Linda sat down at the desk and proceeded to page through her patient's chart. I seated myself beside her.

"In psychiatry," Dr. Hajara told us, "good diagnosis is the cornerstone of effective treatment."

I remembered having heard that in a lecture last year. "It doesn't seem too difficult," I said. "After all, there are only fourteen basic diagnoses in psychiatry."

"Simpler yet," Dr. Hajara said. "Here at Municipal, the patients fall mostly into three diagnostic categories—schizophrenia, substance abuse, and sociopathy. Many patients carry two or all three of these diagnoses. Here, you can use my diagnostic manual."

He pulled a small green paperback out of his coat pocket and put it down on the desk between Linda and me. "I'll let you get on with your work. Tell me when you're ready to discuss the patients."

I opened my patient's chart to the emergency-room report. Tyrone Corbett, a twenty-year-old black male paranoid schizophrenic, brought into the hospital by police the night before. He had apparently quit taking his Thorazine a month ago and since then had become increasingly suspicious. He had boarded himself up in his basement "to keep the devil out." When his mother telephoned, he had refused to answer because he thought she was an agent of the devil trying to destroy his mind through electronic signals from the telephone. The neighbors thought he had a gun, and he had been pulled out of his basement by a SWAT team.

I flipped through the old records, looking for further evidence to support a diagnosis of schizophrenia. Perhaps he would turn out to have some other, more treatable condition, such as depression. I wanted to avoid saddling this patient with an incorrect diagnosis of schizophrenia that he would carry with him for the rest of his life, along with the inevi-

R.T.C. LIBRARY

table stigma attached to that particular label. This I knew: *Once a schizophrenic, always a schizophrenic.* In our medical-school lectures on psychiatry we'd been taught that schizophrenia can't be cured. Aside from truly exceptional cases, I knew this to be true.

The chart revealed that Mr. Corbett met the chronicity requirement for making the diagnosis. He had been continuously ill for three years, unable to work, and barely able to care for himself even when at his best, on adequate doses of medication. I would have to talk to the patient to find out if he had other symptoms of schizophrenia, such as delusions, auditory hallucinations, thought disorder, and inappropriate or flattened emotion. Before initiating treatment I wanted to make sure he was free of depressive symptoms or any other disorder.

I was totally engrossed in the chart, unaware of anything around me, when a dark form burst into the edge of my vision. Linda gasped. I jerked my head up to see our friendly patient back at the window. Through the thick glass his muffled voice begged, "Cigarette, baby?"

"Whew! He startled me," Linda said.

I stood up and closed my patient's chart. Outside the half-door of the nursing station the patients were lining up for their medications. Others stared in at us through the big glass window. The whole scene made me vaguely uneasy.

Linda interrupted my thoughts. "Don't you think it's strange that the patients should have to stand in line to get medicine they don't even want? On the regular medical ward the nurses always bring the medicines to the bedside."

"Yeah," I said vacantly, trying to ignore an unpleasant sensation in my stomach. I was watching the patients shuffle from foot to foot, in their painful struggle to keep still in line. This restlessness, known medically as akathisia, is a paradoxical side effect of the tranquilizing medications. Our pharmacology texts barely mentioned this side effect, but I knew only too well how it could torture the patient.

"Good luck with your first psych patient," I said to Linda. I picked up my black bag and stepped through the half-door into a sea of patients, who moved aside very slowly to allow me to pass.

"When can I go home?" demanded an overweight platinum-blond patient wearing a tight tank shirt and no bra. I ignored the question and kept walking. "Hey, where'd ya get such a skinny ass?" the patient shrieked after me. "Did ya steal it from your momma?"

I turned down a side hallway, looking for my patient's room. It was then that I noticed the pervasive odor. Chronic mental wards all smell the same, I thought. They reek of unwashed bodies, greasy hospital food, and stale cigarette smoke mingled with perfumed disinfectant. The odor aroused deep within me an overwhelming sense of despondency bordering on despair. I had to restrain an impulse to flee.

I shivered. With one hand I pulled the front edge of my white coat close across my chest, and with the other hand I squeezed the handle of my black bag. The feeling lifted. I continued walking down the hall and shifted my thoughts back to the task at hand.

Behind me a voice said, "Hey, are you crazy? Don't walk down that hallway alone."

I spun around to see the orderly striding down the hall behind me.

"This ain't no place for a lady to be walking alone," he explained. "Any patient could assault you or rape you. These things happen here—it's a rough place."

"No kidding?" I said.

"Yep. I've been an orderly here for twelve years. I've seen it all. You'd better let me walk you to your patient's room."

"Thank you. Would you mind staying with me while I examine the patient?"

"Sure thing. That's standard procedure. Here, this is Corbett's room," he said, pointing to a door, "and when I last looked he was in here."

I knocked on the door and said, "Mr. Corbett, are you in there?"

No response. The orderly opened the door and walked in. I followed.

The patient was curled up on the bed, the blanket pulled up over his head. The orderly pulled the blanket down, exposing a lean young black face with piercing eyes.

"Mr. Corbett," the orderly said, "the doctor is here to see you."

The face disappeared back under the blanket.

The orderly yanked the blanket away from the patient. "Now sit up here," he said firmly as he helped the patient up. "This here is Dr. North."

"I'm glad to meet you, Mr. Corbett," I said. "I'm your student doctor, and I'm going to assist in your care while you are in the hospital."

I always said "student doctor," though many of my classmates simply introduced themselves as "doctor." I would have felt like a fraud trying to pass myself off as a physician before I actually graduated from medical school. I would not be a real doctor for another fifteen months, and until then I would just have to be "Student Doctor North."

Without warning, the patient reached for the blanket and pulled it back over his shoulders.

Undaunted, I proceeded with the history. "Why did you come to the hospital last night, Mr. Corbett?"

He said nothing, staring at me with relentless eyes. His face could have been carved in stone.

"Talk to the doctor," said the orderly, leaning comfortably against the doorframe.

A long silence followed, and then the patient said in a Martian-like monotone with a staccato accent on each syllable: "You—are—no—doctor—Carol—North—you—are—the—Devil."

I was slightly taken aback that he had used my first name, then I realized he must have read it off my nametag. That was pretty alert for such a sick patient, I thought.

As he sat on the bed, unclothed to the waist, I studied his lean body. The matted hair framing his face had not been combed in so long that it had formed twin peaks on either side of the top of his head. I thought *he* looked like the devil.

Tyrone was smiling, though not at anything in particular. He was just smiling, a vacant grin. Inappropriate emotion, I noted. A textbook symptom.

"Mr. Corbett, do you know where you are?" I asked. It was important to establish whether or not the patient was disoriented. A patient was considered "oriented times three" if he knew (1) who he was, (2) where he was, and (3) what day it was. Schizophrenics are usually oriented, which helps distinguish them from patients with brain damage.

The patient continued to stare, smiling, clutching the blanket around his bare shoulders.

I turned to the orderly and said, "I can see this isn't going to be too productive. I can interview him tomorrow, but I should at least examine him and record the admission physical in the chart today. Can you help me get him straightened around here?"

The orderly stepped toward the patient. Corbett cringed, pulling the blanket even closer.

I said, "I need to examine you, Mr. Corbett. I need to listen to your heart and lungs, and take a look in your eyes and mouth. Will you let me do that?"

He continued to stare. I opened my black bag and lifted out my stethoscope. As I put the listening piece next to his chest, he abruptly whipped the blanket back over his head and assumed the fetal position on the bed.

Again the orderly pulled the blanket away from Corbett's face.

"Mr. Corbett," I said, "do you understand that I need to listen to your heart? That's all I'm going to do. I'm not going to hurt you, I promise."

The patient squinted at me and said in his staccato Martian voice, "Carol—North—you—may—not—examine—me. I—don't

—have—a—body. I—don't—have—a—heart—or—eyes. You—are —the—devil. All—you—want—is—pussy. Well—I—don't—have —no—pussy."

Wow, I thought, this guy is really delusional. "Mr. Corbett, I promise you I am not the devil. I am here to help you. You came to the hospital because you were having some trouble with your thinking. You will understand this when you get to feeling better and thinking more clearly."

"How—do—you—know?" he asked.

"Believe me, I know," I said confidently.

"How?" he insisted.

"Experience." Much as I wanted to, I could never explain it to him, so I let it go with that one word.

Corbett looked about the room, as if listening to voices.

"Are you hearing voices?" I asked him. I needed to verify the reports of hallucinations in his chart. Auditory hallucinations are a hallmark feature of schizophrenia.

"Yes," he said, still smiling. "And—you—brought—me— here—to—kill—me—and—steal—my—mind."

Just one hallucination doesn't by itself qualify a patient for a diagnosis of schizophrenia, I reminded myself. Other diagnostic criteria besides hearing voices had to be met before the diagnosis could be made. But not only was Corbett delusional and hallucinating, his thoughts seemed all mixed up too. He probably had a schizophrenic thought disorder. I was beginning to believe this patient's diagnosis of schizophrenia. Too bad for him, I thought.

I had always felt that schizophrenia was diagnosed too readily, and what I had read from recent research supported my theory. I viewed the practice of overdiagnosis as unfortunate, because the patient would then have to carry with him for the rest of his life a label that not only was incorrect but was viewed by the psychiatric community as essentially hopeless.

I also knew that schizophrenics need reassurance and reality orientation to help them sort out their delusions and their chaotic thoughts and perceptions. I repeated, "Mr. Corbett, I assure you, I'm not going to kill you or steal your mind."

Mr. Corbett didn't seem to be responding to my reassurances. "Maybe you'll feel more like talking tomorrow," I said as I put my stethoscope back in my bag and closed it.

When I left, Corbett was still lying in the fetal position wrapped in the blanket.

Walking back down the hall with me, the orderly said, "Lady, you sure are one brave doctor. That guy gives me the willies."

I didn't feel particularly brave. "Thanks for your help," I told him, and departed for the nursing station to put a note on the patient's chart.

I saw that Dr. Hajara had already written admission orders for Corbett, including starting the patient back on his high doses of Thorazine. Mr. Corbett was to get an injection if he refused his pills. Perhaps tomorrow after a few doses of Thorazine he would be more able to talk to me.

"I wasn't able to get much of a history or physical," I told Dr. Hajara.

"That's all right," he said. "That happens often. See what you can get from the family. There's no hurry. I have meetings all afternoon today, so we'll have to discuss the patient tomorrow."

In the waiting room I found Corbett's mother. Behind soft-spoken words, her face cried out in pain and worry. I could tell she still loved her son, sick as he was.

"When did you first notice Tyrone was having problems?" I asked her.

"Tyrone was just like any other boy up until about three years ago," she said. "He's always been a good boy, and he made A's at school. He never gave me no trouble till he got into high school—then he stopped seeing his friends, he dropped out of football, and he brought home bad marks on his report cards. At first I thought he might be using drugs or something. Then he started cutting up all the electric cords in the house."

"Why was that?" I asked.

"He said the radio and TV were talking to him. They were giving him special messages. He got so bad I finally had to take him to the hospital. But he won't take his medicine 'cause he says it's evil."

She paused, drew in a long breath, and continued, "Now even his little sisters don't bring their friends around no more 'cause they're afraid of him. I got a whole family to raise, you know? So I got him his own apartment."

"How did that work out?" I asked.

"Not so good. I have to help him keep it up. Oh, he ain't my sweet little Tyrone no more," she said, starting to cry. "I come to his apartment to help him clean sometimes, but he won't let me in. He screams at me and calls me the devil and 'whore.' Sometimes I just can't take it no more."

Tears rolled down her cheeks. Her voice choked. "Oh, Lord, it ain't easy. You can't know how hard it is to see this happen to my son. I pray to God every day to make him better. You just can't understand what it's like."

I felt my own throat starting to choke up. I wanted to hug this woman, but that's not what doctors do. Instead, I put a reassuring hand on her shoulder. I reflected on what she had just said—"You just can't understand what it's like." Oh, lady, if you only knew how wrong you are, I thought.

She talked for another hour, sharing her worries with me, explaining what a financial and emotional drain her son's illness had caused, how it had devastated her family.

"I'm not gonna ask you if you can cure Tyrone 'cause I know you can't," she said. "Thank you for just listening. My son is sick, but I'm sufferin' too."

"Believe me, I understand," I said, catching myself before I said more. I understood, more than she could ever know.

I walked back to the nursing station. Linda had finished

her work and left an hour ago. In the nursing station, the nurses and orderlies were sitting amid their own thick cloud of cigarette smoke, discussing my new admission.

"Strange one, that Corbett is," said a nurse. "He called me the devil. Hah!"

"Sounds to me like he's got a vitamin H deficiency," said one of the orderlies.

I knew enough hospital slang to know that "vitamin H" was Haldol, a sedating antipsychotic medication.

"I'd like some peace and quiet tonight," said the orderly. "If he gets too weird we ought to pump him full of vitamin H. Then he'd be so snowed that even the devil would freeze in the blizzard!" This brought a loud burst of laughter from the group.

One of the nurses looked sideways to see how I was taking their callous jokes. The others were studiously ignoring me.

"We could toss him into seclusion right now," said the nurse. "He won't be alone—he's got his voices!"

More laughter. Mrs. Corbett was right: most people didn't understand, not even the ones you'd expect to understand. I picked up my coat and black bag and walked out of the nursing station to the sound of continuing cackles.

As I let the ward door slam behind me, I reflected that now, for the first time, I was the person holding the key to that door. I had just completed my first day on the *doctor's* side of that door.

CHAPTER TWO

A PERFECTLY NORMAL CHILD

Pop! Something hit against the window screen by my head. Snap! Another one. My eyelids flew open. Terrorized, I sat bolt upright from my sleeping position on the couch. That night, Mom and Dad had permitted me to curl up on the couch with my first-grade reader until I had fallen asleep.

"Mom!" I screamed. "Come quick!"

Two glowing particles materialized out of the night air and hit the screen with two distinct pings.

Mustering an even louder voice, I shrieked, "MO-O-O-O-M! The fire! It's back!"

Mom burst from around the door, Dad close at her heels. By now I was sobbing uncontrollably, so paralyzed from fear that I could not budge from the spot to run away. I had almost wet my pants.

Mom sat down on the couch next to me and cradled my head in her arms. "It's okay, dear. We were right here in the next room. The fire is out. It's been out for hours. Were you having a bad dream?"

Pop! Another spark hit the window screen.

"There! The fire!" I screamed, struggling to break free to run to safety.

Mom pulled me close, so tight that I couldn't get away.

Dad peered out the window. "Is that popping noise what's got you upset?"

I nodded.

Dad looked all blurry through my tears. "Why, honey, that's just the june bugs hitting against the screen. They're attracted to the light in the house, see?"

At first I didn't believe him. Another bug popped against the screen and stuck. It began to crawl up the outside of the screen.

Dad didn't look at all scared. In my mind I knew he was right, that the fire really was out. But I was still scared. The whole house reeked of charred wood. Ghosts of the smoke lingered in the corners. At any moment the fire could spring back to new life, I was certain.

My parents had not yet even finished building our modern 1950s ranch-style home. The house was to have four bedrooms—three upstairs, which were finished, and the fourth, still a skeleton of a room in the basement, which was to be Charley's room. That afternoon the fire had begun in the fresh piles of lumber stacked in the basement corner. After consuming that, the flames had licked at the paneling my parents had painstakingly nailed to the recreation-room walls only days before.

We had moved into our new house only a few weeks ago, but from my six-year-old's perspective, it was my home. This was where I played with my Barbie doll. I was sure the fire wanted Barbie. And it wanted me.

As I sat with Mom on the couch, I felt the floor growing warm under the soles of my feet. The basement below was burning! In seconds we would fall through the floor!

I gripped Mom close, burying my face in her arms. I had

been the first to spot the fire earlier that day, and now I could not stop seeing reruns of the fire scene before my eyes.

Brilliant orange flames, horrible and spectacularly beautiful at the same time, had filled the entire basement. The flames had leaped from window to window, licking against each windowpane as they moved along, and I had stood transfixed in the backyard, staring at my home going up in flames.

For several moments it had been me alone with the flames, stranded in eternity. Then suddenly I had catapulted into motion, tearing off toward the front yard as fast as my little legs could carry me. When I had rounded the corner of the house, I had seen a crowd of neighbors gathered in the street. They've come to watch our house burn down, I had thought. Just then, two fire engines had pulled up, parting the crowd like Moses parting the Red Sea. The firemen put out the fire before it could spread beyond the basement.

Pop! I was startled by another bug hitting the screen. I flinched.

Mom gave me a reassuring squeeze. "It's nothing," she said, stroking my hair. "The fire is out. It's not coming back."

I wanted more than anything to believe her. But she looked tense. It seemed that she, too, was worried about the fire coming back. I didn't realize it wasn't the fire she was worried about—it was me.

"Why don't we get you ready for bed?" Dad suggested. "When you get all snuggled up under the covers you'll feel warm and safe."

The idea didn't particularly appeal to me. But I went along with it because it was inevitable. Sooner or later I would have to go to bed. I would eventually have to be alone with my visions of the fire.

Obediently I slipped into my nightgown. Mom read one of my favorite stories, *Raggedy Ann and Andy*. Then it was time to kneel beside my bed for prayers. I prayed to God to protect our house from fire. I didn't want the prayer to end, because that meant it was time for me to be alone.

Dad pulled the covers up to my chin. Mom kissed me on the lips.

"Good night and sleep tight, sugar," Dad said, just as he did every night.

Out went the light, and Mom and Dad disappeared down the hallway into darkness.

Smack! Something small struck my bedroom window screen. I struggled against an impulse to scream. I didn't want Mom and Dad stomping back to my room to scold me. I knew what they would say. "Carol, cut it out and go back to sleep now, you hear? We're not going to run back to your room every five minutes for this nonsense."

I pulled the covers up over my head. It was stuffy under there, but at least it seemed safer. I drifted into a fitful sleep. The next thing I knew, the house was filled with flames! The smoke was thick, cutting off my air! I thrashed about, struggling to find a way out.

Suddenly there was a burst of light. The hall light had just gone on. Clear as day, there stood Dad at the door of my room, the rays of light streaming past him to dazzle my eyes.

"What's the matter?" Dad asked, rubbing his groggy eyes. "You're awfully restless in here. Can't you sleep?"

Suddenly, to my horror, a hundred Popeye arms materialized out of the air between me and Dad, blocking my path to safety. I gasped.

"Come on, honey," he said. "You can come to me. I'm right here."

I stared at the Popeye arms. They waved up and down like rows of palm fronds in a summer breeze. I couldn't get through them to Dad.

"Don't you want to come?" he asked.

"I can't," I whispered.

"Sure you can," he said, a puzzled look spreading across his face. "Come on—I'm not going to *carry* you."

It was a test: I had to crash through the line of Popeye arms to get to Dad. I held my breath and ran toward Dad, hopping over the arms that I could, smashing through the rest. The Poyeye arms seemed to melt as I traveled through them.

When I reached Dad, he took me by the hand and led me to safety, into his bedroom next door. I sandwiched myself in bed between my parents. Dad didn't seem at all bothered by the Popeye arms. Why did things like that bother me so much? I would have to grow up so I wouldn't be afraid anymore, like Dad and Mom.

"Try not to wake Dad up again," Mom told me. "He needs his sleep, because he has to work hard all week, and his work is very important. He can't do a good job if he doesn't get his rest at night."

I understood. I was just glad to be safe. It didn't take me long to fall asleep.

The next thing I knew, Dad was carrying me back to my own bed. He tucked me in and kissed me on the forehead. "You'll be all right now," he told me.

Then he was gone. I couldn't wake my parents up again. I would have to find a way to get through this night on my own.

I didn't get back to sleep that night. I lay very still under the covers, my eyes peeking out from a little flap I made in the sheets. In this manner I stood guard all night, protecting our house from unexpected fires. After all, someone had to do it. Mom and Dad didn't realize the gravity of the matter. It was all up to me.

An eternity passed before the dim light of dawn began to appear. After that, yet another eternity passed before the sun shot its first rays past the curtains. Finally I heard Mom and Dad stirring in their bed.

When I began to smell the familiar Sunday-morning bacon cooking, I knew it was permissible for me to climb out of bed. Mom served us bacon and fried eggs only on Sundays, because she said it was bad for us to have so much cholesterol seven days a week. My two older brothers, Charley and Ed, insisted on having their eggs over easy, but Mom prepared the eggs sunny-side-up for the rest of us.

I always hated getting ready for church. The petticoats under my starched dress itched, and my pointy-toed black patent-leather shoes cramped my toes. But today was especially dreadful. I was terrified at the idea of being alone in my room long enough to get dressed, because I knew the Popeye arms could trap me there forever, and I could be burned alive when the fire came back.

When Dad went back to his room to use his bathroom, I rushed down the hall right behind him. I zipped into my room next door and threw on my underwear and dress as fast as I could. Dad, unaware of my activity, strode back down the hallway to the kitchen. Panicked, I grabbed my Sunday shoes out of my closet and turned my socks drawer upside down, reaching for the first pair of white anklets I saw. I ran down the hall as if being chased by a hungry bear. When I reached the living room I sat down, breathing heavily, trying to recover from my scare while I fumbled with my shoes and socks.

After breakfast we all piled into the station wagon. As Dad revved the engine, Mom asked, "Does everybody have his Bible?"

Horrors! Mine was still in my room! Mom handed me the house key and insisted that I go retrieve it. I tore through the family room and kitchen and raced down the hall to my room. I whisked the Bible up off the nightstand by my bed and flew back down the hall. The house was full of an evil, ominous presence. It wanted to hurt me. I had to get out, fast.

My heart pounding, I flipped the lock on the door leading back to the carport. Breathless, I climbed back into the car.

Ed remarked, "Wow, what's the matter? Your pants on fire?"

Mom turned to him and scowled. Still scowling, she helped

me shut my car door. She didn't like to be late to church, and I knew I was the reason for the delay. Dad shoved the gearshift into reverse and we backed out of the driveway.

When we arrived back home after church, the house still reeked of soggy smoke. I changed clothes as fast as I could, while Mom and Dad were changing in the next room. Then I took my Barbie and all the other toys I might need that day out of my closet, because I didn't want to have to make a trip back to my room alone later. I set up my toys in the family room, where Dad and Ed were reading the Sunday paper.

The familiar smell of Mom's roast beef filled the house, erasing the memory of the smoke. I was tired of roast beef. Why couldn't we have something different on Sundays, like fried chicken or pizza? Mom also made a batch of her special chocolate-chip cookies. It was my turn to lick the bowl.

Sunday dinner was the only meal at which we prayed. Although we went to church every Sunday, we didn't bring much of the religion back home with us. Dad always said the prayer. Usually it was something short, ending with "Bless this food to our use and our selves to Thy service. Amen." The rest of the week we never heard anything about God, aside from bedtime prayers. I supposed God belonged only on Sundays, just like Ed Sullivan and Walt Disney.

After dinner, I spent the rest of the day playing with my Barbie doll. I made sure I stayed next to a family member at all times. I wasn't going to be the first one to spot another fire all alone again.

All too soon, it was bedtime again. After "Good night, sleep tight" and lights out, I stared into the dark, praying to Jesus and the Father and the Holy Ghost to protect me. Gradually, my eyes adjusted to the dark. I could make out the pink Degas ballerinas printed on the curtains Mom had sewn especially for my windows. I could see my China horses lined up on my dresser. In the dark these favorite things did not seem so friendly as they did in the daytime. I pulled the covers up over my head.

A few hours later, when Mom and Dad came back to go to bed, they peeked into my room. I feigned being asleep. Before long, their murmuring voices grew quiet in the next room. Would this night never end?

A man's voice outside the window broke the silence: "Where's the fire?"

I froze underneath the blankets. Maybe I was imagining the voice.

Then another voice said, "Carol's in bed."

No, this was not my imagination! I leaped out of bed, pulled the curtains aside, and peered out the window. I couldn't see anybody, just Mom's carefully tended flower gardens, the same as always. Could they have gone around the corner to the side of the house? I dashed to my other window and looked out. The yard was empty. Maybe they had guns! I ducked, and crawled on the floor back to bed.

A moment later I looked out from under the covers. Through the dark, I could see that my closet door was ajar. Wait—it was moving! Then a great white ghost emerged from the closet. It didn't make any noise whatsoever. It didn't make any progress, either; it just kept floating out of the closet over and over again.

I knew this wasn't the Holy Ghost, because I could see it. Our Sunday-school teacher had said the Holy Ghost was invisible, so this had to be a bad ghost, like the one I'd seen last Halloween. I thought I would burst from terror, but I managed not to scream. I pulled all the covers over my head and hoped the ghost would spare me.

It was hot under the covers. I started sweating. I was afraid to remove the covers, so I continued to sweat. It reminded me of when I was sick with a fever and Mom said the sweating would flush the bad germs out of my system. And now it was working for this situation, too, because when I peeked out from the covers an hour or so later, the bad ghost had vanished. I had cleared my body of any evil impurities that could have weakened me and made me vulnerable to the ghost. I had discovered a way to protect myself from the evils of my house. Safe at last!

But then I felt something crawl up my ankle. I yanked my feet away from the bottom of the bed, folding my legs up against my chest. There were spiders down there! Suddenly I saw hordes of bugs swarming all over my pillow! I picked it up by its corner and tossed it on the floor. I spent the rest of the night huddled as far away as I could get from the foot of the bed. I wasn't particularly comfortable, but at least I was safe. By morning, my limbs ached from keeping the same cramped position all night.

Mom peeked her head into my room and saw me coiled like a pretzel in one corner of my bed. "Carol, whatever are you doing like that?" she demanded to know.

"My pillow had bugs on it," I told her in earnest.

She took one look at my pillow on the floor. "That's not bugs! That's the flower design on your pillowcase."

Before I knew what she was doing, she had changed my pretty flowered pillowcase to a plain white one. It was to be a constant symbol reminding me of my immaturity through the rest of my years at home, because she never again allowed me to have a flowered pillowcase. I felt terribly ashamed of myself.

Charley stuck his head around the corner. "Baby, a baby!" he taunted.

How I hated being only six years old! I wished I could grow up so I wouldn't have to be such a baby! In three years I would be as old as Charley. Three years seemed impossibly far away.

I hated being the youngest of the four kids in my family. My parents had no idea how they mortified me every time they introduced me to people as "the baby of the family"! Judi was their oldest child, then came Ed four years later; Charley was born four years after that. Mom miscarried her fourth baby and then almost lost me in the middle trimester. I was born three and a half years after Charley. Mom was thrilled to have a second daughter to balance out the family.

When Mom, with her alluring coal-black hair and deep brown eyes, had married Dad, with his perfect blond hair and blue eyes, she had secretly hoped for a child with the rare combination of black hair and blue eyes. But the impartial, random forces of natural gene selection had endowed her with four brown-haired, brown-eyed children. Mom was happy anyhow. By the time I was old enough to have memories of Dad, he had already grayed prematurely. Dad was a quiet man who wasn't good at expressing emotions, yet directly stated his genuine feelings of pride to be the father of four healthy, intelligent, and motivated children.

Mom and Dad had first met early in high school, the year Dad was class president. After graduation, they both attended their Midwestern state college, where they initially drifted apart, only to resume dating later in their freshman year. Dad had to take time off to earn money to put himself through school, and Mom consequently finished college a year before Dad earned his degree in chemical engineering. Shortly thereafter, they married and settled into having a family together and making their dream nest in a nice home. Dad went to work for a small company that manufactured caramel coloring for soft drinks and other food products, which necessitated their moving to the small Midwestern town where the company was located. Over the years, Dad progressed up the executive ranks to become plant manager and vice-president of the company. Mom devoted all of herself to being a good wife to Dad and raising their children right. Our family was the modern prototype of the more stable families of the 1950s and 1960s. Mom was always reminding us of how fortunate we were to live as comfortably as we did, even through the hard economic times they experienced during their early years of marriage and bearing their first children. Every night at bedtime Mom knelt with us by our beds to thank the Lord for His goodness to us. She also took us to Sunday school and services at our Congregational church. Then Dad would pray before our weekly Sunday meal, further reminding us to be grateful to God for all the goodness that we had.

I felt secure. To have my whole world threatened by the ravages of fire was a concept too horrible for my little brain to deal with.

Before leaving for school after breakfast on the Monday morning after the fire, I didn't have the courage to make the long scary voyage back to the bathroom alone. There was no one back in that part of the house, and there wasn't time to wait for anybody to go back there to be with me. I would just have to wait till I got to school, a twenty-minute walk away.

Usually I enjoyed the walk to school. I liked to skip, and I often skipped the whole way, my waist-length ponytail swinging from side to side behind me with every step. But today was different. The sky was overcast, a menacing gray. I sensed danger.

Usually the robins and sparrows sang to me along the way, and usually I liked to sing back to them. But today they were silent. Their beaks jutted out ominously in front of their faces. I passed a house where a man and a woman were standing on the front porch. They were staring at me, and they appeared to be talking about me. Were they going to kidnap me? My mother had warned me about people such as these. I knew all about not taking candy from strangers and not getting into strange cars. I started running as fast as I could. In a few blocks I stopped, breathless, and looked back. I had escaped.

Out of the sky came a sparrow, dive-bombing toward my head! I ducked, and leaped under the nearest bush. Several other birds had gathered forces to tear me to pieces. I crouched under the bush for what seemed an eternity, then I jumped to my feet and began running again. The birds continued to chase me and zoom past my head. I waved my hands in the air, trying to fight them off. I didn't realize how much all this extra activity was delaying me.

When I was still two blocks from school, I heard the "tardy bell" ring. I had never been tardy! I was a model student. How could I ever live this down? Maybe the bell had been rung by mistake. Maybe I wasn't really tardy. I would have to hurry!

When I arrived, class had already begun. Out of breath, I hung up my coat and took a seat at my desk. The first-grade teacher continued writing on the blackboard, as if she didn't notice my tardiness. Perhaps she didn't want to scold me. I I felt I had let her down.

I couldn't concentrate on the spelling lesson. I had to go to the bathroom! The teacher looked like a snippy old school-marm, and I was afraid to ask her permission. She looked evil. I was afraid to bother her.

I couldn't hold it any longer. I tried not to, but I wet my pants. I was mortified.

The teacher made every effort not to embarrass me. She whispered in my ear, "Only two people ever need know about this, and that's God and me." The puddle under my desk was mopped up, and I never heard about it again. But for the next two years I was convinced that all the students in the upper grades were pointing at me and whispering about it whenever I passed by.

I was six years old and afraid of everything, day and night. Getting to and from school was a major task. It wasn't easy dodging killer birds and escaping murderers and kidnappers every day. At night I continued to be tortured by voices, fires, ghosts, and bugs. I started sleeping in Mom and Dad's bed regularly.

One day I overheard Mom and Dad speaking in hushed tones in their room. I couldn't make out their words, yet I knew they were talking about me.

A few days later Mom told me we were going to the doctor. I was surprised when we didn't go to our regular family doc-tor. Instead Mom took me to the local mental health center.

The psychologist we went to see was a tall, thin man with

sunken cheeks. Seated behind his desk, he refilled his pipe while my mother sat down and made herself comfortable. I sat next to Mom, feeling like a tiny bug in the huge armchair.

"Now, Mrs. North, what seems to be the problem with ah"—he referred to a sheet of paper in front of him—"um, Carol?"

My mother crossed and uncrossed her legs nervously before beginning. "Well—it all started with a small fire in our house three months ago. Since then she's been afraid of everything. She refuses to be alone."

Grown-up talk bored me; I didn't try to pay attention. Instead, I stared down at the pattern in the carpet and silently practiced words from that week's spelling lesson at school.

"What kind of child was Carol before the fire?" the psychologist asked.

"She was a perfectly normal child," Mom said. "In fact, her teacher says she's the best student in her class. At home, she has always been well behaved and seemed happy. But she is sensitive."

The doctor raised a curious eyebrow. "Sensitive? How do you mean?"

Mom thought a moment. "She's like the Princess and the Pea. Do you remember that fairy tale?"

He nodded, looking slightly bored. "Yes, wasn't she the one who was so sensitive that a pea underneath a pile of mattresses kept her awake all night?"

"Carol's like that," Mom said. "If there's the slightest bit of mold on the bread she'll taste it before anyone else does. Things we don't notice seem to drive her to distraction. She can't stand the texture of pulp in orange juice. She can't tolerate her socks falling down or her underwear creeping up. And we have to be careful what we say around her so she won't misinterpret it."

"How many other children do you have?" the psychologist asked.

"Three."

He glanced up from his papers, waiting for Mom to say more about them.

Mom took his cue. "Judi, the oldest, is spending this year in Costa Rica as a foreign exchange student. Which is a relief, because she and her younger brother Ed are always fighting—but they're good kids. Then there's Charley. He's the oddball."

Again the doctor glanced up from writing. "Did you say oddball?"

"Well, I mean he's very creative, always trying out his kooky ideas."

"Such as?"

"Oh, things like flipping the switch breakers in the basement just to find out what will happen. But I think Carol's at least as creative as Charley, and her art work at school is very good."

"Mmm-hm." The doctor laid his pencil down on the desk. "Mrs. North, how exactly has Carol been acting differently since the fire?"

"She's so scared. At first she saw fires everywhere. Now she's seeing ghosts in her room and bugs in her bed. She's been so upset that she hasn't slept at all in the last three months, at least not that I've seen. And her teacher called me from school to report that she has been tardy twice. That just isn't like her."

The doctor sucked several short draws on his pipe and asked Mom, "How do you respond to Carol when she's scared?"

"We've been letting her sleep in our bed with us."

The doctor leaned back in his chair and started tapping his pencil against the edge of the desk. "How often is this happening?"

"Lately, every night."

He slid his glasses down his nose and peered over them at Mom. "Well, Mrs. North, I'll tell you what your daughter's problem is. She's looking for attention. And you're feeding right into the problem by paying her the attention she craves every time."

Mom scratched the top of her head. "Am I supposed to just ignore her? That seems cruel. After all, she's only a *child*."

"Not exactly, Mrs. North. But I'll tell you what you can do. Next time Carol gets scared in the night, invite her into your bedroom and sit her on a chair by your bed. Then go back to sleep. It'll cure her in no time at all, you'll see. Then you can sleep in peace."

That sounded plausible to Mom. This was the doctor's advice, and she would do as he suggested, if it could help me get better. I don't remember ever talking to the doctor. He ignored me, asking Mom all the questions.

On the way home in the car, Mom smoked a cigarette. She never talked much when she was concentrating on her driving. I stared out the car window, watching the telephone poles going by, their wires dipping up and down in between the poles. It was an old game I always played in the car.

Every time the line dipped down, a voice that seemed to come from the roof of the car said, "You want a cigar?" A few seconds later when the pole passed by and the line rose to meet it, another voice said, "Here, we'll take it away," and laughed. I never got to see the voices, but I didn't think it odd that there should be voices coming from the roof of our car. I had heard these voices so many times that I just accepted their presence without questioning the finer details. Besides, Mom never seemed to notice them. Today the voices were laughing at me more than usual. They seemed to be enjoying a private joke. It had something to do with me, but I didn't understand it. This was like so many other things: I hoped I'd understand it when I was grown up.

That night when I was in bed, I heard a new voice yell, "Fire!"

I didn't like the tricks the voices played on me. I should have been used to them by now, but when they talked about fire they frightened me. Next, some eerie music that sounded like Chopin's "Funeral March" came floating out of my closet.

I couldn't stand it any longer. I jumped out of bed and tip-toed into my parents' room. For a long minute I hesitated by the bedside. Mom and Dad were sound asleep. I couldn't bring myself to wake them up. They might get mad.

I was torn. I could still hear the funeral music. I tapped Mom's hand. "Mom."

She didn't stir. I tapped harder. "Mom."

She opened her eyes and said in a groggy voice, "What is it, dear?"

She was going to think I was silly, but I had to tell her. Baby or no baby. "There's funeral music."

She didn't even ask me any questions about it. I was glad. She just sighed and said, "Okay, honey. Here's a chair. I'll set it right over here, and why don't you sit on it for a while. You'll be safe now."

I was grateful not to have to return to my room to be alone with the night terrors. Anything was better than that. I sat in the cold protective arms of the chair all night, not moving a single muscle. When the dawn arrived and Mom and Dad woke up, I was still sitting there, eyes wide open and staring.

At breakfast Mom said to Dad, "I feel so *guilty*. How could I have taken that man's advice? He doesn't know Carol. He doesn't understand the problem."

I was busy reading the cereal box. Dad poured some milk into his coffee and stirred it. "What do you think we should do next?" he asked Mom.

"I don't know," Mom said between sips of hot tea. "I think it's more complicated than that. Carol's not just looking for attention. She's *really scared*. It tore my heart out this morning when I woke up and saw that terrified look in her eyes. I'll never be able to forgive myself for leaving her in that chair all night."

Dad straightened his tie. "Why don't we take her to see a

psychiatrist at the university? It's only a three-hour drive, so you could get there and back in one day."

Mom stared into her empty teacup and nodded. She was fighting back tears.

But when Mom called the university, she couldn't get an appointment for three months. Mom needed help soon. So she took me to see Dr. Vandenberg, our regular family physician.

He was a wise old country doctor, and he knew all the tricks. When I had to get a shot, he would say, "Hey! Look over there," pointing to a plastic bird on the lawn outside. It always worked.

This time, Mom and I just went to talk. Dr. Vandenberg directed me to a toy chest on the floor, then he and my mother sat down in chairs to talk. I began digging through the toy chest, pulling out all the Lincoln logs I could find.

"This is your youngest child, isn't she, Doris?" Dr. Vandenberg asked my mom.

She nodded.

"Hmm, six years old now. She's kinda small for her age, isn't she?" He thumbed through my chart. "Ah yes, she's the one I hospitalized several times during infancy for diarrhea and dehydration. She needed IV fluids. Guess we never got to the bottom of that, did we?"

Mom shook her head. "Her appetite never has been very good. And she still gets a lot of stomachaches. But she never was a difficult child, never a behavior problem before now," Mom said. "Though she always has been different from my other children."

Dr. Vandenberg raised his thick white eyebrows. "What do you mean, 'different,' Doris?"

"She's always seemed to require more care than the others ever did. First it was the difficult pregnancy, and then all that awful diarrhea. Then do you remember the time she was four and she had that mysterious fever?"

"Mercy, I won't forget that! Temperature of a hundred six and a half degrees. And no reason for it that I could find."

"I hated calling you out that night. You were so good to come out in the cold. I remember you stayed with her for several hours, and then I sponged her off with cold water through the rest of the night into the next day."

"Strangest thing." Dr. Vandenberg shook his head. "Fever departed just as mysteriously as it came."

Abruptly my mother looked quite serious. "I wish I knew what to do now. She's been terrified ever since the fire in our house last spring. She can't be alone for one minute. She has a wild imagination. I've always thought she was the most creative of the four kids, but now I think her imagination has gone too far. She's been talking about crazy things like fires and ghosts and killer birds."

Dr. Vandenberg gave that all-knowing look of the clever family doctor and walked over to where I was laying the foundation for a Lincoln-log cabin. Squatting beside me, he said, "I'll bet you don't want to be afraid, do you, Carol?"

I shook my head, feeling embarrassed because I knew Mom had told him what a baby I had been recently.

"I'll make a deal with you," he said to me as he reached into one of his desk drawers. "Here is a calendar for you to keep. Every day you're not afraid, your mom will put a gold star on that day. When you've earned thirty gold stars in a row, you'll get a bicycle!"

I looked at Mom. I didn't want to do it, but they hadn't given me a chance to object.

Mom put the calendar under her arm and said to me, "We can pick up some stars at the five-and-dime on the way home."

At least the doctor hadn't called me a baby! And besides, a bicycle sounded great. With a bike, I might be able to keep up with Charley, instead of always being left behind.

Every night at bedtime, after I said my prayers, Mom and Dad asked me if I had been afraid that day. During the first day I had already told Mom about several scary things. I cried because I wasn't going to get a star. But they gave me a free one that first night just to get me started.

The next few nights I continued telling the truth about being scared, and the calendar remained empty. Finally I caught on. I was supposed to lie.

Over the next few weeks I devised strategies for covering up my fears or getting around them without letting anybody know what I was doing. I never made the trip back to my bedroom alone. I waited until somebody else in the family went back there and then I followed, taking care of whatever I had to do at that time. At night I performed my ritual sweating-under-the-covers routine until I was confident that I had purged myself of all impurities, keeping the ghosts and other evil spirits from detecting my scent. I prayed to the Holy Ghost to protect me from the Halloween ghost. When I was most afraid, I relied on my little breathing flap under a mountain of covers.

When I saw ghosts in my room, I told myself, Don't believe it. Even though I see a ghost there, it isn't really there. Like Mom says, it's only the product of my "wild imagination."

I was learning not to trust my own perceptions.

In the daytime I took a new route to school, where the robins and sparrows could no longer find me. My teacher phoned my mother to say that I seemed to be doing better and the tardiness problem was solved. And when I heard voices talking to me, which happened just about every day, I looked around to see if anyone else had heard them too. Sometimes I even asked others if they had heard something, but discreetly enough not to let on what I was hearing.

It didn't occur to me that other people didn't hear voices too. Mom had taught me that there were certain things you just didn't talk about. I thought it was the same way with the voices, that all people experienced them in the privacy of their own homes, but like bodily functions, somehow they were a shameful topic not fit for mention in public. To admit to hearing voices would only disclose how much of a baby I truly was. I learned never to tell anybody I was scared, no matter how scary things got.

Eventually the proud day came when my calendar was completely filled with stars. I remember the day I got my bike as clearly as the day of the fire. It was a crisp fall day, one of the last beautiful biking days of the year. Mom bought me a gleaming blue girl's bike for five dollars at a garage sale right up the street. Mom and I wheeled it home together, steadying opposite ends of the handle bars as we walked. I was going to learn how to ride it that same day.

I thought, Babies can't ride bikes. I must be growing up. When I'm all grown up I won't be scared, and I won't have to lie about it anymore.

CHAPTER THREE

"BABY" NO MORE

R.T.C. LIBRARY, LETTERKENNY

I had always hated to eat. In the fourth grade I was still skinny, and at least two inches shorter than any of my classmates. I looked as if I belonged in second grade. Yet intellectually, I was three grades ahead of my class. I looked like a misfit and I felt like a misfit. Emotionally, I was far behind. I was still battling against the lingering image of "baby." Hence I could never tell anyone that I still saw ghosts and heard voices offering me cigars.

To hide my fears, when I practiced the piano in the basement I played as loud as I could to cover the sounds of the voices. When I was done, I ran upstairs as fast as I could to escape the evil spirits that lurked down there. When my best girlfriend, who was two years younger than I, informed me that Santa Claus was a fake, I was terribly embarrassed that I still believed. Why hadn't my parents told me? They could have spared me the embarrassment.

My brothers were growing up fast. Ed was nearly out of sight—he was ready to leave home to join Judi at college, an-

47

other world. Charley was getting big. If I could keep up with Charley, I would no longer be a baby. I disciplined myself to do push-ups and chin-ups daily. Strong people could not be babies. Charley was strong. I wanted to be like him, to keep up with him. Despite my efforts, three chin-ups was the maximum my toothpick-sized arms could accomplish. Charley could do fifteen in a row.

When his best friend John was busy, Charley would play with me. In our adventures together, I always had to struggle to keep up. Complaining was not acceptable.

"I'm going for a bike ride," Charley told me one day. "Wanna come along? You can, if you'll keep up. I'm not going to wait for you."

Oh, goody, I thought. Playing with Charley was loads more fun than playing dolls. I dropped my Barbie doll, ran straight to the carport, and mounted my bike.

Charley sped off, not even glancing back to see if I was with him. We zoomed down a steep hill, so fast that my bike began to shake. I was scared I would crash. Charley enjoyed speed. He had told me he sometimes got his bike speedometer up to forty miles an hour. He quit doing that, though, after a hornet flew inside his T-shirt and stung him all over his chest, at forty miles an hour. I was home that day when he came bawling into the house.

Charley could pedal faster on his three-speed bike than I could on my one-speed. He edged farther and farther away from me, and I lost sight of him each time he disappeared over a hilltop, only to catch sight of him again when I reached the summit. Finally, he vanished around a corner, and when I got there he was nowhere to be seen. I decided he must have immediately turned another corner, and I took another turn where I thought he'd gone. He wasn't there. Maybe he had turned the corner the opposite way. I changed directions and pedaled several blocks before concluding that I'd lost him for good. I would have to go home and wait for him.

I turned my bike around and headed back the way I had

come. None of the houses looked familiar. I couldn't recall where I was supposed to turn—I hadn't really been paying attention, I had been so bent on catching Charley. I was lost in a new housing development, where the streets all went in funny directions, like a maze in which you could wander for hours and not be able to make any sense out of it.

I decided to get on one street and stay on it. Eventually I would have to come to someplace familiar. The street ended in nowhere, dumping me onto another street I didn't recognize. I followed it to a dead end. I started to cry, pedaling along aimlessly, without any plan or idea of how to get home. The wind in my face whipped my tears away as quickly as they spilled over my eyelids. I feared Mom would be furious if I didn't get home for dinner.

One of my old familiar voices began to give me advice. "Turn right," it said, in a friendly, soothing tone. It didn't scare me at all. In fact, I appreciated the suggestion. I turned right. I stopped crying, even though nothing looked familiar yet.

"Do you want a cigar?" the voice said. No, I didn't want a cigar. I didn't want to play those games. "Don't be a goose," I heard the voice say. I didn't know what that meant. "Seven eight, keep going straight," the voice said in a singsong way. "Turn a corner, Little Jack Horner."

This was getting me mixed up. I wasn't near a corner, so how could I turn? I sensed they were playing with me. I started to cry again.

Suddenly the houses looked familiar again. I was only six blocks from home. I didn't know how I had gotten there because I hadn't been paying attention. Could the voices have somehow changed the landscape and stuck a neighborhood street right under me? I decided it was possible.

"Yup," said the voice, answering my thoughts.

I still had a lot of growing up to do before I could understand the voices, I thought. One day, when I was old enough, I would wake up and automatically understand everything.

I quit crying and dried my eyes. I didn't want anybody to know I had been crying when I got home.

But my childish fears did not fade as I grew older. Although the voices had more or less dissolved into background chatter, their sudden intrusions sometimes still frightened me. Because of the skills I had first learned with Dr. Vandenberg's calendar, I was able to keep most of my symptoms from my parents. Consequently, my symptoms never reached further professional attention. All my parents knew was that I still seemed more fearful than I should for my age, and to help soothe me they got me a dog, thinking the companionship might help me be brave.

Things didn't improve for me in junior high school. The voices began to distract me from conversations. They persisted on words people said, spelling them out or saying them backward. Sometimes while I was talking to other people the voices said bad words like "fuck" or "shit," words I wasn't even supposed to know. Though I didn't know what those words meant, I knew they were bad words. They were so loud I was sure other people would hear them. I couldn't stop thinking the words the voices were saying. I thought the reason I couldn't get them out of my mind was that the voices had some kind of mind-control method by which they could put words and thoughts into my head against my will.

I felt uncomfortable and embarrassed around other people when I couldn't stop the loud thoughts from escaping my brain. The voices would start up during classes, saying things about the person sitting next to me. "Kevin is a creep," they said.

I looked over at Kevin. "Kevin is a creep, Kevin is a creep," they kept saying. My mind picked up on the phrase and continued to repeat it. It wasn't my thought. I couldn't stop it. Suddenly Kevin looked back at me, made a sour face, and turned away. I've got to control these thoughts, I told myself. Everyone can hear them. I could tell by the funny way people began to look at me that they could hear my thoughts. I had always had difficulty reading facial expressions, but something was so obviously going on that I couldn't possibly miss it.

Even my dog could hear my thoughts. All I had to do was think of a trick that she already knew how to do, like "roll over," "sit up," or "speak," and she would carry out the command before I even spoke it. I decided I had telepathic powers. I practiced on the dog, to help gain control over my rampant telepathy. I hoped practicing these mental gymnastics would help me avoid those embarrassing moments around people when the telepathy slipped out inadvertently.

When I felt I had developed my powers of ESP sufficiently on the dog, I shifted my efforts to people. In my classes at school, I sat in a daze, focusing all my attention on the teacher, mentally commanding Mr. Hicks to perform a particular action, such as scratch his nose. As I concentrated, an overwhelming feeling of supreme power came over me, as if I were tapping into some cosmic force. It worked: Mr. Hicks scratched his nose.

In English class I passed a note to my best girlfriend, Joanne, telling her to watch, that I was going to mentally command Miss Peters to drop the chalk. A few minutes later, Miss Peters did drop the chalk. She was so obese that it was an effort for her to bend over and stretch for that piece of chalk. Joanne and I burst out giggling. But secretly I felt guilty that I had caused Miss Peters to experience something unpleasant. I would have to be selective with my powers in the future; otherwise I might cause something evil to happen. After all, I didn't want be an agent of the devil.

I was usually the first kid out the front door after school every day. Although I didn't want to hang around and socialize, I wasn't eager to get home quickly, because I didn't particularly enjoy being there either. Mom had started picking on Charley lately about the way he dressed and behaved, and even though her criticisms weren't directed at me, they bothered me.

I started taking the long way home, circling through a cemetery which was significantly out of the way. I didn't just walk through the cemetery, though; I communed with it. I sensed a spiritual connection between myself and the dead. I never told this to a soul, because I didn't want to dilute my special connections by sharing them with the rest of the world, an insensitive world that surely couldn't comprehend.

I felt my view of the world was justified. On the rare occasions that I had witnessed moments of insight or sensitivity from others, they had typically surprised me by coming from unexpected individuals. During orchestra practice one day, the voices were badgering me with endless taunts and criticisms, further rattling me by singing the music half a bar ahead of where we were playing. I couldn't concentrate on playing my cello. The orchestra played on, while I struggled to reestablish my place in the music. It was too much. Uncontrollable tears welled up in my eyes and spilled over. The more I tried to stop my crying and pay attention to the music, the faster the tears streamed down my cheeks.

My orchestra teacher saw me crying and later approached me in private. "It's all right to cry," she told me. "It shows you're a sensitive person, though I knew that already. Carol, painful as it is to be a sensitive person in this world, it has invaluable rewards. Sensitive people become gifted artists and musicians."

I hadn't expected such insight from my orchestra teacher. I had thought of her only as a crabby conductor whom the kids made fun of behind her back. After that, I frequently reminded myself of what she had said about being sensitive, and this made it easier for me to bear my isolation.

In the cemetery, I wandered for hours, discovering different sections and becoming familiar with all the tombstones. Some were hard to read. It took me an entire afternoon to decipher a weathered epitaph I found on a crumbly tombstone from the 1800s. Its message seemed to speak to me personally. It read:

J. R. Crandell speaks from the tomb.

Remember me as you pass by;

As you are now, so once was I.

As I am now, so you will be.

Prepare for death and follow me.

So, this man knows death, I thought. He knows all about the ghosts and the spirit world. He probably knows the voices that talk to me.

"Who are they?" I said out loud, at the tombstone. "You know—why won't you tell me? Why won't somebody tell me?" J. R. Crandell didn't answer.

One day when I arrived home from the cemetery, Charley met me at the front door. "You'd better watch yourself," he warned me.

Instantly a pang of guilt seized me. Oh no, what had I done wrong now?

"What do you mean?" I said, setting my books down on the hall stand while I took off my coat.

"Mom knows you've been hanging around the cemetery," he said.

My heart began to thump hard against the inside of my rib cage, like a little animal trying to get out.

"How does she know that?" I asked him.

"She knows everything," he said. "She's a snoop." Then he turned and descended the stairs to his room.

I picked up my books and retired to my room to study. I shut my door tightly behind me. I didn't want Mom snooping on me. Charley was right: Mom did seem to know everything. Maybe the voices were talking to her and filling her in on my activities. Or maybe she was mind-reading. That could certainly be possible, because sometimes I couldn't control my thoughts, and they seemed to float out across the air. A person with special abilities might be able to pick my thoughts out of the air. That could explain those times when Mom gave me those long, funny looks that made me feel so uncomfortable. This was horrible: it meant I had no privacy at all.

I opened my math book and began to do my homework problems. My mind wandered. If Mom was really reading my mind, I would have to find a strategy to counter her mind-reading. I would either have to avoid thinking any thoughts, or else police my thoughts to keep them from escaping my control. Or I would have to jumble up my thoughts to keep anyone from being able to make sense out of them.

Just then Mom poked her head through my door. "How hungry are you? Do you want me to fix you one or two pork chops for dinner?"

"Just one," I said. Why had she chosen this very moment that I was thinking about her reading my mind to come into my room? Did she know that I knew? I glared at her.

In return, she gave me a puzzled, troubled look that felt like pins and needles raining down on me.

A terrible sense of urgency seized me. I needed some distance. Go away, I thought. Just go away and leave me alone.

It seemed like forever before she said, "Dinner will be ready in forty-five minutes," and disappeared back down the hall. I got up and shut the door again. Damn! I was certain now that Mom was reading my mind. It would be necessary to control my thoughts at every moment. This was not going to be easy.

In high school, classes and music and dance lessons kept me busy, and in tenth grade I added church activities to my already overloaded schedule. My best friend, Joanne, whose parents attended our church, was the one who had gotten me so interested in church.

"You should come to Sunday school and the senior high youth group," she had told me. "It's going to be totally different now. We have a new Sunday-school teacher and a new assistant minister to lead the youth group. I've been a couple of times, and it's really neat."

It sounded interesting. I thought I'd give it a try. The leader of our Sunday-evening youth group was a young student minister from a nearby seminary. At our meetings we read from the Bible and participated in organized lessons and discussions of religion. Then we would pray and sing, and hold hands and pray some more. Praying became an emotional experience; we prayed for each other and for the world's problems. After the meeting we usually ran around the church and played tag or other games, or made popcorn. Often we participated in community service projects, like visiting the shut-ins. In time, our youth group expanded to fifteen or twenty members, including a few of the most popular kids from my school. Everyone in the group was accepted and loved, no matter how unpopular or "weird" he or she was considered at school.

This total acceptance by my peers affected me intensely. Here was a group of people who wanted to explore the spiritual realms, people who seemed to understand me and who were interested in the things that interested me most. I began to find religious explanations for my unusual experiences. The Bible was full of bizarre experiences such as voices of spirits and demons talking to people, faith healing, and gifts of the Spirit. My experiences were not so unusual; the Bible proved that. Although no one else in our group mentioned hearing voices, I thought of the voices as a sign of religious maturity. When the others had put in enough effort to get that far in their spiritual growth, they might get to experience the same things I did.

I carried my Bible everywhere, and read it avidly whenever I got the chance. I didn't care if the other kids at school thought I was weird, because now I had a group of friends who all felt the same way I did about religion. It was the most important thing in our lives.

I lived for Sundays. I went to church at eight in the morn-

ing for Bible study, then stayed for Sunday school at nine
and church service at ten. After I came home for Sunday-
noon dinner, I often went back to church to spend the afternoon with the group at various church-related activities, such
as car washes to help raise money to donate to the poor over-
seas. At six in the evening our youth group met, and then
we all hung around goofing off or finishing up various tasks
like making posters for the next Sunday sermon we had to
give. Sometimes I didn't get home until eleven o'clock at
night.

At church I met CJ, a woman from the Methodist church
who had volunteered to be a chaperon for one of our youth
group's overnights. CJ had two teenage children of her own,
and she had terrific rapport with adolescents. From the very
first moment I met her, it seemed to me our thoughts shared
the same wavelength. She could recite from memory numerous Biblical passages referring to gifts of the Spirit such as
speaking in tongues, faith healing, prophecy, and casting out
of demons. I wanted to know more. Here was someone who
might be able to help me unlock the mysteries that were so
confusing to me. CJ knew more about gifts of the Spirit than
anyone I had ever talked to. I listened to her for hours, pum-
meling her with endless questions. Did spirits communicate
with her? Did she hear their voices too? Yes, she felt that
God and numerous spiritual entities, both good and evil, attempted to communicate directly with her. She believed that
by praying and reading the Bible, she could strengthen her
faith to allow for heightened communication with the Holy
Spirit.

Instead of visiting the cemetery after school, I began going
over to CJ's house. She was like a second mother to me, ac-
cepting me despite my faults and helping to steer me in a
noncritical manner through my confused world of spiritual
chaos. The warmth of her smile felt wonderfully protective.
I tried to emulate CJ's strength. I already felt that we shared
the same sensitivity: when she hurt, I hurt; when I felt joy,

she felt joy. We seemed united in a common spiritual bond charged with emotional intensity that words could not describe.

CJ warned me, "You must be careful, because by getting yourself more in tune with the spiritual realms, you open yourself up to evil influences as well as holy ones." Then she cited several Biblical passages about demons and evil spirits that possessed people.

I was awed. I had never before met anyone who was so knowledgeable about and sensitive to the subjects that interested me most.

"Have you ever spoken in tongues?" I asked her, referring to something I'd read in the Bible.

"No," she said, "although once I felt as if I was on the verge of doing it. It was during one of my prayer group's meetings. The group's members get so fervent in prayer that they automatically start speaking in tongues, and the words flow effortlessly from their mouths. It happens regularly at our prayer meetings."

"Wow," I said. I tried to imagine what it would be like to speak in tongues.

"Would you like to come with me to my prayer group this week?" she asked me.

"Oh yes," I said eagerly, "if that's all right." I was simultaneously excited and frightened by the idea of seeing the gifts of the Spirit.

"Be at my house at six-thirty Thursday night," she said.

I told my parents simply that I was going to a prayer meeting. I was afraid if I told them what kind of prayer meeting it was, they wouldn't let me go.

CJ and I arrived late to the prayer meeting. When we entered the room—it was someone's living room—I saw about thirty people praying, silently yet fervently, in a circle on the floor. The air in the room seemed to vibrate with spiritual power.

Suddenly a woman on the far side of the room broke the

silence, gushing forth in a foreign tongue I didn't recognize. Across the room, a man raised both his arms and said, "I understand what you are saying, praise be to the Holy Spirit! Saint Mary is speaking through your tongue, telling us that we are to construct a church according to the following strict instructions from the Lord! Praise the Lord!"

The woman continued babbling her strange utterances, which she apparently couldn't interpret herself. The man broke in every few seconds with further interpretations. The message was a set of detailed instructions describing how the church door was to be constructed, right down to the carved wood patterns, gold-leaf designs, and even the type of screws to be used in the doorknob. I thought it was odd that such an awesome gift of the Spirit should be used to communicate such trivial information. I would have thought the Spirit would be sending more important messages via the tongues. But, I thought, far be it from me to question the Holy Spirit.

When the first woman finished speaking in her tongue, several other people began speaking in other tongues. Each tongue sounded different and unique; no two were anything alike. I decided that these people had the ultimate personal relationship to God, because of their intensive prayer and spiritual sophistication. This should be the goal of my spiritual quest. When I had grown strong in my faith I would be able to share in these gifts also. After all, I was sure that I possessed special spiritual sensitivity.

The people speaking in tongues gradually grew quiet, and the prayer ended. The group broke up into smaller groups for discussion and further prayer.

A young man in my group turned to the man next to him and said, "Harry, were you here last month when that new guy came to our group?"

"No," Harry said, "I must have missed him."

"His faith was weak," the first man said. "During our prayer he started moaning and thrashing around. He let the devil get inside him—a horrible sight. We all prayed over him while he kept thrashing and spitting and cursing, but we couldn't drive the devil out. We had to make him leave, and I heard that after he left here he got real crazy. The devil's still in him."

Harry shook his head. "This is dangerous business. People who are weak in their faith or who don't know how to direct their spiritual powers shouldn't be here. Just like what happened to that guy—they could tap into an evil spirit. Those evil spirits are so jealous of our relationship with the Holy Spirit that they can't wait to find an opening to get at us. The stronger we get, the more anxious the devil is to get in."

I realized I was in jeopardy. My faith, like that of the man they had mentioned, wasn't strong enough either. I wanted to believe everything, but I still had doubts.

Suddenly I heard a voice that clearly wasn't anywhere in the room say, "Get behind me, Satan!"

I realized I would have to fortify myself against unwanted spiritual influences. Silently I began to repeat the words *Thou shalt love the Lord thy God with all thy heart and soul and strength* over and over, trying to immerse myself in love for God. Still, I couldn't dismiss the doubts. I hadn't entirely believed that everything I had witnessed that evening was true.

I thought to myself, How can I know this is all true? I was instantly surprised by the loudness of the words I had just thought. My thought had accidentally escaped from the privacy of my mind and flowed out into the room. The other people in the room, all of whom were obviously sensitive to psychic phenomena, had undoubtedly heard my words and begun to realize that I was the one in the room with the weak faith. I wanted more than anything to believe. It was crucial at this moment. Surely the doubts had been placed in my mind by a demon. They couldn't have been my own.

Before anything bad could happen, the meeting ended. CJ patted me on the shoulder and said, "Did you enjoy the prayer meeting?"

"Oh, yes," I said. I didn't want to tell her that I was scared out of my mind.

Only when we were securely buckled into the seat belts in her Volkswagen and heading back home did I feel safe. I never returned to another meeting of that particular prayer group. Shortly after that, CJ's husband was transferred to another job in another state, and I lost track of her. I missed CJ. She had been more than a good friend and second mother to me—she had been a teacher, priest, and spiritual adviser. Now I was more confused than ever. CJ had introduced me to a new world, and I wasn't sure whether I was properly interpreting it on my own, without her help.

The leader of my church youth group graduated from seminary and left to take a job as pastor of a church far away. The group subsequently lost its vitality. Then the seniors graduated, changing the group's membership, especially as a new group of sophomores joined.

I drifted away from my friends. I dropped music lessons and dance classes, then quit orchestra, and finally dropped Spanish, which had previously been my favorite class. I was otherwise absorbed in trying to keep communication with God going at all times, so that no demon could overpower me in a weak moment.

"Be good," a voice told me.

"Do bad," another voice advised.

"Stand up," said a voice.

"Sit down," said another.

I was confused.

I imagined I would have to maintain purity of self to keep free of their influence. Life is a prayer, I repeated to myself frequently. Live it that way. Whenever I felt vulnerable I whispered, "Lord Jesus, be with me."

More and more, my thoughts escaped my control, diffusing out from my brain for others to hear. I increased my efforts to police the contents of my thoughts at all times. It wasn't easy trying to *not* think thoughts, but it was something I knew I absolutely had to do. Most of all, I wanted to keep my mother from hearing my thoughts. Whenever it seemed she was tuning in on my thought waves, I purposely substituted nonsense words for my true thoughts, or intentionally scrambled the words as they came to me. But in the process, my thoughts sometimes got so hopelessly jumbled that I needed to write them down to straighten them out for my own comprehension. To keep anyone from being able to read the thoughts I was writing, I invented a private code of original characters symbolizing letters, words, phrases, and tenses all mixed up in such a way that no one could possibly break it. On paper it looked like endless columns of nonsensical symbols.

My thoughts weren't the only thing giving me trouble. My perceptions had changed. I had become vaguely aware of colored patterns decorating the air. When I first noticed them, I realized I had actually been seeing them for a long time, yet never paid attention to them before. I thought that everyone saw them, that they were a visual equivalent to background noise, like a fan's hum that goes unnoticed. These patterns, composed of tiny spicules and multicolored squiggly lines, wiggled and wormed their way around and through each other like people milling in a crowd. The patterns looked like what I imagined the visual equivalent of radio static to be, so I called them Interference Patterns. At times they intensified, sweeping across the front of my eyes like a veil, madly decorating everything I looked at.

Occasionally the Interference Patterns reflected visual sounds, altering their conformation to the changing quality of, say, the sound of a lead pencil scribbling across paper. A sneeze or a door slamming might release an explosion of associated designs and colors into the air. By an odd coincidence of the senses, I was actually *seeing* sounds. I doodled endlessly in the margins of my school papers, trying to reproduce the intricate shapes of the Interference Patterns I saw. I labeled the drawings "Sneeze" or "Door Slamming" or what-

ever it was that had provoked the particular pattern. Although
the titles on my drawings were perfectly understandable to
me, they would have been total nonsense to anyone else.

Seeing sounds was unlike anything I had ever experienced
or even imagined. This phenomenon had to be cosmic. I decided I must have done something to evoke a leak from other
planes of existence, allowing cosmic Interference Patterns to
spill into this world. But I could discover no connections. I
was baffled. I would have to accept the interference as another of life's many mysteries.

I was surprised that the voices offered no comments to explain the interference phenomenon. Surely they understood
what it was all about. All they would say, in a taunting manner, was "Things are not what they seem." The voices knew
the truth: my schoolteacher was indeed a kidnapper, sparrows were really attack birds, my mother was a mind reader.
No, nothing was quite what it appeared to be on the surface.
All existence was merely a thin membrane covering a greater,
hidden reality. The voices and the Interference Patterns represented leakage from a greater, parallel plane of existence
pouring into the ordinary experience shared by most people.
Except most people weren't attuned as sharply as I had become to picking up supernatural clues. Given the right tools,
such as faith, prayer, and awareness of the farthest extremes
of life, one might have occasional glimpses into the wonderful world that lay beyond. I was convinced that I was on the
verge of something big.

One night I was awakened by a man calling my name. A
powerful presence filled my bedroom. I opened my eyes.
There was Jesus, standing over me, right next to my bed.
Next to Jesus, I felt so minuscule that I couldn't even *begin*
to comprehend Him, much less appreciate His greatness.
The intensity of His presence horrified me. I wasn't ready
for Him yet. I was too weak. "Go away," I said, pulling the
covers over my head.

When I peeked out from under the covers a few minutes later, Jesus was gone. I threw off the covers and sat up. I was shaking. My pajamas were soaked with sweat. The intensity of this experience reminded me of the Popeye arms and ghosts I had seen as a child. It occurred to me that maybe Jesus could have explained some of life's mysteries to me. I would have liked to talk to Him, but I had been too scared. Why had such a potentially positive experience terrified me so? Probably because my faith was still defective, I thought. I would have to work on it.

Life is a prayer, life is a prayer, life is a prayer. The thought consoled me. I would seek to live every moment as a prayer, full of pureness and holiness. That way, no evil forces could possibly penetrate my life.

I became further preoccupied with trying to understand the greater reality that I thought existed. I didn't know what it was, but I was convinced it was there. I felt compelled to comprehend it and to try to integrate it with the rest of my experience. It monopolized all my thoughts all the time, whatever I was doing. In class, my eyes would lock into a comfortable stare, and off I would drift for hours, my mind traveling in search of far dimensions.

My distant stare became so habitual that when I talked to people, I would stare at them, unblinking, not moving or glancing away every few seconds as people normally do. At those moments, I felt that I penetrated the inner spirit of the other person and connected with the greater reality of the universe. Then the Interference Patterns would sweep across my visual screen and break everything up.

My classmates whispered about me. "She's weird," they said. "Like, wow, you know, she's *intense*."

My experiences seemed to confirm that vestiges of the greater reality of the universe, as I thought of it, lay immediately in front of me, right in this world. To find them, I merely had to be alert and look for them. They were disguised in subtle nuances of ordinary perceptions, in the form of Interference Patterns, voices, and hidden meanings. My wordly understanding was clearly changing, growing.

When Charley came home from his freshman year at college during spring break, I could see that he too had changed. At college, free from Mom's disapproval, Charley had let his hair grow down to his shoulders, and he was now wearing faded bell-bottom blue jeans and paisley shirts. He looked just like pictures of college campus hippies I had admired. I knew that hippies were into drugs, but Charley didn't want to talk about that. I wanted to be like Charley. I bought a pair of hip-hugger bell-bottom blue jeans and a wide leather belt, then topped off the outfit with an embroidered headband to hold my long, straight brown hair in place.

I was curious about drugs. Drugs users claimed they got new insights about the universe during their drug experiences. Scared as I was to try drugs, I had to know. I bought two marijuana joints from a school acquaintance and tried smoking them alone in the woods near my house. The smoke seared my eyes, burned my airways, and made me cough, but I didn't experience anything I thought would resemble a high.

One day when Mom came upstairs from the basement she said to me, "It smells strange down in the laundry room, like burned rope. Do you think Charley is using drugs down there?"

"Oh, no," I said. "I'm sure Charley would never use drugs." I didn't want to rat on my brother if that's what he was doing. I knew *I* wasn't smoking pot in the basement. But perhaps she was smelling an odor lingering on me from when I had used the marijuana. After all, if my thoughts could drift into her brain, then maybe odors could, too.

"Well," Mom said, "I've never smelled anything like that before."

I told Charley about the incident.

"It's uncanny," he said. "She knows everything. It's like she's a mind reader."

I didn't tell him I knew for sure Mom was a mind reader. He wouldn't have believed me unless I explained to him how I knew, and I wasn't prepared to do that.

A school classmate, Michael, had told me that he smoked pot regularly. When I expressed interest in trying it, he promised he would let me know when he got hold of some good pot. One evening when Mom and Dad were out, Michael called.

"Hey, ya wanna get high?" he asked.

"Tonight?"

"Yeah," he said. "I've got some *hash*. It's really good shit. It's so good I think maybe it's laced with opium or something."

I was intensely curious. I didn't tell him I'd tried marijuana once before and failed to experience anything. If he had strong enough pot it might get me high—yet the idea of such strong drugs also scared me. My curiosity prevailed, and I said, "All right! Do you think I'll get stoned my first time?"

We drove around town in his car while inhaling hits off his homemade hash pipe, then we went to his house to listen to records. This time I did get stoned, with no difficulty. Gradually, my perceptions grew excruciatingly intense, and the experience turned frightening.

As we listened to the Beatles singing "Here Comes the Sun," I saw a glowing sun mushrooming out of the darkness. It switched back and forth between being a good sun and an evil sun threatening to engulf me. The sun seemed cosmic, oozing into this world from a parallel plane of existence.

"It's all right now," the Beatles sang, momentarily reassuring me. I was relieved every time the music stopped after a song to give me a chance to recover before the next one.

I glanced over at Michael. He was leaning back on his bed

with his eyes shut, apparently lost in enjoyment of the music and the high.

I was glad he wasn't talking, because I didn't think I could coordinate my speech to respond. Stoned on pot, I found even simple physical movement—standing, sitting—to be amazingly difficult.

Being stoned made things seem different in an indescribable way. The feeling that *things are not as they seem* permeated everything. Even trivialities like the shape of a dirt mark on the wall exuded a sense of such overwhelming significance that, I imagined, underneath all this immediately apparent meaning lay far deeper Meaning. I had discovered Meanings beyond Meanings, all pointing to a cosmic dual reality. I had no idea what the meanings were, but I sensed their presence intensely. Although I'd vaguely felt this way before, I'd never experienced it quite like this. My marijuana-aided insights confirmed my impression that there truly was a greater reality beyond everyday comprehension.

By the time Michael took me home, the drug effects had faded. Exhausted from the marijuana, I fell into bed and dropped right off to sleep.

The next day I felt more normal, although a certain sharpness to my senses still lingered. The Interference Patterns seemed brighter or somehow more prominent than usual. The feeling that *things are not as they seem* remained with me. My ordinary awareness had been heightened by the marijuana experience. Yes, there really were things going on in another plane of existence. And drugs could open the door to that other existence.

Alone, I "smoked up" a few more times. I learned to be aware of the early signs of being high, so that I could quit smoking before I was stoned out of my mind and scared. Each time I got stoned I felt I came closer to understanding the ultimate reality. I fully expected that one of these times I would suddenly awaken to Enlightenment.

When stoned on pot I became very quiet. If I said anything at all, it felt to me like lengthy discourse. People sometimes surprised me by remarking how quiet I was at times when I wasn't aware of being overly quiet, even when I wasn't stoned. I decided I'd had enough of drugs for a while. Anyway, it seemed that I'd gained all the insights I was going to get from smoking marijuana. I had no further interest in it. My brain, now drug-free, continued to rev away in neutral, producing no spontaneous material. Eventually my thoughts thinned out so far that I could find nothing at all to say. Meanwhile, my perceptions magnified. My mind, a vacuum, slipped into a state of Pure Perception; environmental stimuli constantly bombarded my senses with unrelenting, nearly unbearable intensity. The rustling of a book's page turning produced paroxysms of Interference Patterns materializing out of the air, capturing my total awareness.

I was puzzled that changes in my perceptions were still occurring when I wasn't smoking marijuana. At school, trying to maintain a normal external appearance despite my secret perceptual confusion required my constant attention. For years I had been practicing mental gymnastics and developing special techniques to appear normal to others, when in actuality nothing had been normal. I had devised elaborate schemes to check things out to determine whether or not they were real without seeming obvious to others. I had also learned to be careful not to talk back to the voices when other people were around. Up to now my techniques had been nearly flawless. I had managed to integrate my special private experiences into the mundane routine of daily living, without much friction. But now, with my advancing internal chaos, I would have to strengthen and refine my skills in order to succeed in the ordinary world. The regular world still meant a lot to me, and I would have to work harder to fit my new experiences into it smoothly.

The voices, reflecting my confusion, kept up running commentaries among themselves. Usually they stayed in the distant background, chattering away nonsensically, like people at a cocktail party in the next room. I generally didn't pay their conversation much attention, but when I heard them talking about me I couldn't help listening in.

"She's in here," I heard one of the voices say.

"She's on that side," said another voice.

What side? I thought. I knew they were talking about me, but I didn't understand what they were saying. I strained to hear every word. I didn't want to be last to know the ultimate truths.

"Come to our side," one of the voices enticed me. "You're confused. We know. We have the answers."

How did they know all that? If they really did, then they must have cosmic connections. Their words rang of the truth.

"What do I have to do?" I asked.

"Dispense with life as you know it."

"Why?"

"You won't need it, there's so much more."

"But how?"

"Pull the plug on the machinery."

"What?"

"Your body. It's a machine . . . lean . . . green . . . obscene . . ."

Rhymes or no, I hadn't thought of it that way. They knew all too well. I needed relief from the weight of cosmic significance swirling through my brain. I would have to do it. My current existence was frighteningly painful.

"How do I do it?" I demanded to know.

Silence. I understood their silence to mean that I was supposed to think of a way on my own. This was my territory, not theirs. Their job didn't start until after I had accomplished my mission.

I didn't have the guts to resort to violent means such as jumping in front of a speeding train or leaping from a tall building. I didn't have access to pills or guns. All I could think of was a razor blade in a hot tub. I remembered having heard about that method, maybe on TV or in a magazine. Without thinking anything through, I locked myself in the bathroom. The details wouldn't matter once I had achieved my objective.

I drew the razor edge swiftly across the inside of my wrist, creating a thin red line in my skin. The line fell partway open and filled with blood. There was sharp pain.

Blood! Pain! I hadn't expected this. Much as I tried, I couldn't continue. I was chicken.

"Stupid," the voices criticized. "You blew your chance."

I began to cry. I couldn't even kill myself properly. A drop of blood ran down my hand and fell into the tub. It looked so real; in fact, it looked more real than real. It was so intense it was frightening. I felt the intensity of my own action, the intensity of everything in my life, come crashing down on my head without mercy. I didn't know how to bear this.

Suddenly I realized that if I had killed myself, I would have smashed through reality to the other side, whatever it was. Perhaps I might even have met God. I wasn't ready for that kind of intensity yet. I was only a seventeen-year-old girl. I wasn't prepared to confront the mysteries of the universe directly. I would have to wait until I was more sophisticated to try to comprehend infinity.

I covered my wrist with a bandage, hiding it under long-sleeved blouses. In a few days the cut healed. My parents wouldn't have to know. I could never explain what I had tried to do.

For several days afterward I was despondent. I knew I was afraid to plunge into infinity, yet I was scared to keep on going the way I was. There was no way out.

I couldn't concentrate on my schoolwork. It was insignificant next to the cosmic matters I was facing. I felt trapped, and there were no solutions. I went to my school counselor.

"I don't like my classes" was the most I could manage to tell her.

"What kind of problems are you having?" she asked.

"Mostly problems with my parents," I told her.

It was true; I thought my mother was reading my thoughts. I often glared at my mother with hostile eyes. She glared back at me. I had been practicing thought-scrambling so much at home that now my thoughts were starting to come out scrambled spontaneously, and I didn't even have to try anymore to produce nonsense. And sometimes when I couldn't produce any thoughts at all, I blamed my mother for stealing them right out of my mind. Yes, I was having problems with my mother.

Just then the voices opened the door to the counselor's office so fast they couldn't be seen, said "Go to hell!" and shut it again. I whipped around to face the door. The counselor looked, too.

"What was that?" she asked.

"People I know," I said. "But I didn't get to see them."

The counselor referred me to a psychiatrist.

I knew very little about psychiatrists. I pictured a middle-aged man, someone who couldn't possibly understand the mysteries that were troubling me. But then I considered that a psychiatrist must have completed at least eleven or twelve years of schooling. He would be one of the most educated people anywhere: a learned man. And with all those years of schooling, he ought to know as much as anyone about the far reaches of the universe. He might have some information that could help me. But I had to be careful how I said things. A psychiatrist might view people who try to kill themselves as mentally ill. I was certain I wasn't mentally ill. There was a distinction: mine was a case of torment caused by my selective sensitivity to planes of existence beyond ordinary reality. The point of my actions hadn't been expressly to kill myself—that wasn't what was important. The real issue was my need to break through to the ultimate reality. I would approach the psychiatrist for answers, while couching my real concerns in discussion of suicide. It was worth a try. I didn't know what else to do.

"What kind of problems have you been having?" Dr. Marshall asked me.

"Problems with school and problems with my parents."

Dr. Marshall looked puzzled. "Can you tell me more?"

This was going to be tough. I didn't even know how to start to explain my real concerns. I didn't know what questions to ask. After a very long pause, I said, "I haven't been able to tell anyone this before." I was trying to buy another moment, hoping I could formulate my questions.

Dr. Marshall looked impatient. "Well, why don't you try telling me."

I didn't know how to start. How do you tell an ordinary human about something so extraordinary as awareness of a parallel reality?

Before I was able to answer him, he interjected, "Do you have any friends you can talk to?"

I shook my head.

"Well, who do you talk to about what's bothering you?"

I shook my head again. I couldn't seem to start talking. I didn't think I could possibly tell him I talked to voices. Already it seemed that this meeting wasn't going to be too productive. Dr. Marshall asked me several questions about my friends, school, and family. I answered each question briefly, as accurately as I could, trying to avoid exposing any of my scrambled thoughts. No, I didn't socialize with a lot of friends; other people didn't seem to understand me. No, I wasn't in serious academic difficulty at school, I just couldn't concentrate on the work. Yes, my parents were a problem; my mother was critical of everything. I couldn't seem to find a way to crack the barrier to the important issues.

"How old are you?" he asked.

"Seventeen."

"Hmm." He scratched his head. "I'd like to prescribe you some medication, but since you're underage, I can't do it without your parents' consent."

"I can't tell them about this," I said. I was adamant.

"Come back and see me in a month," Dr. Marshall said.

A month later nothing had changed, and he still wanted to prescribe medication. I still refused to allow my parents to know I was seeing a psychiatrist.

"Well then, I can't help you," he said. "You need medication."

I didn't think I needed medication. Dr. Marshall wasn't going to be able to give me the help I needed. I thanked him and left, never to return to his office. But I was genuinely grateful to him for having spared me some of his valuable time.

Years later when I read my medical reports, I saw he had diagnosed me as a "schizoid personality." Schizoids are loners who lack the capacity to express warm feelings. Psychotic symptoms such as delusions and hallucinations do not occur in schizoids, as they do in schizophrenics, who are far more severely ill individuals. Schizoid tendencies by themselves would not automatically make a doctor think of schizophrenia.

Dr. Marshall hadn't asked me about hearing voices, and I didn't know how to tell him. So he never obtained sufficient information even to consider schizophrenia.

Despite my difficulties, I continued to achieve. I was chosen as one of the few students of my junior class to join the National Honor Society a year early. Even so, I felt I should be doing better. Since I was studying as hard as I possibly could, I should have been making straight A's. But no matter how hard I tried, I couldn't avoid an occasional B.

I had always known that I wanted to go to college. From what I'd observed, being a housewife wasn't for me. I didn't want to spend my life attending to screaming kids and cleaning house, day in and day out. I could find something more meaningful to do with my life. Mom and Dad had both gone to college, and somehow I felt that was expected of me. Judi, Ed, and now Charley had all gone to college. Judi and Ed had both graduated Phi Beta Kappa. I couldn't imagine doing that. But I knew that I wanted to succeed on my own merits, not those of some future husband. I planned to build a career of my own to provide personal satisfaction and direction for my life.

I was grateful to graduate ninth out of my high school class of five hundred. It was the very best I could do. I had earned a cumulative 3.82 grade point average. I wished in the worst way that I could have made a perfect 4.00.

"We're proud of you," Mom and Dad both told me. And they meant it.

All I knew was that I was glad to graduate, because soon I would be able to get away from home to go to college, out from under my mother's watchful eye.

CHAPTER FOUR

COLLEGE

To me, merely graduating near the top of my high school class didn't mean all that much, especially since Riverside High was an ordinary school in a small town. Besides, I didn't consider my difficulties with the Parallel Dimensions to be a handicap. It didn't occur to me to think I'd done anything out of the ordinary in achieving good grades despite the distractions of the voices and Interference Patterns and all their attendant phenomena.

School was supposed to get harder the farther you advanced. I couldn't imagine anything more difficult than high school. So I didn't expect that I could possibly do as well in college, competing against so many brilliant minds. But I knew I would have to work even harder, if that was possible. I was prepared to do that.

"You should try to do your best," my parents had always said. "Then no matter how things turn out, you can always be proud of yourself."

I'd never felt my best was sufficient. I lived under self-imposed pressure to do better than my best, to excel no matter what personal sacrifice might be required. I didn't feel as capable as I imagined my peers to be. I didn't see myself as abnormal or handicapped, but simply as not intelligent enough. To succeed, I felt I had to make up for my deficits by working hard. That would mean no parties, no drugs, no drinking, and no lying around—instead, grinding away at the books every spare minute to get ahead while everybody else was out partying. That was fine with me. The way to get ahead in life was to keep being tough long after the softies had given in. I'd never been afraid of hard work; I thrived on it.

In August my parents drove me to the state university in Cedar City. Now that I would be ninety miles away from home, I hoped my mother would no longer be able to read my mind. And I hoped the voices had remained in Riverside.

I opened the door to my new dorm room. Feet propped up comfortably in front of the television, an overweight girl sat staring at the screen, munching potato chips between puffs on a cigarette.

"Hi, I'm Carol," I said.

"I'm Mary Ann," she said, pulling herself away from her soap opera. "Well, c'mon in and unload your stuff."

My parents helped me move in all my clothes and boxes of belongings. Then they kissed me and left for home.

I sat down to chat with Mary Ann. I hoped we would be good friends. After a while I went shopping and bought several pairs of blue jeans. Now I was equipped for college.

The following day I went to registration for my classes. Most of the classes I signed up for were required courses. I'd taken a pass-out exam the year before. (If you passed, you were "out" of the course.) Because of my scores, I was exempted from all but one science requirement; to fulfill it, I chose astronomy. I was still interested in learning more about the universe and the worlds beyond.

The next day I bought all my books and went to my new

classes. The auditoriums—bursting with five hundred students or more—were overwhelming. I wondered how I could ever match up to all these brilliant people.

My last class of the day was modern dance. Stripped down to my leotard and tights, feeling self-conscious and exposed, I entered the gym. Several young women clad in leotards had already congregated in the middle of the room. They stood primping in front of the mirror, warming up and stretching out, pointing their toes, practicing fancy steps they knew, pulling the elastic of their leotards over the tops of their hipbones. Others sat cross-legged in a circle at the edge of the room, talking, looking very prim, their hair done up in neat little buns. They appeared to be friends from classes together last year. Their voices bounced strange echoes off the two-story ceiling, imparting a surrealistic touch to the whole scene. Suddenly I felt I'd made a mistake, that I didn't belong here in this class.

"Last year I danced with the Elmont Carroll Dance Company in New York," said one woman.

"Oh, lovely," said another. "I've danced in New York for twelve years. Now I want to go to San Francisco. I'm starting up my own company there."

Wow. I didn't tell them I'd danced for ten years in a tiny dance studio in my hick hometown. My stomach was tying itself up in knots. I was going to look foolish trying to keep up with these other dancers. Yes, signing up for this class had clearly been a mistake.

The teacher entered the room and clapped her hands. "Okay, let's get started," she said. The pianist began to play, and we began to dance. After so many years of studying classical ballet, I found it awkward trying to turn my feet in instead of out, and to flex my ankles instead of pointing my toes. But I'd studied some jazz dance back home, so at least the departure from strict ballet principles wasn't totally foreign to me. And I possessed enough flexibility and balance from being so well grounded in ballet that I had no trouble kicking my feet high into the air and executing the complicated turns. The workout was difficult, but I found I could do it, just barely. My flexibility would allow me in time to learn to contort my body into all the weird modern dance positions with ease. Several of the dancers appeared to be having considerably more difficulty than I was. I didn't feel so bad now. If I worked to my maximum, I would survive modern dance. Every day after dance class I practiced my new routines for two hours back at the dorm before hitting the books for the evening.

At a party after the first week of classes, I met a terrific guy, a junior named Steve. He was from Riverside, too, and had even gone to Riverside High. We were crazy about each other and soon became inseparable. I spent more time in Steve's room than in my own, and soon I even began sleeping there with him. Evenings, we ate supper and studied together till he had to go to work at one of his two part-time jobs and I had to go to rehearsal for *The Music Man,* the annual campus musical, in which I was a dancer. After rehearsal I'd study a while longer till Steve got off, and then we would meet at the bars and drink till closing time, eventually staggering back to the dorms. Women weren't allowed in the men's dorm after midnight, but Steve would sneak me in and then we would smoke pot half the night in his room and I'd stay till morning. His roommates were usually staying out all night with different women. Between studying and going out with Steve, I probably averaged only four hours of sleep a night. I felt exhausted, but incredibly happy to be able to do all my schoolwork and have a good time too. Mom seemed to be out of mind-reading range, and I felt truly on my own for the first time in my life.

During my first few weeks at college, the voices were curiously absent. I was beginning to think they had remained back home, along with the Interference Patterns. I decided that mature college women didn't hear voices or see patterns in the air, and now I had become one of those mature women. I later realized I hadn't left the voices at home at all, that they were still with me, mumbling softly while I was concentrating on my books, or chattering away to each other in the background. In the midst of all the new campus stimulation and excitement, I'd mistaken the voices for conversations of nearby students. I didn't pay them much attention, because they weren't talking to me and thus constituted only a minor distraction.

One evening when Steve and I were lying around in my room watching TV, drinking beer, and smoking pot with Mary Ann, the unpleasant feeling that *things are not as they seem* crept over me. The television blared away mercilessly, blasting the gunshot noises and tense music of a late-night western movie across the room at me. I glanced over at Mary Ann and Steve. The flickering white light from the TV screen bathed their faces in cadaverous shades of pale. I realized that special relativity had seized the world (I'd been studying Einstein's Theory of Relativity in astronomy class), and transported all people through time and space into the realm of the dead. Only somehow I hadn't made it; I had been dropped off prematurely in limbo, in a parallel existence where I was able to see what had happened to everyone else and yet was incapable of doing anything about it. The presence of evil filled the room, surrounding me on all sides.

Perhaps I had allowed this to happen by weakening, by allowing evil influences to enter the world through me to establish their control. I mentally tried to switch everything back to its usual state, the way in school I'd learned to flip fuzzy objects in and out of focus on the microscope by adjusting my eyes. No matter how hard I tried now, things remained *not as they seem*. Maybe this wasn't in my mind. It had gone beyond that now.

The TV continued to blare away. I was unable to change things back to normal. There was nothing I could do. When

I tried to move, I was overcome by a sensation of falling into a bottomless pit. I continued to lie there on the bed, bombarded by the TV noise, passively watching everything happen. This was more real than real, too horrible for words. I was caught in Pure Perception, where external stimuli overwhelmed my senses, rendering my brain incapable of producing thoughts or initiating movements.

I fought to overcome my state. Summoning all my effort and more, I whispered faintly, "Steve."

He didn't hear me.

"Steve," one of the voices taunted.

I managed to repeat, louder, "Steve."

Steve turned his head toward me. "What is it?" he said softly.

I didn't want to tell him, but I had to. "I'm scared," I said.

He looked puzzled. "Scared? What of?"

I didn't know what to say. I was scared of the TV, the evil forces, the Man from Glad on the commercial. I didn't know how to tell Steve. "Please make it all stop," I whispered, not particularly to Steve, but in prayer to the universe.

"Make what stop?" he said. "The TV? Is it scaring you?"

I nodded. I couldn't say anything more.

Steve looked over at Mary Ann, who was lying silently, very still, on her bed. Her eyes appeared to be closed. "Mary Ann," Steve said into the room's darkness, "are you awake?"

No answer.

"Mary Ann, do you mind if we turn off the TV set?"

Still no answer.

"Do you want me to turn the TV off?" Steve asked me.

I was too frightened to talk, so I just nodded.

Steve got up and flicked the off button. "There," he said. "Now that's better. What a noisy movie."

I agreed. Maybe now the quiet would allow me to gain more control over my mind, to gather strength against the world's evil.

Steve and I lay there quietly for a long time, holding hands. He was my strength, my protector. When Steve was around, my physical barrier against evil tripled in thickness.

Finally he said, "I should go now. I have to get up at six to get to my cafeteria job."

He kissed me and slipped out the door. For a long time, I lay silently on my bed, still in my clothes, praying to God to protect me from evil. The voices talked back to me, mostly muttering incoherent phrases. I was sure they were evil. Finally I fell asleep.

The next morning when I awoke I was still feeling vulnerable. I got out of bed, pulled on my coat, and threw an extra pair of jeans and a shirt into my backpack. Even though it was before visiting hours, I went over to Steve's room and pounded on his door. He had just returned from his cafeteria-line duties. When he opened his door, he looked surprised to see me. "Hi, what's up?" he said.

"Can I stay here with you for a while? I'm still scared."

"Sure," he said. He didn't ask any questions, he just accepted my wish.

I decided not to smoke any more pot or drink any more liquor. I wanted to clean up my system, to strengthen myself against evil. I would need all the help I could get, and getting stoned seemed only to make things worse. So when Steve smoked and drank, I just sat there.

To my disappointment, my sobriety didn't do anything to diminish the excess meaning or to silence the voices. One voice in particular spoke to me in an excessively reassuring manner, telling me that everything was going to be okay. I didn't know whether or not to trust this voice because it seemed so reassuring, *overly* reassuring, as if for some purpose of its own. The smooth tone of this voice reminded me of the computer Hal in the movie *2001: A Space Odyssey*. I remembered from the movie that Hal was devious, not to be trusted. The voice I was hearing now gave me that same gut feeling, but I shrugged the feeling off, instead sucking up his reassurances and ignoring my initial distrust.

For weeks I was unable to get to classes without Steve's support. Finally, he suggested, "Do you think you ought to see a psychiatrist?"

The thought hadn't occurred to me. I didn't consider psychiatrists to be particularly helpful individuals. "No," I said. "This doesn't involve my mind. This is far more serious."

"But how are you going to prepare for finals?" he said. "You can't seem to study at all."

He was absolutely right. I was horrified at the idea of not being able to study for finals. If I couldn't keep up in school, I would wreck my future. Somehow, I had to pull myself together so I could study. I agreed to go see a psychiatrist.

Steve called for an appointment with the psychiatry department of the university medical school, then he accompanied me to make sure I got there all right.

My "doctor" was a third-year medical student. "I'm Dr. Smith," he introduced himself, and then he took me into a little interviewing room where he asked me questions for an hour and a half. He seemed especially interested in the intimate details of my sex life. Then he performed a pelvic examination, the first I'd ever had. I was mortified. I was glad he had a nurse helping him, because she could understand what I was going through and she held my hand through the worst parts. Finally, he administered a written examination with six hundred and forty true-false questions, then sent me home with a bottle of Valium pills. Once again, I hadn't been able to reveal my deepest concerns to the doctor. All I had been able to tell him was that I was scared and unable to study well.

The Valium only made things worse. It made me so sleepy that I couldn't even read the first paragraph in my text before falling asleep. I quit taking it after two days, and without it I managed to study, though not very effectively. I tried to compensate for my inefficiency by working extra hard.

My final grades were all A's except for a B+ in religion. I was absolutely exhausted. Steve took his exams and made all A's and B's. Together we went home to Riverside for the Christmas holidays.

Steve and I spent Christmas Eve with his parents, sitting around the Christmas tree watching TV and playing cards. The voices chattered away in the background with suggestions of which cards to play, but I ignored them because they were stupid suggestions. I found Steve's parents just as friendly and engaging as Steve, and I couldn't help but like them. Later, Steve told me his parents thought I was "awful cute."

Steve and I spent Christmas night at my house with my parents. We sat around the fireplace listening to *Lawrence Welk Brings You a Merry Christmas* on the stereo. Steve was polite around my parents, and he talked in his usual stimulating way about many topics. As usual, I was impressed with him, and I hoped my parents would be, too.

Later, Mom told me, "I don't see what you see in Steve. Don't you think you could do better than that? He doesn't seem too bright, or too motivated to make much out of himself. Philosophy is interesting, and photography's a nice hobby, but neither one's a very realistic career for a college person."

"*Mom!*" I yelled at her. "How could you say such a thing? Just because he's not making straight A's? He's a lot smarter than I am! He's majoring in Eastern philosophy. He's holding down two jobs to put himself through school, and he's earning money with his photography! His parents are too poor to help him!"

She didn't say anything more.

I was sure that my mother was still reading my mind, uncovering my awful secrets. I didn't know why she didn't just confront me. Perhaps she was in cahoots with the Evil

Forces. She darted evil looks all around. I darted hostile looks back. Christmas vacation was no fun. Things seemed so much worse at home that I wished I were back at the dorm, where the atmosphere was at least more neutral. Unfortunately, classes wouldn't start for another ten days. I kept thinking that if I could get back to school early maybe I could reinforce myself against the next onslaught of sinister events.

Finally, I announced, "Mom, Dad, I want to go back to school now."

Mom looked aghast. "But your vacation isn't even half over yet. Why would you want to do that? There's nobody back there at school now."

I just shrugged, not knowing exactly what to say. "Guess I'm bored here," I lied. "I could do some research in the university library and get a head start on next semester's term paper."

They didn't argue with me. Mom did nothing but frown at me the next few days. It appeared that the Evil Forces had permeated her. I had to get away. It was a relief to hop into Steve's dirty, beat-up '63 Plymouth two days later for the ninety-minute drive back to school. On the trip, Steve cranked up the radio, but I noticed that not even loud songs could entirely drown the voices out. He lit up a pipe and passed it to me. I drew the smoke into my mouth, being careful not to inhale, held it for a while, then exhaled. Shrouded in the thick fog of marijuana smoke in Steve's car, we tooled down the interstate highway at eighty-five miles an hour, not fast enough to suit my desire to get back to school right away.

I found comfort in the quiet desolation of campus my first few days back before the students returned from Christmas break. Without all the noisy confusion and raucous parties, I began to relax.

In my more casual state of mind, I began to notice things in a more sensitive way than I ever had before. Campus evergreens burst into the most intense contrasts of lights and darks and shades of greens that I had ever seen. I wandered around campus looking at everything I possibly could with great wonderment, as if I were seeing it all for the first time. Like the fire in my childhood home, the sights were so intense that they were both horrible and spectacularly beautiful at the same time. Weighted down with the burden of Pure Perception, I had to move slowly and carefully. I spent hours marveling at the texture of the bricks on the buildings, at the intricate moving patterns of the moonlight on the river, at the folds of bark on trees, at designs dancing over the ballroom carpet in the Union, even at the fine weave in my jeans. These were no ordinary designs and patterns; they were pregnant with meaning, meaning that I didn't yet understand. I marveled that all this wonderful richness had actually been there all the time, but I had never appreciated it quite like this. It all pointed back to the familiar concept *things are not as they seem.*

I became so immersed in what I was doing that I didn't realize how ridiculous I must have looked bending down to examine and touch ordinary sidewalk cement. What no one else knew was that the cement had been secretly transformed into a wondrous substance, full of grains and lines, hieroglyphics, messages from worlds beyond, messages that I felt compelled to try to understand. The significance of my discoveries made how other people viewed me unimportant and irrelevant, in the way someone running to catch a bus doesn't care if his hair falls out of place. Late afternoons, I walked back and forth across the bridge over the river, basking in the sensation of the shadows from the railing bars flickering their patterns until the sun dropped too low in the sky to make crisp shadows.

I became so engrossed in perceptions that I forgot to move. Brush designs in the paint on the walls fascinated me for hours. The meaning of life had shifted. True meaning lay not in this world, but in the complex systems and parallel universes that lay beyond.

Steve came and went, eating meals and working at his jobs. Each time he arrived back at his room, he found me still lying there on the bed, staring at the wall, not moving a muscle. I didn't even have to change my gaze to change what I was seeing; the Interference Patterns did it all for me, crawling over everything, creating new designs in swirls and colorful fluxes with every changing moment of my environment. At times, I couldn't discern whether the voices I heard were merely extensions of my own thoughts or my old voices taking on new disguises and mimicking my present thoughts. The soothing Hal-voice remained with me constantly, offering up his false reassurances.

"Carol, what's the matter?" Steve asked.

"Nothing," the voices answered him for me.

Wow, what a trip I thought. Now I don't have to talk. They're doing it for me. I don't need to move or do anything. Everything's being taken care of for me.

"Carol? Won't you talk to me?"

Of course I'm talking to you, Steve. My thought waves were bouncing all over the room. This was a new advance in communication.

"Carol, let's go back to the hospital and see that doctor again. I think you need help."

I didn't try to disagree. He sat me up and helped me put on my socks and boots. Every new touch, every sensation on my skin sent paroxysms of patterns sweeping over the room. I let Steve guide me across the river to the hospital. I didn't need to command my walking; my legs moved like machines. The voices had programmed them for me. All I had to do was go along for the ride. Yes indeed, this was interesting.

Dr. Smith asked me a whole new set of questions. "Any problems with your toilet training? How's your sex life? Do you masturbate?"

I didn't need to answer him. The voices were providing all the answers, saying my own thoughts before I could even think them. They were taking care of everything.

The doctor looked at me. "Hmm, you're not being too helpful today." Then he disappeared and came back with a prescription for some antipsychotic pills.

Steve led me over to the pharmacy, then pocketed the bottle of pills and led me back to the dorm. "Here, take one of these," he told me. "No, take two, you need them."

I gulped down the pills with a sip of water. Before long, I felt enormously drugged. The patterns faded, my eyes closed, and I fell asleep without even taking off my boots.

The next day Steve accompanied me to registration for the spring semester. I declared dance as my major and signed up for another semester.

Before long, I was again lost in contemplation of the Interference Patterns I saw everywhere. I could barely move, hardly speak.

"I'm losing you, Carol," Steve said. "Please don't go away from me like this. I love you, I don't want you to leave me. I'm going to have to take you to the hospital. Don't be mad at me—I don't know what else to do."

No! Don't! Just let me lie here. If I move I'll fall into that time warp forever, and everything will be lost. Please, no!

He couldn't hear my silent screams. Kneeling beside the bed, he wrapped my arms around his neck. "Now, put your legs around my waist," he said, hoisting me onto his back piggy-back style, then standing up. I was powerless to resist. My limbs were petrified on his back, in rigor mortis. There would be no letting go.

Steve toted me down the three flights of dorm stairs and outside into the January night air. His breath formed ghosts that floated away on the air; my breath did nothing, proving that Steve was still here but I had departed to the Other Side. My God, I was no longer here. I would lose Steve for good. I felt I might cry, but I had no tears. My emotions were empty. I must have left them back in the regular world.

A campus bus pulled up to the corner, its thick black letters spelling out the familiar "CAMBUS" across its side. I had ridden the Cambus across the campus a hundred times; but this was not the Cambus I knew. It was the Cambus to infinity. Steve stepped up onto the bus with me.

When the driver saw me clinging to Steve's back, he said, "Aw, now ain't that cute—lovebirds!"

Steve sat down sideways in the first seat. Because he couldn't make me unlock my legs from around his waist, we rode the whole way like that. The other passengers tittered and snickered at the spectacle. I didn't feel embarrassed as I normally would have; it made no difference in the world to me, because I was no longer in this world. None of that mattered now.

CHAPTER FIVE

"PSYCHO"

The bus doors slammed shut behind us. Steve picked his way across the front lawn toward the old brick psychiatric hospital building that loomed ahead through the darkness. Steve struggled through the snow, carrying me toward the ghostly white light that illuminated the hospital's front door like a beacon for the lost. He was breathing heavily, each expired breath forming a crystal rainbow against the light before drifting away. As we approached the light at the end of the sidewalk, I could see swarms of dried-up ivy crawling around the edges of the ancient wooden door.

Wait, this is no hospital, I thought. This is some medieval mistake.

Steve rang the front bell. A woman in a blue short-sleeved jacket opened the door and welcomed us. Her eyes sparkled against the door's light.

We're here. I hope they can help. I hope to God the hospital is immune from the Evil Forces.

The walls engulfed us at funny angles. Even inside the

hospital the air was saturated with that colorful cosmic granularity and with the Interference Patterns. Steve unloaded me onto an easy chair in the waiting room, unwrapping my stiff arms and legs from around him.

Steve, where are you going? Don't leave me, I'll fall off. I'm on the edge of this precarious cliff, don't you see, and if I move one muscle fiber I'll fall off into the endless time warp. Steve, stay here, and hold up my world.

Far away my nose is itching. Never mind, it's only an existential itch. I left the real itch off at the last bus stop with my tears.

Itch. Who said that? Not I. It echoes in here it echoes in here it echoes in here.

"Carol, is that your name? Carol?" Snap, a man in white snapping rubber fingers right in front of my face, twelve colors radiating off them like sunrise in the Grand Canyon.

I screamed in my thought waves, *Damn it, stop that, stop killing me, here I am torn by terror into billion dimension-spaces and you are doing a cosmic watercolor in front of my eyes.*

Now I was a hunk of red meat bumping along on a butcher cart under long rows of white lights and institutional ceiling tiles flashing by, accelerating to the speed of light and beyond, into special-special-special relativity. A set of double doors swallowed me headfirst. *Is this the entrance to Infinity? Here goes . . .*

"She's not with it," I heard someone say. "Let's get her clothes off."

Hey! Wait a minute! I'm modest! I didn't say that . . . did I? Hey! Stop it!

Ignoring my silent screams, the man in white unzipped my jeans. *No, don't move me, don't send me over the brink! Steve, help me! Where are you?*

"Don't you worry," said one of my voices. "We're here with you. We've taken care of Steve, too." The voice laughed hideously.

"Aw, shuddup," a second voice answered the first. Then to me the voice said, "Don't listen to him. Listen to me."

Yet another voice said, "Three hundred milligrams in five see-sees water oughta do it." It sounded like the man in white talking, though I couldn't be sure. I was getting all these voices mixed up.

"Okay, let's stick the medicine in her vein now," he said.

No, no drugs, please. I haven't done anything bad!

My last words bounced around the tiny examining room, garbled over by everything else being said by many voices.

Ow! Someone jabbed a needle into my right arm, on the inside of my elbow. They'd done it now, they'd pushed me off the edge into infinity. . . .

I closed my eyes and waited for the trip. The room began to twirl.

Next I felt a hand pinching my right eyebrow, hard. A husky voice connected to the pincher-fingers said, "Are you with us?"

I looked up to see an overweight, gray-haired, bearded doctor staring into my face from six inches away. The voice sounded closer than before. "We're going to help you sit up now."

Things didn't look any better from the vertical perspective. The room was still turning.

"How do you feel?" he asked impatiently.

I reached up and touched my hand to my face, and it felt normal. No sunrises, no Grand Canyon, no echoes. "Okay," I said timidly. Still no echoes.

"What happened to make you like this?" he asked.

"Where's Steve?" I was afraid he was lost somewhere in another universe.

"We sent him home," he said. "You're going to have to stay here awhile."

I touched my face again, just to make sure it was still real. I hadn't fallen over any brink. "What did you do? I'm better. . . ."

"We gave you a little medicine to help you move. Now, can you tell us what's going on with you?"

I looked around at those surrounding me: the doctor in his long white coat, the orderly in whites, three nurses—all staring, as though I were on display. Drugged, my eyes faded out of focus, and the world drifted into double images. I let my eyelids droop shut and my head fall forward. The world disappeared.

"Carol, wake up." I felt hands jerking on my arms. "Talk to us."

I opened my eyes, and everything looked the way it did when I had drunk too much. I tried to read the nametag on the doctor's white coat pocket, but it wouldn't come into focus. On the wall, glassed-in cabinets held all sorts of terrible-looking equipment: syringes, tubes, glass bottles, swabs, scalpels, speculums, devices that looked fully capable of medieval torture.

"Merry Christmas to you," said one of my voices.

I looked at the doctor, then at the nurse. Neither of them appeared to have said anything. I looked behind me, to see only blank wall. So—it wasn't that easy to get rid of those voices. I smiled.

The doctor looked at the nurses; the nurses looked at the doctor and nodded.

"Are you hearing voices?" the doctor asked.

I smiled again. He would never understand all the cosmic significance filling up the world. There was no point in trying to explain it.

"Tell him no," one of my voices told me. "He could use that information to kill you."

The voices knew best. I shook my head no. "I'm ready to go home now," I said, unable to keep from slurring my words.

"Sorry," said the doctor. "You'll have to stay here. We need you to sign this voluntary admission form." He handed me a clipboard and a pen.

What I really wanted was my clothes, and to get out of there.

I looked at the paper on the clipboard. The words blurred and floated into doubles across the page. "Where do I sign?" I said.

"Sign here." The doctor made a big X on the page. I signed by the X.

An aide popped in the door and asked me, "Is your boyfriend a tall blond guy named Steve?"

"Yeah," I said. "Where is he?"

"Well, he hasn't left after all. He's still out in the dayroom. Would you like to see him now?"

"Yes."

The nurse helped me off the examining table. "Here are your clothes."

The doctor said, "While you're getting dressed, I'd like to catch a few words with Steve, okay?" Then he departed.

It took an eternity to get my pants buckled up and get my shirt on straight. I was so drugged that I needed help from a nurse, who then led me out into the dayroom. The doctor had finished talking to Steve and had left. I found Steve sitting in the dayroom on a black vinyl couch decorated with old cigarette burns. I sat down next to Steve, and he put his arm around me and kissed me. "You'll be okay here," he reassured me. "They're going to help you."

"What did the doctor say to you?" I wanted to know.

"Not much. He wants you to take some medicine."

Steve wasn't telling me what the doctor had really said to him.

"What's the matter with my girlfriend?" Steve had asked.

Without looking directly at him, the doctor had said, "She's a catatonic schizophrenic." The doctor felt an obligation to answer Steve honestly, whether or not it meant transgressing my legal right to confidentiality as a mental patient.

"Schizophrenic?" Steve repeated. "You mean, like a split personality? I don't think she's like that."

Still looking past Steve toward the far side of the room, the doctor explained, "Schizophrenia isn't a split personality. It's a split from reality, and believe me, buddy, your girlfriend's got it bad."

Steve stared at the buttons on the front of the doctor's white coat, as though getting a visual grasp on the buttons would help him grasp the doctor's words. "How bad? What's her prognosis?"

The doctor looked him right in the eye. "You really want to know? I'll be frank. Your girlfriend's never going to get better. She's probably going to be this way for the rest of her life, or worse. She'll probably end up permanently institutionalized."

Steve swallowed, hard. The swallow stuck in his throat. He was momentarily unable to speak.

The doctor laid a heavy hand on Steve's shoulder. "Look, if I were you, I'd forget her. If you want my advice, that's it. You ought to get out now, before you get in too deep. Her situation is essentially hopeless. Sorry, I've got other work to do now." He turned and strode away.

Steve stared at the diminishing white figure until the doctor stepped through the door and it closed solidly behind him. Did the doctor maliciously wish to destroy the last vestiges of hope for me and those around me? Or did he think he was doing Steve a favor in giving him some privileged information and advice?

Now as I sat beside Steve, he lied to me. "The doctor said you're going to be okay," he told me. "With time and with therapy." He gave my shoulders a squeeze with his arm. He was trying to convince himself just as much as he was trying to reassure me.

Suddenly a nurse interrupted us. "That kind of behavior isn't permitted in the dayroom," she said curtly.

Steve took his arm from around my shoulder and moved a few inches away from me on the couch.

"I hope this kind of behavior won't repeat itself," she said, then marched away to monitor other patients' activities.

A small thin man, unshaven and wearing only a hospital robe, stepped up onto a footstool in the middle of the dayroom and began to sing "Glory Hallelujah!" at gradually increasing volume and intensity. He seemed unaware of anyone else around him. "I'm Christ," he said, to no one in particular.

The nurse returned and pulled him down from the stool.

"Where is my crown of thorns?" he yelled as the nurse and two orderlies dragged him out of the dayroom and off down the hall toward the Quiet Room.

"Visiting hours are over," the nurse said when she came back. "And it's bedtime. You will have to abide by the rules here."

"Guess I'll have to go," Steve said. "I'll be back to see you tomorrow." He kissed me. The nurse walked him to the door.

I got up and followed them. I wanted to go out and watch Steve fade off into the snow at the start of his long trek back to the dorm.

The door had locked behind him. Did you have to have a key to get out? Was I locked in? When I had signed that paper, I hadn't been aware that locked doors were going to be a part of the deal.

"Come away from the door," the nurse said. Then, smiling, "Don't you know you're on a locked ward? You won't be going anywhere tonight." She reached down and jangled the set of keys clipped to her belt. "You look tired. You want to go to bed now?"

I cooperated, backing slowly away from the door, because I didn't know what else to do. I didn't want to break any rules.

"Would you like a tour of your new home?" the nurse

said. "I've got some time now. Is there anything I can get you? A toothbrush?"

I avoided looking at her, avoided answering any questions. Obediently, I followed her around on the tour. She led me down each of the three different hallways that took off like spokes from the hub of the dayroom.

"Here's your ward," the nurse said, pointing to a large open room with about twenty old-fashioned steel-framed hospital beds lined in rows along the walls. "The second bed is yours."

I walked over to the bed, and discovered the word "PSYCHO" stamped over the bedspread in large black letters. I pulled down the cover to find "PSYCHO" stamped on the pillowcase and on each blanket and crisp white sheet.

"Here's a hospital gown for you to wear to bed," the nurse said, handing me a folded gown. I unfolded it to reveal a traditional open-in-the-back hospital gown with "PSYCHO" stamped across the front in the same large letters.

"I'll show you the rest of the ward," the nurse said. She led me to the women's bathroom. Three toilets and two showers stood exposed in their open stalls, without any doors. No privacy here.

Next she led me past the nursing station with its open half-door. "This is where you'll line up to get your medicines," she told me. Across the hall, the cafeteria was closed and dark. "Mealtimes are precisely at seven, eleven-fifteen, and four-thirty," she told me. "Don't be late to meals, because we lock it up as soon as everyone is finished, and you won't get to eat till the next meal."

It was becoming clear to me that here you had to eat when they told you to, sleep when they told you to, get up when they told you to, maybe even go to the bathroom when they told you to.

At the end of my tour, the nurse led me back to see the isolation rooms. There were two of them. In one, the Jesus

Christ man was still singing "Glory Hallelujah" at the top of his lungs, beating his fists against the inside of the door's small thick window. Behind the heavy steel door, his noises sounded muffled and far away.

"I believe the other Quiet Room is empty," the nurse said, unlocking the door with a thick three-inch-long key suspended from her belt on a long chain. A small plastic mat occupied the middle of the cement floor of the cold, eight-foot-square room; the walls were of green ceramic tiles. I shivered. I hoped they would never stick me back here, to be forgotten forever.

After my tour, I retired to my bed. I didn't feel safe. Even three-inch-thick steel-clad locked doors wouldn't protect me from the Evil Forces. It would be safer to sleep in my clothes than to undress and put on the hospital gown, and that's what I did.

Early the following morning, a handsome young doctor approached me. "Hi, I'm Dr. Falmouth," he said. "I'm going to be your doctor here in the hospital. I'd like you to come to my office with me so we can talk."

He sat behind his large desk, and I sat in a straight-backed armchair by the desk. Next to me stood an enormous fish tank filled with blue-green water, the bottom lined with multicolored pebbles. Big exotic-looking fish lazily swam around a diver figurine blowing bubbles on the bottom of the tank. Those little bubbles making their verticle lines to the surface captivated me, and, hypnotized, I could have watched them for hours.

Dr. Falmouth interrupted my bubble-gazing. "What brings you into the hospital?" was his first question.

Oh, no, here we go again, I thought. Where was Dr. Smith? Why couldn't Dr. Falmouth just read Dr. Smith's notes. I turned my head to stare at Dr. Falmouth. Sitting there in his long white coat, he looked like an ad for a men's fashion magazine. I imagined his picture featured on the glossy cover of a magazine, the title "Fashion Doctor" emblazoned at the top. His blond hair was full-bodied and very straight; he wore it attractively long over his ears at the sides, and long enough to touch his collar in the back. He combed his hair out of his eyes with his fingers while stroking his full, neatly trimmed beard with the other hand. His trousers were carefully tailored, and all his clothes were shades of beige, tan, and brown to contrast with the blond color of his hair. He wore a button-down shirt with a stylish wide necktie, and expensive but casual leather shoes. Smoking a pipe, he looked *too* comfortable. Anybody who looked like that couldn't possibly understand my discomfort. I tried to imagine he was smoking a joint rather than a pipe.

"Well, does he or doesn't he?" the voices asked me.

"Does he *what*?" I asked, somewhat irritated at the cryptic nature of their questions.

"Smoke pot!" they answered.

Dr. Falmouth waited a few seconds before saying," I didn't understand your question. What did you want to ask?"

I shifted uncomfortably in my chair. "I don't know," I said. I drifted back into gazing at his fish tank, then watching Interference Patterns crawling around his office. He asked me a lot of questions, but I couldn't concentrate on them, so I just said "I don't know" a lot. Sometimes the voices chimed in answers, but Dr. Falmouth didn't seem to be picking up on their answers.

"I'm going to start you on some medicine," Dr. Falmouth said. "It's called Stelazine. I hope it will make you more active. It seems like it's a big effort for you to move. Is that right?"

It was, but I didn't put forth the effort to answer him. After the interview, I went back to my room, and an hour later the nurse called me to the nursing station for my pills. I spent the rest of the day lying on my bed, snoozing intermittently, feeling drugged. A nurse finally came back and told me to get up: hospital rules. Patients were not to lie on their beds during the day.

I went out to the dayroom and sat. The colorful cosmic granularity in the air held my interest. I tuned everything else out, sitting there motionless for hours, staring at the air. The voices jabbered away in the background, and I listened intently.

"We're here, Carol," Hal said in that sugary-sweet, smooth voice of his. "We're here to help you win the battle."

"Don't believe him," said another voice in a raspy tone. "He doesn't know."

Another voice said, "We know you know about the Other Side."

The Other Side. Yes, I remembered. It had something to do with the Evil Forces. Somewhere, there was a parallel existence, a whole other universe on another plane of being. Sometimes bits of it spilled into ordinary life. That was where the voices came from, and the Interference Patterns too.

"Carol is safe," said a woman behind my head.

I turned and looked. There was no one standing there. I decided the woman was probably another one of my voices.

"No, she's not safe," said Hal. "I'm safe, you're safe, we're safe, she's not safe."

"You're out!" said the cigar voice. "Do you want a cigar?"

I smiled. I hadn't heard that one in a while.

Faintly, I thought I heard Steve's voice drifting among the others. I knew better than that: Steve wasn't here.

There was a tap on my shoulder.

Never mind, it's more voices, I thought. If I looked, the hospital staff would think I was crazy and want to medicate me even more. I had to avoid looking crazy. I sat very still, trying to ignore the tapping.

"Carol," I heard Steve's voice saying right next to my head. "Can't you hear me? What's the matter?"

Slowly, so as not to look too suspicious, I turned my head toward the voice. There was Steve, standing right next to me.

If the voices were playing games with me, this was cruel, because I did want to see Steve in the worst way.

Steve came around the end of the couch and sat down beside me. I was so happy to see him, I tried to smile, but my face felt dead. I still hadn't found those emotions I'd dropped off at the bus stop. Steve took my hand and rubbed it between his hands. They were cold.

"Is it cold out?" I managed to ask.

"Yes, it's twenty below."

It could be two hundred below, I didn't care; I was safe now that Steve was by my side. "Take me back to your dorm," I whispered. "Protect me."

Steve looked as if he was going to cry. He still didn't tell me what the admitting doctor had told him the night before. He had spent the entire night walking around the campus, thinking over the doctor's advice, weighing the pros and cons of leaving me versus staying with me. Finally, he had decided that his love for me was more powerful than any set of circumstances, no matter how seemingly impossible. He couldn't leave me, especially not now that I needed him more than ever. Someday I would get better, those doctors would see, and I would regain my freedom and finish college, and he would marry his girl. He had seen a glimpse of me as a real person before I had faded completely into the fog of the Other Worlds.

"You're going to get better," he told me. "Just be patient. I'll wait for you. No matter what, I'm not going to leave you."

With devotion like that, I couldn't help but be inspired. I would get better for him. Again, I tried to force a smile against the wooden texture of my face.

We sat there gazing into each other's eyes for about two hours. He tried to liven me up by talking to me, but I was having difficulty concentrating on his words against all the background noise of my voices. Finally he had to leave in order to get to his job on time, and besides, the supper bell was clanging.

R.T.C. LIBRARY

I marched into the cafeteria behind the other slow-moving, shuffling patients. As I sat down in a vacant chair at one of the tables, I heard a lady with an infantile voice asking, "What's for supper?"

"Meatloaf," said a young man across the table from me. He was unable to get very close to the table because his huge potbelly prevented him, and he had to stretch his arms to reach his plate. I couldn't imagine existing in such pathetic physical condition as either of these two people. I didn't belong here. I wasn't one of them.

"Meatloaf, oh goody," the infantile-sounding patient said, not bothering to mop up a gob of slobber sliding down her fat, greasy chin.

Gross, I thought. What a slob. I couldn't stand to look at her for more than a second or two.

Unfortunately, she decided to plunk herself down at the table right next to me. She shoveled a triple-sized portion of meatloaf onto her plate. She dove right into the pile of meatloaf with her fingers, bringing a handful up to her mouth. When she had gotten the bulk of the food into her mouth and started to chew, she used the back of her other hand to wipe her mouth, smearing meatloaf grease across her cheek, over the layer of grease that was still there from lunch. I wondered if after I'd been in the hospital for a while I might end up like her.

This wasn't helping my appetite. It was all I could do to force myself to break off a bite of meatloaf with my fork and lift it to my mouth. But there was something peculiarly wrong with the texture of the meat, something sinewy churning around with it in my mouth. I stopped chewing and reached in two fingers to pull out whatever it was.

The greasy lady looked over at me and said, while managing to drop several bits of food out of her open mouth, "Ooooooh, icky, a Band-Aid."

Yes, there it was, a Band-Aid, cooked to perfection. Right in the middle of the meatloaf, just waiting for me to chew on it. For a split second I felt I might vomit; then I recovered, stood up, and turned in my plate of food at the dirty-plate window.

After supper, I sat quietly in the dayroom trying to watch TV. The medication was slowing me down considerably, and even the simplest movement seemed to take forever.

The voices gathered behind me, keeping up a running commentary on everything that was happening.

A nurse breezed through the dayroom on her way down another hallway. "There goes the nurse," said a voice.

A flash of light zoomed across the dayroom, burning out and disappearing into thin air. Had I really seen that?

"There goes another comet," said a voice.

Okay, I did see it. This could only mean one thing: further leakage of the Other Worlds into this world. The comet had been a sign.

"It's all right," Hal reassured me with his sugary voice. "We're here with you."

Interference Patterns began to materialize in the air. I stared at their colorful swirls, watching new patterns emerge in response to every sound in the room. When the voices spoke, the patterns shifted, just as they did with other sounds. It was like the vampire test: vampires don't have reflections in mirrors; nonexistent voices shouldn't affect the patterns the way other sounds did. That was scientific proof that the voices were just as real as everything else in the world; actually, they seemed even more real.

Frightening. I didn't know whether existence in the Other World would be divinely magnificent, beyond human description, like heaven, or whether it would be like the worst imaginable hell. I was ambivalent about whether I wanted it to happen. On one hand, I didn't want to stop the emergence of goodness, yet if it threatened to be hellish, I would have to try to prevent it.

I froze, not wanting to produce further patterns from the stimulation of my bodily movement. I didn't want to be responsible for encouraging such change in the world. Live your life as a prayer, I reminded myself.

I heard a news announcer on TV parrot my words: "Live your life as a prayer."

Yes, that was good advice for the world to know. The newscaster had broadcast my own thought. The communication systems brought in from the Other Worlds were incredibly sophisticated, more than I could understand. The whole world was now praying with me.

A nurse sat down next to me on the couch and put her hand on my arm. "Carol, what's going on with you? You're just sitting there doing nothing. Are you bored?"

The sound of her voice created new waves of Interference Patterns, sent hurtling through the air in front of us.

Hush! Don't you understand what you're doing? For God's sake, don't help the Other Side.

She shook my arm gently. "Why, Carol, I believe you look scared. Am I right?"

Oh, no, now you've done it, you've inadvertently hurled us into that bottomless pit. With the force of your movement you've made us start to fall again.

The nurse got up and went for help. She returned with two male aides, who picked me up off the couch, carried me to my bed, and left me lying there alone in the dark. The whole time, the patterns swirled through the air, crashing over my head like a tidal wave. Would any of us survive this ordeal?

On my bed, undisturbed, unmoving, I applied the powers of my concentration, gradually settling the turbulent waters of the Other Side. The Interference Patterns began to fade back into the air. If I could only lie still indefinitely, I might have a chance.

By morning, only dim vestiges of the patterns remained. I had survived that battle, preventing the Other Side from taking over more than a little chip of the world.

Later that morning, a social worker visited me. "I need to

call your parents and notify them that you're here," she said. "Can you give me their phone number?"

"Please don't call them," I said. I didn't want to make them suffer. I hadn't been filling my parents in on recent events. This would come as a shock to them. Things like this just didn't happen in *our* family.

"Would you prefer to call your parents yourself?" the social worker asked.

No, I couldn't possibly do that. I didn't have the strength to face hurting my parents this way.

"Well, it's got to be done," she said. "Either you do it or I'll have to."

I gave her my father's work number. I thought he would be calmer receiving this kind of news than my mother would be.

The social worker returned to her office to make the call.

I didn't know the details of the social worker's conversation with my father until years later, when he described to me what a shock her news had been to him.

"Mr. North," the secretary's voice blared over the intercom, "there's a woman on the phone who says she's a social worker and it's urgent that she speak with you right away. She won't tell me what she wants."

My dad set down his pen. "Put her through," he said, shuffling papers to the side. This unimportant call couldn't take too long—probably just somebody asking him to do some PR work again, or something like that. Still gazing at the papers, he picked up the phone and said hello into the receiver.

The connection sounded hollow, like long distance. "Mr. North," came the voice from the other end, "are you the father of Carol?"

Abruptly Dad looked up from his paperwork. "Yes, I am. What can I do for you?"

"I'm calling to inform you that we have your daughter as a patient here in the psychiatric hospital in Cedar City," the voice crackled on the other end of the line.

"No, I don't see how that could be," Dad said. "There's nothing wrong with my daughter. Are you sure you've got the right number?"

"I think so, Mr. North. Is Carol thin, with short brown hair and deep-set brown eyes?"

"Yes, that sounds like Carol. But how can this be? She was just home at Christmas and she didn't look sick then. Are you sure?"

"I'm sorry, Mr. North, I'm sure this must come as terrible news for you, if you didn't know your daughter was ill. She's apparently been having serious emotional problems for quite some time. Weren't you aware anything was wrong with her?"

"No," Dad said, his voice wavering slightly. "Is she all right? What's the matter with her?"

"Mr. North, I don't know how to tell you this—but your daughter is seriously ill. We're not exactly sure what her problem is yet, as the initial psychiatric workup hasn't been completed. Right now it looks as though she'll need to be here in the hospital for a long time. It's possible she may never recover from her illness."

Dad paused a long time, thinking. Thinking of how I had looked the last time he had seen me, trying to imagine what could possibly have gone wrong. Then all his thoughts blurred together. "She was fine a month ago," he repeated, trying to convince himself as much as anyone else. "I can't believe it's as bad as you say. What's she like now?"

"She's been drifting in and out of a catatonic state, not even moving or speaking at times."

"Can we see her?"

"Mr. North . . . " She paused, trying to think how best to tell him. "Right now might not be the best time. But if you insist on visiting her so soon"—she paused again, drawing a deep breath—"then you should be fully prepared to see a daughter who may not even be able to talk to you. She's a very sick girl."

"All right," he said. "We'll call her before we come—but I'm sure she'll want to see us." He cleared his throat, one of his nervous habits that indicated he had something further on his agenda, something that was making him uncomfortable. "Um—may I ask you a favor?"

"Yes?"

"Please don't call my wife. Let me break the news to her. I'm afraid this is going to devastate her."

"I understand, Mr. North."

"Thank you for calling. We'll come just as soon as we can—after we talk to Carol."

"Have a safe trip, Mr. North. Goodbye."

Dad set the receiver back in its cradle and buried his face in his hands. He would call me that night, after he'd talked to Mom.

Back on the ward, Dr. Falmouth had arrived for the day. He strode importantly through the dayroom on his way to the nursing station, his long white coat flowing impressively behind him. To me, he appeared distinguished, unapproachable, Freudian. After checking my chart in the nursing station, he emerged and led me to his office for a therapy session. In his office he took copious notes on a clipboard that he was careful never to let me see.

"What was your childhood like?" he asked, stroking his beard.

Using the fewest words possible, I tried to explain all my history to him. Excess words would only invite further displays of Interference Patterns. I was still slowed down from all the medication. At key therapeutic moments in the interview, Dr. Falmouth interjected appropriate mm-hmms. He asked me all kinds of questions about my sex life, masturbation, and my childhood toilet training. His questions embarrassed me, but if I had to tell him all that stuff to get help, I supposed I would. He seemed to be trying to find some early perverse sexual experiences which, I supposed, would explain all my problems.

"And after the fire in your house," he asked, "when you were six, you did what? Oh, so you slept in the parental bed. Mm-*hmmm*." More scribbling on his clipboard.

"We're here, you know," Hal reminded me softly, in the background.

The doctor didn't appear to have heard the voice, and I wondered if he was at all aware of the Interference Patterns or any of the other phenomena from the Other Side. "Do you see the patterns, too?" I asked him.

He scratched the back of his neck. "What are you talking about?"

That was my answer: no, he wasn't at all aware. There was no point in discussing these things with him. I was beginning to lose hope that he might help me.

"Do you see things?" he asked me.

"No."

"Then what are you talking about?"

"I don't know." The pauses between my thoughts were lengthening, until finally I wasn't talking at all. My body processes were slowing down, my mind grinding to a halt. My thoughts had been stolen away, even my subconscious ones. I wondered if perhaps Dr. Falmouth had borrowed them for a scientific paper he might be writing.

Dr. Falmouth terminated the interview.

Later, one of the nurses herded me into a medical conference in a small room stuffed with an audience of about twenty people—doctors, medical students, nurses, aides. Most were smoking, and their cigarette smoke hung in the room in a dense cloud. The patterns crawled all through the smoke, spreading their fear into my brain. The doctors bombarded me with the same old questions about toilet training and sex. I feared stirring up further chaos in the room's air from the force of my words. I spoke as little as possible.

"It appears that questions about sex frighten you," Dr.

Falmouth said from the audience. He looked rather pleased with himself for having suggested the connection.

I rolled my eyes upward, trying to make sense of the psychological ramifications of his observation.

"When I ask you about sex, you look frightened. Am I right?"

I shrugged my shoulders. I'd never thought of it that way. He knew every slant on sex to talk about, even the slants on the slants.

The interview was brief, and afterward I went back to the dayroom to sit, knowing that they were discussing my case over cups of coffee and more cigarettes, trying to arrive at the correct diagnosis. I didn't want to be diagnosed; a diagnosis could not adequately define my problem. My problem was special, like no one else's in the world; in fact, it was out of this world.

Later, Dr. Falmouth informed me that he was going to increase the dosage of my Stelazine. I didn't argue.

"When can I go back to classes?" I asked him. If I missed much more school, I'd flunk out, and that would only compound my problems. I had seen other in-patients who were also university students leaving for class in the mornings and returning to the hospital at night.

"We can give you passes to go to classes," he told me. "Do you think you're up to it yet?"

I didn't know; all I knew was I had to try. I nodded.

Even though the prognosis for my recovery was considered grim, the medications might improve my control over my symptoms enough to allow me to resume classes while I was still being treated in the hospital. The doctors were doubtful of my ability to function in school in the future, yet they had observed that some schizophrenic patients can keep up many of their regular activities, though at a reduced level. Only time could tell whether I would ever be able to handle school again.

That evening, my parents phoned. Getting my words out demanded considerable effort. My mind was producing thoughts at the speed of continental drift.

"What are you doing in a hospital?" Mom demanded. "You don't belong in any hospital. You're not sick, you've never been sick. I know you better than that."

I didn't know what to say. A long, uncomfortable silence followed.

"We can come see you tomorrow," Dad said. "I can take off work."

"Please don't," I said. "I'm not ready yet." Granted, I didn't view myself as sick either; but they obviously had no idea of the dimensions of my problems.

"Carol, don't be ridiculous," Mom said. "Let us come over and take you out of there. We can take care of you."

"Don't do that, Mom. What are you trying to do, kill me?"

The tone of Mom's voice came across the wire as sinister, matching the evil, critical nature of her conversation. It was becoming apparent that Mom was no longer a free entity with her own will. She had come under complete control of the Evil Forces. And perhaps I'd even caused this by allowing her to read my mind, which had provided the Evil Forces free access to her mind.

"Well, when do you think you'll be ready to see us?" Dad asked. "We can come whenever you want us to." Dad had always been a strong voice of reason. Reason was what I needed now. The more logic, the better, to help me figure my way out of my mess.

"Wait till the weekend," I said. "Don't take off work. Just come on the weekend."

They agreed. I would have three days to pull myself together.

When I got off the phone, I found Steve waiting for me in the dayroom. He had brought me my homework assignments. I'd missed only a few days of classes, and I might be able to catch up on the work. The only potential problems were my dance and art classes, where you had to be there to do the work. Steve had taken care of that; he had spoken with the professors, both of whom had been completely understanding, offering to be helpful in any way they could. It was a huge relief to know that I could continue with my classes in spite of the time I'd missed. I would have to avoid missing any further time, though.

The next morning, the nurse unlocked the thick outer door for me, opening it up to the outside world. Bundled up against the cold, with my backpack full of books on my back and my blue Stelazine pill nestled in my stomach, I walked through the door and into the hospital lobby. My first taste of free air in days was indescribably good. There stood Steve in the lobby, my prince waiting to sweep me up and walk me to class. I kissed him on the lips, and we went off to my class together, arm in arm, plowing through a typical Midwestern January snowstorm raging outside.

Inside me, I felt equally snowed from the medication. My head spun with dizziness; my legs were heavy oaks trudging through the snowdrifts.

Steve kept squeezing my hand. "Come on, smile," he kept telling me. "Things aren't so bad. You're free now, and I'm with you."

I tried to smile, but my face still felt wooden, dead.

In class, I still couldn't concentrate, even though the voices had faded, sounding faraway and unimportant. Trying to think was like trying to turn over a car's engine at twenty degrees below zero. How was I ever going to get my schoolwork done if it was this hard to think?

After classes, Steve walked me back to the hospital, about a mile away, before returning to his dorm. He grinned, telling me, "All this walking back and forth to the hospital is making my leg muscles get big and strong—feel them. I don't mind the extra walking at all."

His devotion continued to inspire me. Steve, too, seemed to have unusual determination, all the better to help him understand my motivation. If there was any possible way to get through this thing together, we'd find it, and stick to it till we succeeded. This was our unspoken plan.

Back at the hospital, I made myself comfortable in a day-room easy chair, propping open my literature text on my lap. There was plenty of time in the hospital to study; there was nothing else to do. All of the Evil Forces and Other Worlds could do whatever they wanted, fly all around me and throw themselves at me; yet I would sit here and study, regardless. Nothing was going to stop me from getting my work done, not until the final disintegration of the world and my body into Infinity.

I had finished writing one page of an essay and had started on the next when my right thumb began cramping up. The thumb seemed to have a mind of its own, beyond my control. It refused to grip the pen, instead going into spasm, straightening and extending like a hitchhiker's thumb until the pen slipped out of my hand, dropping to the floor. I retrieved the pen and repositioned it in my hand, but before I even finished the end of the line, my thumb had popped back up, dropping the pen again. I massaged my thumb and tried again, but I got only three more words down before the same thing happened, and not even one word on the next try. It was going to take me all night to get this essay written.

What was going on here? Had an external force taken control of my thumb? Or was some hidden, vile sexual impulse deep within my own subconscious mind expressing itself through these uncontrollable thumb movements? Dr. Falmouth would have a field day with this one. Why had my anxiety expressed itself in my thumb? Why not in my toe, my stomach, or even my head—in a muscle-tension headache, or neck pain? What was the special sexual significance of the thumb? I decided not to tell Dr. Falmouth. I didn't think I could face the embarrassment of having to hear the Freudian interpretation of my thumb spasms. I didn't tell the nurses about my thumb, either. They would think I was either totally nuts or else just making it up.

I kept writing, looking around to make sure nobody was observing what was happening to me. My essay stretched on for three pages, and it took probably a hundred drops of the pen and repositionings before I had finally finished. The pages looked messy, but I didn't think I could do any better, so I just left it.

Studying was now a monumental task, as it had never been before. My writing was coming slowly, but far worse, my thoughts were coming even more slowly. I hoped my molasses brain would straighten itself out soon, or I could be headed for serious academic trouble. That panicked me. I tried not to think about it, fearing that the increased anxiety from such horrible thoughts would only provoke my thumb to go further out of control.

I put away my books and joined in a game of cards with two other patients and an aide. I held my hand in my lap underneath the table, to hide my spasmodic thumb.

A young woman from Activity Therapy who didn't look any older than I was came around asking who wanted to go to a movie. Patients who were not too sick were given privileges by their doctors, which included opportunities to go on trips with hospital staff to sports events, concerts, movies, the recreation center, the bowling alley, the swimming pool, and so on. Certain patients whose behavior was undesirable had to earn privileges; this was a kind of therapy called behavior modification. It seemed cruel and archaic to me, like being a young child all over again and having your parents punish and reward you.

Since I couldn't study, I decided I'd exercise my privileges and go to the movie. I was loaded onto the hospital van with ten other patients and three staff members. Bumping along the street in the crowded van, I reflected how odd it felt to be stuffed into this hospital van with a bunch of crazy people, like sardines in a can. I hoped that going places with these people didn't mean I was crazy too.

Standing in line at the movie, I was embarrassed to be seen with people who were unmistakably mental patients. Even worse, I was mortified to be ordered around by the hospital staff in public. In the theater lobby I saw two students I knew from my religion class last semester, and I tried to hide on the far side of the group as we walked through.

After the movie, we dutifully made our way back to the van parked four blocks away, and now I, like the other patients, used the only available means of self-propulsion—that slow, overmedicated shuffle. In the second block, my toes began to curl under inside my boots, making it impossible for me to walk normally. I stopped, bent down to take off my boots and straighten out my toes, and then put my boots back on. After another half block, my toes curled under again, and again I stopped to pull them straight. Each time, they curled under sooner than the previous time, until finally I resigned myself to walking on the uncomfortable lumps of my toes curled underneath my feet. I was careful to tell no one about this, feeling all the while much worse about the unmentionable sexual impulses from my subconscious mind that I imagined were making me do this. Determined to handle this problem on my own, I decided I would have to establish more self-control.

The next day was Saturday, the dreaded day my parents were supposed to visit. It was worse than I anticipated. Even from a distance, I could clearly see that my mother's face looked strained. When she came close, I could see her eyes were red from crying. Mom and Dad both hugged me, and Mom handed me a box of her special chocolate-chip cookies, looking away to hide her expression of pain from me. She gazed all around, critically examining the ward to determine if it was a reasonable place for her daughter to be. I saw disapproval written all over her face.

Dad was jingling the loose change in his trousers pockets, a habit I knew he did when he was feeling nervous or uncomfortable. He cleared his throat, as if to announce that he was about to say something difficult. "Look, Carol," he said, "we've asked around about this hospital. I don't think it's the place for you. Are you sure you even belong in a hospital?"

"What's the matter with this place?" I asked, irritated. Here I was doing everything I could to get better, enduring considerable discomfort and sacrifice, and my parents were about to dump a huge load of criticism on my head. I felt it coming.

Mom said, "We've found out that this place has a reputation for drugging people up so much they don't know what they're doing. The doctors don't care about the patients here. They just drug 'em up to shut 'em up. Do you want to turn into a zombie like these other patients?"

Mom stared off across the room at the hospital inmates shuffling through the dayroom or sitting in chairs staring off into space with vacant facial expressions. Just at this inopportune moment, the greasy meatloaf lady came running through the dayroom without a stitch of clothing on, sat right down on top of a depressed fat lady who was passively vegetating in an easy chair, and then urinated right on the poor lady's lap.

"I want to eat now!" the greasy lady yelled.

Two male aides came running in and hauled her away, still screaming, to the Quiet Room.

"Let us take you out of here," Mom said. "Let us take you anywhere, but don't stay here in this awful place. It can't be good for you. You're not like them."

"We could take care of you just fine at home," Dad said.

There was no doubt in my mind that in my current state of confusion, I would crumble under the emotionally charged atmosphere at home. "No," I said firmly. "No way. Don't interfere with my treatment. I've got to cooperate, so I can get over my problems."

"We're only saying this because we love you," Mom said.

"Don't you know that? We only want what's good for you."

They were upsetting me, but no emotion could escape through the wooden surface of my face. The medication had made my voice heavy and rendered my feelings hollow. I wasn't able to make my point. Although superficially my parents appeared to be right, I couldn't yield to their demands. It was crucial to stop their resistance, because they were undoubtedly linked up with the Evil Forces.

"I don't want to discuss it" was all I could manage to say.

"All right, honey," Dad conceded. "We don't have to talk about it until you feel up to it."

"We just want you to know that you don't look like yourself," Mom told me. "You're starting to look like those other zombies, all drugged up from the medicine, can't you see? Your eyes are dull. You don't look healthy. We love you, and it hurts us terribly to see you like this."

To my relief, Mom and Dad finally dropped the subject. They took me out on pass to dinner at a restaurant, inviting Steve to join us. Although they had ceased talking about wanting to take me out of the hospital, I sensed it was still foremost on their agenda. When I went to the restroom, my parents pulled Steve aside and pleaded with him, trying to enlist his help in persuading me to leave the hospital.

My parents secretly wondered if Steve had contributed to my illness. They suspected my involvement with Steve had somehow influenced me, planting in my mind the idea that I was unable to cope and needed to go into a psychiatric hospital. I'd never been like this before I'd met Steve, and from this they drew a causal connection. From their view, all they could see was a black box: in one end goes Carol completely intact with considerable talent and potential, and three months later out the other end comes Carol a total mess and a mental patient. The only element they could associate with the black box was Steve. Although they avoided telling Steve their suspicion of him, their feelings were so intense as to be obvious.

Later Steve told me he had felt terribly uncomfortable over dinner with my parents. "I don't think they like me," he said.

"Nonsense," I lied to him. "There's nothing wrong with you. They're just upset because they don't like the hospital."

My parents were critical of Dr. Falmouth, too. Mom complained that in their conference he just sat there mysteriously smoking his pipe, stroking his beard, writing on his clipboard, avoiding telling them anything, not answering any of their worried questions about how he was going to help me or how and when I would recover. "He doesn't seem to have any human warmth," Mom said. "He's a cold fish."

I was relieved when my parents had gone. I wanted to make up my own mind about things.

"I'm going to change your medicine," Dr. Falmouth told me. "I don't think the Stelazine is helping you. I'm going to discontinue it and start you on a new drug, Haldol."

I would cooperate with him. Although I wasn't feeling any better with Dr. Falmouth's treatment, I felt I must trust his ability to cure my problems. Simply being a doctor qualified him in my mind to be highly intelligent, educated, and devoted to helping people get over their problems. From childhood, I had learned utmost respect and awe for the abilities of doctors—starting when Mom had taken the psychologist's advice so exactly, sitting me in that chair all night. And now Dr. Falmouth was my last hope. I was totally dependent on him for my ultimate survival. He knew what was best for me.

"Carol's not doing so well," I heard one of the aides tell a nurse. "Do you think she'd do better in the Quiet Room, away from all this stimulation?"

I felt hands on me, picking me up, carting me off to the Quiet Room. The nurses stripped off my clothes and handed me a hospital gown before locking me in the Quiet Room. The room was grossly underheated. As I lay there on the floor my bare legs and feet began to turn blue.

I'm here in the hospital, but I also have one leg in Infinity, and the events in this world make no difference whatsoever. The chill isn't real. The only thing that's real anymore is HyperReality, the Infinity.

I lay motionless on the plastic floor mat for hours, till my limbs grew stiff from not moving. The drain in the center of the concrete floor belched up rough voices that laughed at me and called me foul names that reverberated back and forth between the puke-green tile walls several times before dying away. Intermittently, ghoulish faces appeared on the other side of the door's window to observe me as they might observe a reptile behind glass at the zoo. At first I thought those faces belonged to the aides coming back to check on me; then I thought maybe they were really the faces of the voices, finally showing up to meet with me. Later, I wondered if maybe the faces weren't there at all, but just another product of my troubled mind.

I was caught in a limbo or maybe a purgatory, awaiting my place in the Other World. Oh, how I wished something would happen to break up the events and end my discomfort.

Magically, the three-inch-thick door swung open.

"Carol." Dr. Falmouth's voice. "I'd like to talk to you."

"Talk . . . walk, balk, chalk, gawk, squawk," the voices echoed, rhyming Dr. Falmouth. That coded message meant we were now traveling toward the sun with supervelocity. We had emerged from special relativity into special-special relativity. My body was electric, buzzing: a sixty-cycle hum, serving as conductive material in a communications network that allowed forty billion messages to zoom back and forth between parallel universes and Other Worlds. Without me to transfer their messages and hold them together, all of these systems would fall into chaos. Dr. Falmouth would never be able to hold strong against the awesome powers before us.

Dr. Falmouth raised my arm into the air.

My fingers bolted themselves into a new mold, ready for firing off ray beams into multidimensional space.

The doctor left, and I held my new position.

Lunch arrived on a tray. Someone dribbled lukewarm milk over my lips and down my chin. My fingers remained bolted. Lunch left on its tray.

One minute later supper arrived on a tray. There had been time for just one message between lunch and supper. The feeding spoon chinked against my teeth, emitting an electric sensation. Supper left on its tray exactly as lunch had.

One minute later breakfast arrived on a tray. Amazing, how time accordioned itself in these HyperReal Dimensions. Orange juice trickled down my neck and into the folds of my gown.

"Carol, I know you can hear me."

Ah, the doctor's voice again. He unbolted my still-suspended fingers and rested my aching arm on my stomach.

"Dr. Falmouth," a nurse whispered, "she hasn't moved a muscle in twenty-four hours. She hasn't even gotten up to void."

Void: wow. I'm transcended. I'm so far beyond it all that ordinary things like bodily functions no longer matter. What is important is that with the slightest interruption of my trajectory through space, I could be hurled into the dark void of Infinity forever. It is up to me to hold the world and the universes together with the strength of my will. If I fail, these people will disintegrate along with me. I will try to hold on.

"Let's put some medicine in her vein," Dr. Falmouth said to the nurse. "Bring me the drug kit."

I felt a distant pricking sensation on the inside of my right elbow. These impotent hospital people were foolishly trying to save everything by shooting their drugs into my veins. It wouldn't work. They had no understanding of what was going on.

I took a deep breath, sucking up all the air molecules in the entire room. I continued inhaling until I had all the air molecules in the hospital captured in my lungs.

"In goes the medicine," I heard Dr. Falmouth say.

"Pretty corny," one of the voices answered back.

I let my breath out, bombarding the doctor's face with my captured air molecules. The particles moved away from my nostrils with such velocity that they turned blue. I was falling again.

It appeared that I was not really there, despite how I looked to everyone else. I had really departed to another dimension, to observe from a great distance all the things that were being done to me. It was all over now. Their medicine wasn't helping me—though I didn't expect it to. It was too late now. Dr. Falmouth was starting to disintegrate, I could hear his skin starting to tear apart. I wanted to tell him to run, to get away from the falling systems, but I couldn't find the correct circuit in the communications network to send him the warning.

I heard Dr. Falmouth's voice again. "Let's try some more medicine."

Whoa, I feel drunk. The drug has already flooded the crevices of my brain.

Dr. Falmouth helped me sit up. I looked around the room, feeling so woozy from the medication I thought I might pass out.

Hey, I'm thinking thoughts again. I've gotten out of the Pure Perception. I must have done something right.

Later, Dr. Falmouth asked me, "What did you think when the first dose of the medicine didn't make you feel any better?"

"It was horrible," I said. "I thought it was my last chance, and that I was lost forever. What happened?"

"That first dose I put in your arm was saline," he said, watching me to see my reaction.

"Saline? What's that?"

"Salt water. A placebo, a fake. What do you think of that?"

"Why would you do such a cruel thing as that to me?"

"To see what it would do."

I never trusted Dr. Falmouth after that.

My parents drove to Cedar City every weekend to visit me. They took me out on gate passes to go shopping, ride in the car, and eat real food in restaurants instead of the tasteless hospital fare. Anything to help keep me active, they thought. Coming to visit me was painful for my parents, especially my mother. To see the way the medications were increasingly turning her daughter into a zombie made her feel sick inside, and she didn't see that the treatment was helping me at all.

My parents felt helpless, and even if they'd had the means to change things, they wouldn't have known how to help me. Feeling alone and confused, they phoned Dr. Falmouth for information, and for the support they hoped for. "He's so cold and distant," Mom complained. "And he never tells us anything." She told Dad, "Carol needs a doctor who cares about her. Dr. Falmouth doesn't look like he's got a caring bone in his body. I thought psychiatrists were supposed to be the most caring doctors of all, to help people deal with their very sensitive problems."

Again, my parents suggested taking me out of that hospital and finding another one. I took that suggestion as personal criticism. I didn't want to leave; I wanted to stay in Cedar City and continue in school. My parents were trying to wreck everything for me, I thought.

I tried to keep going to classes and studying. I was now missing entire days of classes, instead remaining in the hospital, moving not one muscle while totally absorbed in the Interference Patterns and the voices. Trying to study was becoming increasingly difficult, though I couldn't understand exactly why. I felt restless inside, as I'd never felt before. I felt as though I had a motor inside my chest, a motor that would never shut off. It was incredibly difficult to sit and study when I felt that motor running inside my chest. Never in my life had I ever felt bored before, but now I was beginning to wonder if boredom might be my problem. It was so hard to study now that I worried that the cause might be that

I was losing my motivation. I would have to reach deep down inside me to find the strength to keep going in school.

As I sat in the hospital dayroom chair reading my literature book, I noticed a tenseness in my right shoulder, as if it was trying to raise itself by its own volition. No matter how hard I tried to prevent it, the shoulder tightened further, until it was touching my ear. I must be really nervous for this to be happening, I thought. It must be those vile sexual thoughts again.

I kept reading, trying to relax, trying to ignore my shoulder. I reached up with my other hand and tried to push it down, but it wouldn't cooperate. I must be going crazy, I thought, from being around this crazy atmosphere so long with all these lunatics.

Still, I couldn't make the shoulder relax.

Glumly, I closed my literature book. Studying was too difficult. I was indeed slumping into a state of no motivation. I'd never felt like this before, and it was beginning to panic me. If this kept up, I'd never be able to finish school.

I walked back to my bed to put away my book. Walking seemed to help, but as soon as I stopped, the shoulder cramped up again. I would have to keep walking. I walked back and forth down each hallway leading from the dayroom, but eventually the shoulder popped back up again. I walked faster, and that seemed to help. Each time, the problem with the shoulder caught back up to me, and I had to walk even faster to make it relax. Finally, I had to increase my pace to a trot.

"We're winding up your muscles," I heard one of the voices say. "Tighter and tighter and tighter, till they'll tear away from your bones."

I started running.

A nurse stopped me in the hall. "Carol, you shouldn't run here. What's going on?"

"I guess I'm nervous," I told her. "And scared." I wished I had more control over my physiological processes. Nobody could help me with this, nobody could possibly understand.

"Why don't you go back to your bed and lie down," the nurse suggested.

Lying down only made things worse. Next my head pulled itself backward until I was looking at the headboard. My eyeballs fixed themselves as high up as they would go in their sockets. I'd never experienced anything like this before. I decided this must be rock-bottom in mental illness.

"Help," I told the nurse. "I'm out of control."

"Let's give you a warm shower," she suggested. "That's good for relaxing people."

It sounded like a good idea. Anything to relax.

She didn't make me undress. I stepped into the shower fully clothed, feeling the warm gushes of water spraying over my head and eyes, cascading onto my shoulders. For an instant, my shoulders seemed to relax. Relief.

When I stepped out of the shower I still had on all my clothes, now totally soaked. No one seemed upset that I was dripping all over. Two nurses rubbed me with dry towels. But before long, my shoulders went into spasm again, even harder. No matter how I tried, I couldn't keep them down.

"I've got to keep moving to keep ahead of this thing," I told the nurses. I tore myself loose from them and started walking in circles, then I broke into a run.

"Stop it, Carol," they told me. "If you're going to behave like that, you must stay on your ward in your bed."

I went and lay down on my bed, but I couldn't hold still. I got up and started running around my bed in little circles.

"This is ridiculous," one nurse said to the other. Then to me she said, "If you'll lie quietly, we'll page the doctor on call."

Obediently, I climbed back onto my bed. I hoped the doctor would be able to give me something for my nerves, if only I could wait till he got here. Still, an overwhelming urge to keep moving, to run, coursed through my body, and controlling it every second was a horrible effort. As I lay there on my bed, the largest muscles running the length of my back spasmed hard, retracting my back into a painful arch till I was suspended over my bed like an acrobat, my eyes glued to the tops of their sockets.

"This is your own silliness," the voices told me. "You brought this punishment on yourself. Be good, or more will follow."

I wondered what I had done to cause this, to weaken myself to their influence.

"Stop it, it's hurting!" I screamed at them. "Please, just stop it!"

My shoulders underwent a new wave of contraction, and my back curved further, making it difficult for me to expand my chest to get enough air into my lungs. I wondered if I could suffocate this way.

"Where does it hurt?" The voice came from a doctor who had suddenly appeared at the side of my bed.

Oh sweet relief, he was going to help me relax.

I couldn't twist myself around enough to get a good look at him. I moaned, "My back, my shoulders, it's my muscles."

He put his hand on my legs and said, "Here, lift up against my hand."

When I tried to do that, a sharp pain shot up my abdomen, and it went into spasm. "Aargh, that hurts," I gasped.

"Okay, it looks like you're having a drug reaction to the Haldol. I'll give you some new medicine for it," he said casually as if he made the diagnosis at least six times a day.

He wrote the order on my chart and left. A nurse gave me a shot in my buttock. Within twenty minutes, the muscle contractions stopped entirely, to my great relief.

The next day, Dr. Falmouth stroked his beard and told me, "I'm going to stop the Haldol. Your body is apparently very sensitive to it. I'll be starting you on another drug, Mellaril."

After my first dose of the Mellaril, I began to feel dizzy. Especially when I first stood up, my head would twirl, and

I would have to hang on to the furniture for a minute until the dizziness passed. I didn't tell anyone about feeling dizzy, because I was embarrassed about this new symptom and what it might mean. Besides, I didn't want to complain. Dr. Falmouth hadn't explained to me that dizziness is a major side effect of Mellaril, and I worried that my dizzy feelings represented further chaos erupting from my subconscious mind.

When I awoke the following morning, I felt more groggy than I had ever felt in my life. Far off, through the haze of my mental fog, I heard a nurse telling me, "Carol, get up out of bed, please, and come to the nursing station for your medicine."

I opened my eyes, but my eyelids fought hard against me to close again, and I didn't have the spunk in me to keep them open. The world melted away.

"Carol!" the nurse said, more insistently this time. "You must get up! Hospital rules! What's the matter with you today?"

I sat up and swung my feet to the floor. My head felt as if a two-ton weight were sitting on it, pressing on my brain. The room was twirling, fading into deepening shades of gray. I struggled against my dizziness to pull on my jeans. The nurse stood by my bedside to make sure I didn't fall back into bed, as I wanted to do. Just sitting up required the effort of shoving an overloaded garbage truck up a steep hill.

"All right," I said, "I'm ready now." Then I stood up, too quickly.

Feeling dangerously light-headed, but quietly trying to fight the dizziness, I walked down the hall, the nurse beside me. After about twenty steps, the world turned gray, then black, and disappeared completely. My legs went rubbery. I grabbed out at a stretcher parked in the hallway. The next thing I knew, there were three nurses beside me, one of them shoving me onto the stretcher and another one wrapping a blood-pressure cuff around my upper arm. I felt the cuff squeezing tighter and tighter as I drifted out of consciousness. The nurse laid me flat on the stretcher, and I began to feel a sensation of liquid running in my ear canals, accompanied by sounds of water rushing through tunnels in my head and crashing against my eardrums. I was getting nauseated.

I lay there awhile, and the fog gradually faded until I could see again. I heard the nurse saying, "No wonder she's dizzy—her blood pressure is only sixty over twenty. I didn't think people could even stand up with pressure that low."

I spent the rest of the morning sitting in a dayroom chair, struggling to stay conscious against the dizzy feelings.

"Hmm, you're sensitive," Dr. Falmouth said, with more stroking on his beard. "We'll have to back off and go up more slowly on your dose. You'll get used to the side effects."

I missed another two days of classes because I was too dizzy to get there. The next day, the exertion of dance class made me so dizzy that I had to lie down during the exercises. This just wasn't going to work. I was beginning to wonder how I was ever going to get through the semester.

My dance teacher was so kind and understanding about it that she made me feel like crying. "It's all right," my teacher told me. "Just do what you can till you can get adjusted to your medicines. I won't hold it against you."

Steve came to the hospital religiously every day to bring me class assignments. He was my bridge between the hospital and the campus outside. "I'll never stop loving you," he told me every day.

I loved Steve. He was so wonderful that I felt like crying, but I couldn't find the tears. Inside, my emotions felt flat, vacant. I reassured Steve that I loved him. I was amazed at how Steve could remain untouched by all the evil that surrounded me. He wasn't at all bothered by the voices that troubled me so deeply.

Over the next few weeks Dr. Falmouth continued increasing my medicine till I was again so dizzy I could barely get out of bed in the mornings. I was losing my battle to stay in school. Finally, I couldn't hang on any longer. I had to admit defeat. I was devastated. I called my parents and told them I had to drop out. They drove to Cedar City, canceled my semester's registration, and moved my things home. Now I had nothing to do, since I was no longer studying. Every day I shuffled down to Occupational Therapy and Recreation Therapy with the other patients; on the ward, I tried to play cards and watch TV or knit.

The medication was putting weight on me. I ballooned out with an extra fifteen pounds. For the first time in my life, I could feel a roll of fat around my waist, and I could no longer pull my hip-hugger jeans shut over my hips. I'd never felt like a blimp before. I couldn't imagine ever being able to dance again; only weeks before, I couldn't have imagined *not* dancing. I was losing the things that were most important to me: dance, school, my physical well-being.

Dr. Falmouth phoned my parents to tell them I was only getting worse, not better. He advised them to start thinking about long-term institutional care. Again, he avoided answering any of my parents' questions about the specifics of what was going on with me. He offered no support or reassurances. My mother became upset, later telling my father that she was sure there was something wrong with Dr. Falmouth, she didn't know exactly what, but she knew he was not the right doctor for me.

My parents were tormented with worry about my welfare. They agonized over what to do, but they couldn't think of any way to help me. They were so anguished that they couldn't talk to anyone. When their friends asked about me, my parents retreated into privacy, merely saying I was doing fine and abruptly changing the subject. Their friends quickly got the message that my parents didn't want to talk about me, and before long they quit asking about me, only to wonder in private. They couldn't understand why my parents wanted to be so secretive. My parents then wondered why their friends didn't show any interest in our tragedy, interpreting their friends' silence as coldness. They wondered why nobody in their bridge club ever asked about me, not even the member who was a psychiatrist and from whom they would have expected more understanding.

When family members asked about me, my parents told them only that I was still in the hospital, nothing more. Even my sister and brothers weren't privileged to any more information than that.

Isolated from family and friends in this way, my parents suffered alone. They still visited me every weekend, determined to get through the major Midwestern ice storm that descended over us one weekend in April, with all the usual accompanying travel advisories. After each visit, they went back home thinking how much worse I had looked and fretted for another week.

In desperation, they went to our minister for support. He showed no understanding of their plight at all. He didn't seem to recognize my illness as a medical entity with so much suffering attached. He intimated that my problem was due to weakness of the will and defective faith. My parents didn't call on him again. Each week in church when the minister went down the list of church members who were ill with cancer and heart conditions and other horrible diseases and said a prayer for each of them, my name was not among them.

My mother told my father, "If Carol had a brain tumor, or multiple sclerosis or cerebral palsy, it would be different."

Dad nodded, realizing that if I had a debilitating medical illness, the support of the church and their friends would be right there, to comfort them. It seemed that no one cared. My parents were certain that people in town knew about my problems and were gossiping about us. My parents suffered doubly, first with my sickness, and then with the social stigma of mental illness. It didn't seem fair.

"Why, God, why all this? Why do you make us suffer?" my

mother said in her prayers. Even God didn't seem to understand or care.

Meanwhile, the medicine that had made me quit school was now causing me severely uncomfortable feelings of restlessness and agitation—called akathisia in medical terminology, and a known side effect of antipsychotic tranquilizers. I couldn't sit still for five minutes. I could no longer pass the time by watching TV or knitting. I watched the clock hands endlessly traveling around in their slow circles. The medicine counteracted the catatonia; instead, I was being motorized. I felt as if I had an unstoppable motor running in my chest, twenty-four excruciatingly long hours a day, making me unable to sit or lie down or relax. The motor-chest made me walk. Hours on end, I paced from one end of the hospital to another, wearing trails down each of the hallways leading from the hub of the dayroom. I had never experienced restlessness like this before. It was so intense it was worse than pain. It felt like a live worm growing inside my chest, and as soon as it got big and strong enough it would burst right out of my chest. In the meantime, it wiggled around inside of me, giving me the wiggles too.

"What's the matter?" a nurse asked me. "Can't you go sit down? Why are you pacing like this?"

"I've got the Walkies," I told her. "I can't help it."

The hospital staff adopted my term. Every patient with akathisia from high doses of antipsychotic tranquilizers had the Walkies.

I couldn't imagine how any doctor could be so cruel as to first lock people up, and then fill them with huge doses of medications that made it impossible for them to sit still to pass the time. It was slow torture.

And it got worse. Before long, I was running uncontrollably down the halls.

Two orderlies tackled me, then hauled me back to the Quiet Room for another night.

The next morning Dr. Falmouth visited me in the Quiet

Room. He looked more distant than ever, even irritated. He seemed as if he didn't want to have anything to do with me anymore.

"Things are going to change around here," he told me in an indifferent tone of voice. "We're going to take away all your privileges and start over. That means you lose your private room and go back to sleeping on the ward; you can't go to activities, and you can't have visitors."

"No!" I said. "Why?"

"Your behavior. It's not good. I want to see if you can control it. This will give you an incentive. If you start acting right, then you'll win back your privileges one by one."

He turned around and strode out of the room, the long tail of his white coat last to disappear from view. I sensed he had given up on me. I had been a naughty little girl, and now I was being punished.

No one on earth could possibly understand my suffering, I thought. I tried harder to behave better, to not respond to the voices, to keep quiet even when I was most frightened. I tried to sit still in spite of the Walkies. I suffered through my pain in silence. It was the most difficult thing I had ever done. I sank into despondency.

For days, the nurses turned Steve away at the door when he came to visit. No one would tell him why this sudden change of routine. "Doctor's orders" was all the nurses would say.

That's it, she doesn't love me anymore, he thought. He decided life wasn't worth living without me to make him whole. He told me later he had considered hurling himself off a bridge, but then had decided to hang on, hoping he might somehow get back with me. I missed him horribly.

Gradually, I learned how to become a good actress, pretending that I was a normal person in spite of my symptoms. I recalled the cover-up skills I had developed back in childhood with Dr. Vandenberg's calendar and gold stars. Now I worked to apply and refine my old techniques. I learned to restrain myself from answering back or even looking around when the voices talked to me. I forced myself, in spite of the excruciating pain of the Walkies, to sit quietly and watch the catatonic clock hands go around and around all day long, at their snail's pace. The motor-worm in my chest felt increasingly closer to bursting, yet I continued to sit still.

My mother was right. This place wasn't going to help me. Now I was stuck, and in order to get out I would have to pretend to get well. Cooperating with Dr. Falmouth's behavior modification was demeaning, but I had no other choice. It was the only way I could get free, and I had to do it.

Gradually, I began to win back my privileges. Steve was allowed to see me again. Next I was permitted to go to Occupational Therapy and make ashtrays and potholders. Eventually I earned out-trips in the hospital van with the other patients, to see movies and ball games. Through the whole process, the agony of the Walkies persisted, preventing me from enjoying any of my privileges. I just wanted out.

To Dr. Falmouth, my "improvement" on his behavioral-modification program proved that I hadn't been sick at all, that I had merely been acting bad. He glowed over his clever success at making me behave. Yet he contradicted himself by continuing to increase my antipsychotic medication.

Before I won back my private room, Dr. Falmouth decided I was well enough to leave the hospital. He seemed bored with me, longing to be rid of me. He phoned my parents and told them I was ready for discharge. I was more than glad to leave. At least on the outside, I could act to alleviate my irrepressible urge to keep moving constantly.

Accompanied by my parents, the voices, and fragments of the Other Worlds, I returned home to Riverside to recuperate. My self-esteem was shattered. I grieved over having ruined my education and my future. Since the school semester hadn't yet ended, Steve would have to stay in Cedar City for another month, and we would be separated. I didn't see how things could possibly be worse.

CHAPTER SIX

COLLEGE: NEW GOALS

I was miserable back home. I felt so discouraged over how I had devastated my life that I didn't feel like doing anything. Yet the Walkies continued to tear at me. I had to do *something*. So I quit taking the medication. Over the next few weeks the akathisia died away, but the voices grew more clamorous. Even so, I felt more comfortable without the medicine.

My parents were appalled that I had stopped the medicine. Although they didn't like what it did to me either, they insisted I should be in treatment. They took me to see a psychiatrist in another state, a doctor they'd heard prescribed vitamins in huge doses—megavitamins, which at the time was the new remedy for mental illness. The doctor told my mother I had chronic schizophrenia and that my case was really severe. He prescribed megavitamins, but also insisted I take large doses of antipsychotic medicine along with them. I became an expert in the art of pill-taking. I learned to swallow a handful of up to fifty vitamins at once, without even gagging (though it took several gulps of water to do it).

Back on the antipsychotic medication, I gained more weight. The voices faded, but not entirely, and I could hear them calling me fat. I decided I would have to do something about the weight gain. I retrieved my bicycle from the cobwebs in the corner of the garage and started cycling vigorously every day for two to five hours at a time. I had always enjoyed riding my bike. I had purchased it unassembled, at a local discount store, with my own money. I had named it Clepto, because I believed it stole parts of the environment to bring to me to enjoy. Whenever I pedaled hard toward a bright blue sky I noticed a colorful design in the air, a moving, churning blob about two and a half feet in diameter continuously imploding kaleidoscopic designs on itself. It remained suspended in air, a constant three feet in front of my face, guiding me on my way. I called it my Guiding Pattern.

Because of the effects of the medicine, trying to cycle or exert myself in any way became so burdensome that at times I simply couldn't. It took a mountain of effort first to overcome my drugged, motivationless state, and then even more effort to plow through the sedation that enticed me with the sweetness of sirens to give in to fatigue and give up the fight.

Falling back on the strength of my marathon determination, I managed to persist with my rigorous bicycling program. But in spite of all the exercise I was still gaining weight. I placed myself on a strict diet, religiously limiting my intake to only six hundred calories a day. Despite this, I wasn't losing weight, but merely holding steady. It didn't make sense. Anyone taking in so few calories and burning off so many should be losing weight. I decided the only explanation could be the medicine. Gaining no reward for all my extra effort was so frustrating that I finally quit exercising and quit taking the antipsychotic pills, though I continued the vitamins. Within a month the extra twenty pounds around my waist had magically melted away, and I began to feel better about myself. The voices could no longer call me

Fatty. I realized that though the antipsychotic medications dulled my symptoms, they also dulled my mind and thus weakened my ability to function. My goal was to function, at all costs. If my refusal to take the pills meant I wasn't cooperating with my treatment, then so be it.

My mother went out of her way to be nonintrusive and pleasant. Her attitude helped, and I became more relaxed, forgetting that she was reading my mind. She signed me up for an art course at the Riverside Junior College, and I sailed through the course with an A, inspired with new confidence that despite my symptoms, I could still achieve.

Everything was better when Steve got back to Riverside for the summer. He worked at his usual factory job, which he hated. I talked to Dad about it, and he hired Steve on at his plant for the less boring chores of manning the loading dock and scrubbing out steel tanks. Over the summer, Steve and I started talking about getting married someday. It seemed inevitable; we got along so well together. I thought marriage would be great if it didn't interfere with my career plans. I didn't want to start having babies right away.

Although my future plans with Steve looked bright, the other spheres of my life still seemed bleak. My self-esteem remained pathetically impoverished. Repair of my damaged selfhood would by definition require restoration of my career, because I felt I couldn't be a whole person until I was a successful professional woman. Constant uncertainty over whether I would be able to handle college and a future career ate at me. I decided that I would have to adopt an attitude of trying to survive one day at a time. Eventually the grueling summer wore to an end.

At the start of fall, Mom and Dad once again loaded up the family Oldsmobile with my stuff and moved me back into the dorm for a go at a new semester. My new roommate was a lively, warmhearted physical education major. I knew we'd get along great. When Mom and Dad departed, I went right over to Steve's dorm and we smoked some pot to welcome in the new semester. The marijuana didn't give me any trouble, and I took that as a harbinger of success for the semester ahead.

I registered for a heavy load of classes, including several advanced dance classes. I also auditioned for the annual university musical, *Cabaret*, and was accepted for that. Steve and I fell into our previous year's groove of studying like crazy, working and rehearsing, then partying whenever we had time.

I was so motivated to succeed this semester and so fearful of flunking out that I severely overcompensated. I studied every possible moment. I took a book to read while I stood in the cafeteria line at every meal; I read another paragraph every time I went to the bathroom; I even buried my head in my class notes while walking to and from classes. I made it through the first set of exams with all A's, which gave me new confidence. I believed that even if I should experience a return of symptoms so overwhelming that they began to impair my functioning, I could outmaneuver them, overachieving by working harder than anyone else possibly could. I was going to survive, and that's all there was to it. I came to realize that surviving would require avoiding drugs. Drugs only created mental chaos for me, and I knew I would need to keep my mental faculties in top condition to help me deal with what lay ahead. If that's what it was going to take, I could do it. I would do whatever I had to do. I didn't want to take any chances with my education.

The voices had rejoined me back at school, talking and buzzing in the background most of the time, but at least that's where they stayed. I decided not to let myself be distracted by them.

One beautiful sunny Saturday afternoon when I was walking down by the Cedar River, I heard a loud, chopping sound, the sound of helicopters flying close overhead. They stirred up the air, their vibrations alternately flapping and sucking against my eardrums. I covered my ears tightly with my hands, but that didn't seem to stop the air vibrations. As the helicopters came closer and closer, the chopping noise began to echo through the air, joining Interference Patterns that began pulsing in rhythm to the chops. It was horrifying. The chopping noise became so great that it blocked out all other sounds, and the patterns grew so intense in front of my eyes that I couldn't make out the ground. When I tried to climb a flight of stairs, the thick patterns swirled in front of me to block my view, and I nearly tripped. In the next minute the patterns partially cleared to reveal the individual steps, which were dancing back and forth. As I tried to climb on them, their edges rapidly shifted back and forth, unbalancing me until I had to sit down. Within a few minutes, the helicopters faded, and the Interference Patterns calmed down. I was left sitting on the stairs, trying to overcome a sensation of nausea.

I assumed the helicopters had come from the Parallel Worlds. I began hearing them from time to time. Whenever I heard them, I rushed outside to try to get a glimpse of them, but I could never spot one directly. They were sneaky.

The echoing quality I heard in the helicopter vibrations began to filter into everyday sounds. Ordinary noises began to take on an echoing tat-tat-tat quality, and when this occurred in lectures, it was next to impossible to decipher the words of my professors. The echoing sounds spilled into my visual perceptions, creating a "trailing" effect of multiple images sliding off the backs of moving objects. The helicopter noises heralded further swirls of Interference Patterns that filled the air so thickly that they jumbled my view.

All of this was terribly confusing, making it more difficult for me to do even the simplest thing, like crossing a street. The added campus stimulation further contributed to my confusion. I took to wandering around late at night, trying to figure things out in the quiet of the night when most students were asleep in their beds. Many times I stayed up and studied while Steve slept through the night. I forced myself to get along with as little sleep as possible—not that I didn't feel tired, I just thought that sleeping was a waste of time and self-indulgent. By controlling my urges to sleep, disciplining myself to fight fatigue and study instead, I felt I was being strong, and compensating for my deficits.

One night I took a study break and pattered barefoot down to the vending machines in the dormitory basement to get a snack. As I stood at the machine, I felt the whirring of its motors vibrating across the floor and up into my feet. I'd learned about this phenomenon in science classes. It was called resonance frequency—a vibrating object causes a nearby object to vibrate merely because the second object measures the perfect length corresponding to that sound frequency. I decided that in accord with this scientific principle, there must be machines in my feet answering to the machinery in the vending machine. The mechanism that created the phenomenon didn't even involve anything cosmic, it just adhered to ordinary laws of science to produce the unusual effect. That in itself seemed cosmic.

I abandoned my quarter in the vending machine and wandered through the dormitory basement, still feeling the hum of the machines working in my feet. I wondered if they might somehow be connected to the machines from the helicopters. That, too, would be cosmic.

My bare foot just missed stepping on a broken Coke bottle. There was a message here. I was supposed to use the glass edge to rip away the flesh of my feet to get a view of the machines inside, which would provide a parallel view into the workings of the Other Dimensions. The helicopters were using the resonance frequency in the machines in my feet to tap into my own intelligence and suggest the idea. Although the connection was subtle, I was astute; I could see the master plan here. I was standing on a cosmic junctional point where Other Worlds crossed through ordinary existence, and the broken glass was my ticket to a great seat in the auditorium of Infinity. This was so exciting that I forgot my fear.

Eagerly I sat down and began to carve into the top of my foot with a piece of green glass. It wasn't easy, because the glass was so rough. I was surprised at the toughness of my skin. I made several gouges, not even slicing through the long tendons running the length of the top of my foot. A few drops of blood oozed forth, then the wounds just sort of lay there doing nothing. I poked around in them with my finger, trying to get beneath the skin edges to probe into the machinery inside, but the skin was tenacious and hung tightly to my underlying flesh. I pulled the wounds as far open as they would stretch, but I couldn't see any machines inside. The humming stopped. I had missed my chance.

Then I heard the distinct chopping of the helicopters in the distance. I rushed up the stairs from the basement to the outside to try to get a look at them before they disappeared. Outside, a new snow was falling; the ground was already covered with two inches of fresh powder. The wind blew the snowflakes all around, muffling the chopping sounds. Still barefoot and dropping small red splotches of blood in my snowy footprints, I ran down the snow-covered sidewalk beyond the building to get a better look at the sky. By now the helicopters sounded even farther away.

"Come back!" I yelled after them. "Don't leave! I'm here!"

"I'm here, you queer," Hal said softly.

The helicopter noises faded completely into the snowstorm.

A footstep sounded behind me. I jerked around to see two policemen following me. Out of nowhere burst a squad car, its red lights flashing without sirens. I bolted.

The two policemen tackled me. One of them reported to his radio, "We've closed on the girl creating the disturbance. She looks like a college coed, that's all. Just some loon running around barefoot in the snow."

I struggled against them. I was sure they had descended from the junctional point to hold me in a dangerous spot until another, more sinister Parallel World arrived at the spot.

The next thing I knew, I was an involuntary passenger in the backseat of the squad car, forced to lie still by the two cops sitting on top of me holding me down. All around I could see twirling red lights flashing silently across the tops of buildings we passed. This was the end of the world. Terrified, I awaited my destiny.

The cops carried me, still struggling, into the same psychiatric hospital I'd been in, where they met the psychiatry resident on call. Their voices sounded all echoey with the Helicopter Effect.

"Helicopters?" I said.

"We've got Steve, too," said one of the cops. Odd, he spoke without moving his lips.

"Steve!" I called out. I wanted to see him. I didn't understand why they were doing this. Then I realized I was hearing the voices, not the cops talking,

The psychiatrist didn't say a word to me. He stuck a needle in a vein of my arm and shot in some medicine. Everything whirled, and I thought I might pass out. The voices diminished, the echoes stopped, and all the people in the room faded. By now my foot had quit bleeding, and since even the deepest laceration was a clean slice, my foot escaped notice during all the excitement.

When I regained my equilibrium, I was told I would have to stay in the hospital. I was too drugged to argue. I was locked into the Quiet Room for the night, and fell right to sleep under the influence of the drugs.

I'd never seen this psychiatrist before. Undoubtedly he had access to my hospital records, but he never indicated he had read them. I was just glad I didn't have to see Dr. Falmouth. He was working at another hospital.

By the next morning, the voices, helicopters, and patterns had faded. I would have to gain my freedom right away to get back to classes. I was determined not to fail this time. I tried to appear as normal as possible to the hospital staff. Using the skills I'd perfected in the hospital last spring, I very carefully ignored all the voices, echoes, and helicopters. I tried to engage in normal conversations, concentrating hard on sounding as rational as possible. I made it very clear that I needed to get out and go back to school and my studies. On questioning, I admitted that I had been hearing voices the night before, but then I fudged a little and told the hospital staff that the voices were all gone and everything was back to normal. In a few days I earned my freedom.

Back at the dorm, I phoned my parents to reassure them I was okay, even though I wasn't so sure of that myself. As I suspected, they had received a call notifying them of my latest hospitalization. I knew they would be anxious to hear from me, and worried sick, particularly Mom.

"Look, Carol," Dad said, "we think you need better psychiatric treatment."

"Don't you agree?" said Mom. "You can't keep bouncing in and out of the hospital. You need a psychiatrist to help you *before* you get that bad."

After a brief silence on the wire, Dad said, "I got the name of a doctor in Welmington. Even though it's an hour's drive, I could get off work and take you. He's supposed to be pretty good."

Mom added, "We've heard his approach is totally different from the Cedar City doctors'. He's not so quick to pin bad labels on patients and then give up, and he doesn't prescribe such large doses of medicine. He helps people by talking to them and allowing them to work through the problems bothering them."

I was still skeptical, but on Christmas break I agreed to appease them and go with them to Welmington, hoping to relieve their uneasiness. I decided I could tolerate the doctor only if he didn't try to pin a label on me or control me by drugging me up.

I was surprised: I immediately liked Dr. Black. He was totally different from Dr. Falmouth. He seemed to really care. Dr. Black's neatly trimmed beard was salt-and-pepper-colored, and he didn't stroke it. He maintained a quiet, calm unassuming air. "Call me Paul," he said. "All my patients do." I found I could talk to him with no difficulty, and he seemed to understand practically everything I said. He didn't say "Mm-hmm" or scribble on a clipboard, either.

Paul told my parents after the interview, "I don't have to tell you your daughter is very sick. I'd like her to come into the hospital for treatment, but she refuses to do that. I guess I can appreciate how anxious she is to avoid further interruptions in her education. She's not agreeable to taking any medications right now either, because she's afraid they'll interfere with her ability to study and go to classes. I can understand those feelings after her experience last spring."

"What should we do?" Dad asked.

"Keep an eye on her, and bring her to see me for psychotherapy every month."

Dad said, "What if she gets too out of control?"

"Then bring her here for a brief hospitalization, and she can return to school as soon as she's able. I tend to agree with Carol on the importance of her staying in school, and I'll do everything I can to help her in that endeavor. Even though she's pretty sick, she's intensely motivated, and that's allowing her to compensate. She's on the edge, but I think she can do it."

"Will she be all right staying in Cedar City?"

"Just for security, I'd recommend she go to her university's counseling center and find a counselor she can talk to on a regular basis there between appointments with me—she needs someone who can keep a closer eye on her."

On the way home in the car, my parents discussed Paul, agreeing that they both liked him—especially the sense of warmth and compassion he communicated. He seemed practical and down-to-earth, attributes my parents valued. At last, someone was interested in helping their daughter. If he could truly help, they would be eternally grateful.

I appreciated not being forced to take medicine. I quit the

megavitamins; six months had been a long enough trial. Following Paul's recommendation, I went to the counseling center and started therapy with a counselor there. A graduate student in counseling, he was a small, quiet young man who seemed genuinely interested in helping me stay in school. His reserved, timid manner reminded me of a rabbit, as did his physical appearance. I began to call him Rabbit, affectionately. He liked that, and his colleagues at the center picked up the nickname too. With Rabbit's support in weekly psychotherapy sessions, I plunged into the next semester's work. The following week, grades from the previous semester were announced, and I was pleased to learn that I had gotten all A's except for a B in literature, which had always been my worst subject. Although Steve had helped me survive the last semester, my problems were obviously too much for him to handle alone. He was relieved that I had found a counselor who could help ease his load.

Rabbit helped me explore the reality of my delusions. He didn't insist that there weren't any helicopters or voices or Parallel Dimensions. I wouldn't have believed him. Instead, he explored possible alternative explanations with me and helped me work on my survival techniques. When I lapsed into periods of Pure Perception and began staring at the wall for hours stretching into days without moving, he advised me that I needed to reduce unpleasant stimulation, to get away from noisy crowded places where the voices confused me, yet maintain contact with the real world by talking to someone I trusted, like Steve. Rabbit encouraged me to test my ideas, check things out, see if other people confirmed my impressions.

Rabbit's commonsense advice was more helpful than any medication I had ever taken, certainly more than any Quiet Room. He saw my case as chronic and difficult, and he didn't have unrealistic expectations of curing me; thus he avoided getting his ego tied up in performing heroics. He aimed toward more modest goals like helping me adapt to my chronic illness and keeping me functioning at the highest possible level. Between my appointments with Paul, Rabbit kept me going. Between my appointments with Rabbit, Steve kept me going.

Eventually my symptoms became too great for Rabbit to handle. Over several weeks the helicopters began to bother me more, and the voices became more insistent. Despite having Steve at my side, I began to panic. I couldn't study. I slipped into Pure Perception, so far gone that I didn't move for days. I was totally absorbed in watching the Interference Patterns swirl all around me while I listened to the echoes bouncing all over everything and the voices talking away at me in the background. After a while the incessant stimulation numbed me, as though I were being tossed around on a carnival ride that I didn't want to be on.

Steve called Rabbit, and Rabbit sent me to Welmington, where I was admitted to the psychiatric locked unit. Since I hadn't been eating, Paul nourished me with intravenous fluids for a few days. The medications he used were milder than the ones I'd received in Cedar City. Gradually, the Pure Perception experiences faded back into their more indistinct state, and I started moving and talking again, feeling more under control. As soon as I was able, I wanted to get back to school. I was missing midterm exams. I wasn't well, but I'd managed to get myself under enough control to make everybody think I could manage school again. I knew better than to talk about the voices or the helicopters to anyone.

Before he discharged me, Paul told me he thought I should stay longer for more treatment. He intimated that by uncovering my deeply buried conflicts and talking to me to help me resolve them, he could help me get well. I felt that although it would be nice to do that, I didn't have the time. I had to get back to classes. Paul's professional expertise undoubtedly told him that a patient as sick as I was should remain in the hospital, yet his heart told him how much I needed to keep forging ahead with my life on the outside.

He didn't want to hurt me. Allowing me to leave the hospital so soon was a calculated gamble. He later told me he had come to this decision because he was impressed with my unusual determination, greater than that of any other patient he'd ever seen. This attribute, coupled with my learned techniques to stabilize myself in the presence of symptoms that would totally incapacitate other patients, presented a unique combination of abilities he thought might allow me to succeed in spite of my disability. I sensed that in letting me go, Paul was putting his trust in me. He was counting on my making it. I would not let him down.

Once again in Cedar City, I wasted no time getting back to my books. I studied intensely, averaging eighteen hours a day. If I could just find a way to stop wasting my time sleeping, I could study twenty-four hours a day. I spent as much of my study time with Steve as I could, but I didn't have time to see much of my dormitory roommate or anyone else. The voices continued their running commentary, no matter what I was doing—eating, studying, showering, walking to classes. I was beginning to resign myself to spending the rest of my life with the voices. Sometimes I liked them because they said such funny things, but I didn't like all the tricks they played on me.

The stress of school piled on top of the stress of my symptoms again became almost more than I could bear, but I managed to hang on through finals. That semester I earned a B in religion and A's in all my other courses. I'd proved that with my determination, I could achieve my goals. By taking an overload of courses both semesters of my sophomore year, I had managed to make up for the semester I'd lost while in the hospital, acquiring just enough semester hours to qualify for starting my junior year next fall. I was exhausted.

That summer, back in Riverside, I became increasingly uncomfortable around my parents, particularly my mother. I didn't realize she was worried sick about me. I interpreted the strained look on her face as evidence of evil intentions toward me. She was reading my mind and feeding my thoughts to the Other Side. I maintained a psychic barrier between myself and my mother, holding her at the farthest distance possible by darting hostile, paranoid looks her way, and acting irritable when she came too close. To keep my thoughts private, I increased my efforts to scramble them. Before long, I was mixed up myself.

In desperation, my parents took me back to Welmington, and Paul kept me in the hospital for six weeks. Then Paul went on vacation, and his partner Gilbert, a clinical psychologist, took over my psychotherapy. I told Gilbert all about how evil my mother was and how she was slowly destroying my mind.

Gilbert allied himself with me against my mother, a psychological technique to help strengthen my ego. When my parents came to visit, he had a session with them.

"What's Carol's problem?" Dad asked him.

"You know—the same thing as always. We don't like to apply diagnostic labels to people here, but since you're pressing me, and since her diagnosis is so clear, I'll tell you. She's got schizophrenia. And she's got it bad."

"What causes it?" Mom asked, as she had asked doctors in the past. "I've heard it might be due to a chemical abnormality in the brain."

"That's nonsense, Mrs. North. Does anyone else in your family have schizophrenia?"

"No."

"See, that proves it. Her illness is not genetic. Mr. and Mrs. North, there is absolutely nothing chemically wrong with your daughter. All our laboratory tests are normal, except for a minor disturbance on her brain-wave tracing."

"What are you telling us?" Mom said.

"Carol's making herself ill—she's doing it all herself. She's gotten psychotic by indulging herself. She *enjoys* being psychotic. That way she can escape the pain of reality. I think she can control the psychosis, and that's what I'm here to help her learn. She needs to face up to it."

"You mean she can snap out of it when she chooses to?"

"Exactly."

"Well, then, what's preventing her?"

Long pause. "You."

"What?"

Gilbert found this to be a perfect opportunity to apply to my case the traditional concepts on the psychodynamic origins of schizophrenia as described in psychology texts. "Mrs. North, you seem like a very distant, overly critical woman," he said. "Did you ever show Carol you loved her when she was growing up? Her upbringing was too rigid, and you as a mother were always too quick to condemn. She never got the acceptance she needed. You set up a damned-if-you-do-damned-if-you-don't situation for her—confusing and ambiguous—and that kind of atmosphere for growing up produces disturbed individuals. Carol is very disturbed, and it happened over a long period of time when she was growing up."

Mom was shocked. His unexpected remarks devastated her. It would be years before she would be able to talk about it. She loved me, and now this man was accusing her of not loving me, of having psychologically abused me. She went over the conversation again and again in her mind, trying to figure out exactly what horrible things she had done to me during my childhood to make me turn out so sick. Raising me hadn't been easy. No one had rewarded her for her persistence and dedication in raising a difficult child to the best of her abilities. She felt as if she'd been kicked in the face.

Mom talked it over with Dad. "Honey, you know how much I love Carol. You know I would never do anything intentionally to hurt her. All these years I thought we did so much to try and help her, I had no idea I was damaging her so. I wish now that she had miscarried during the pregnancy when I was hemorrhaging. If I'd known she was going to be so sick, and have to suffer so much, I'd have let her die then."

"Doris! You don't really mean that, do you? You're just reacting emotionally. Look, honey," Dad went on, "the doctors are doing all they can to help her. If we want to help her now, we're going to have to swallow our pride and go along with it. We've got to be strong or she's not going to get better. It's the only thing we can do." He dried the tears off Mom's cheeks.

Mom said, "You're absolutely right, dear. I don't know what got into me. Those men are her doctors; they know what they're doing. At least they're better than Dr. Falmouth. I just wish it didn't hurt so much." Mom had decided she could and would tolerate the pain, to help me. She would have to sacrifice her personal integrity. If she had to admit she had raised me all wrong in order to help me get well, she was prepared to do it. She would do anything, no matter how painful, if it would only help. She would gladly even take on my illness herself to spare me.

I was about to start my junior year at college, and it was time to think seriously about my major. I heard a cryptic message from the voices concerning clarity of vision into far realms of existence. I interpreted that literally to mean that I was supposed to become an optometrist. That fall, to meet the pre-optometry requirements, I changed my major to general science and registered for basic science courses—freshman chemistry, freshman biology, freshman physics, and calculus, the same classes the premeds had to take. With hard work over the next two years I could fulfill all the pre-optometry requirements and complete my new major, then apply to graduate optometry programs. I also signed up for two dance classes, just for fun.

I moved into a single dormitory room, to ensure better conditions for studying. Though Steve had graduated from college the previous spring, he had remained in Cedar City to work for the department of philosophy. I was glad to be back in town with him.

I contacted Rabbit to continue our weekly therapy. I foresaw a difficult semester ahead and knew I would need reinforcements. As I feared, the science classes initially overwhelmed me. The huge auditoriums overflowed with hundreds of nervous-looking students, mostly freshmen aspiring to become doctors and dentists, the rest largely science majors headed for graduate school. Circulating rumors of discouraging failure statistics for medical-school admissions, accompanied by unimaginable horror stories of individual medschool applicants, had contributed to the student anxiety.

"Just wait till you get to organic chemistry," someone had told me. "On the first day of class the auditorium is so full that students are sitting in the aisles and standing in the back of the room. The professor gets up and announces that by midterms there will be a seat in the room for everyone—half of those present on the first day will drop out, and half of those left will fail the course. Eventually, of the remaining students who survive to apply to med schools, only a fraction are accepted. People are committing suicide over failing organic chemistry and having their applications to med school rejected."

I was glad I wasn't a premed. I didn't think I could handle that kind of pressure.

My freshman chemistry professor explained to our class of well over a thousand students that this semester he was offering a new "self-paced" program he'd personally designed—for a limited number of students. Dr. Sands said he would accept the first two hundred students lined up outside his door after seven o'clock the next Monday morning; the rest of the students enrolled would remain in the regular program. The self-paced program would allow students to take each exam whenever they felt they were ready, and if they weren't satisfied with their scores, they could keep retaking the exam an unlimited number of times. The exam questions would come directly from material in the book, so all we had to do was study, and we wouldn't even have to attend the lectures if we didn't want to. The course was designed for those self-motivated students who could discipline themselves to do the work on their own. He'd written a computer program to generate exams made up of questions from an enormous data base he'd been collecting. The computer would create a unique exam for each student.

This arrangement was tailor-made for me. The material to be learned was finite, all of it contained in one book; my determination was infinite. If I could manage to get into the self-paced program I would be virtually guaranteed an A, simply through my usual hard work and persistence. I planned to be the first student outside Dr. Sands's office early Monday morning. I would arrive at five o'clock and wait two hours. The other students couldn't be that dedicated, even if they did happen to realize what a terrific opportunity this was.

Early Monday morning I emerged from the predawn blackness to enter the Chemistry Building through the front door. There I encountered a long line of students—certainly over two hundred, it seemed—already gathered and waiting. I was so appalled and disappointed that I nearly turned around and walked back out the door. But since this was so important, I decided I had to stay, on the slight chance that there might not be two hundred ahead of me. It turned out I was the 187th student, and I went home elated to be signed up for the program.

Later that week, I went to Dr. Sands's office to sign up for my first set of exams. "I want to take the first five units," I told him.

He looked at me as if I were crazy. "Five units! You can't possibly be ready for the first five exams after only one week!"

"But I've been studying hard," I said. "I'll be ready." I had been studying chemistry and nothing else for eighteen hours a day all week. I had completely memorized the first eight chapters of the book.

"I hadn't expected anyone to request five exams so soon," Dr. Sands told me. "To be honest, I've only prepared the first two exams. Could you settle for two units this week? That's the maximum I will allow any student to take at a time."

The next day I was one of a handful of students to show up at the first exam session. I didn't know it, but the computer program had gone haywire and generated its questions from the *eighth* study unit. The material in the questions looked foreign to me. Oxidation potentials? What were those? I hadn't seen those in the chapters I'd studied. How was I supposed to know about them? Had I made a mistake and read the wrong chapters, or possibly even the wrong book? Was there additional material I didn't know about that I was supposed to have studied? I looked around at the other students. They were all busily calculating and writing, and they didn't look the least bit distressed. I had obviously missed something. I struggled with the questions for an hour, and finally the proctor made me hand in my exam before I had finished. I felt like I was about to cry. I tried to pull myself together for the five minutes between the two exams while the proctor passed out the second set of questions. There was only one other student staying to take the second exam.

The second exam was even worse than the first. Crystal field model? What was that? Hybridization? Coordination constants? Acid-base titrations? I had to make wild guesses at almost every question. At the end, I turned in my answer sheet, feeling hopeless. There was no way I could have passed.

The answer sheet was posted in the hall outside. Dejected, I went to check my answers. All the other students had left. Standing alone in front of the answer sheet, I counted up my wrong answers and computed my scores. I'd gotten only thirty percent right on the first unit, twenty-five percent on the second. That was only slightly better than random. I needed ninety percent to get an A.

I couldn't stop the tears from streaming down my face. I ran back to the dorm and locked myself in my room. I didn't call Steve, because I was too upset to talk, even to him. I opened my chemistry book, not knowing where to start. I wondered if talking to Rabbit might help, then decided he couldn't possibly make a difference in my situation. Nothing could help.

Trying to study chemistry only made me feel worse. I closed the book. I could never force myself to get through the material again. I had performed to the maximum of my marathon ability, and failed miserably. How could I ever do better than that?

"Coordination constants," Hal whispered softly in my ear.

"Don't remind me," I said, feeling desperate for relief from my despair.

"Kill yourself," Hal whispered, reflecting my thoughts.

I was still amazed that Hal had access to all my private thoughts and feelings. But he was right. I could see no other way out of this mess. I couldn't make it here on earth. Maybe I would be more successful in the Other Worlds.

"We're here," said one of the voices. "Next stop: Jupiter."

The Other Worlds frightened me, but right now I was even more terrified of this world. The time was now perfect for my leap to the safety of the Beyond. But to break free of my body, I would have to dispose of it. The last time I'd tried, when I'd sliced my wrist back in high school, it was painful and I'd botched it. Since then, I'd had increasing feelings that my body was being slowly converted into machines that were undetectable and that functioned identically to the human body. I didn't know exactly why or how this was happening, but I knew it had to be part of my otherworldly connections. Machines don't feel pain. Death couldn't hurt too much now. This time I would succeed.

I didn't have a gun or pills. I wasn't violent enough to leap in front of a truck. Perhaps I could hang myself.

I looked around my tiny dorm room for a rope. The best I could come up with was a ball of yarn. I tested its strength, and it broke easily. It would never do. I dug through my drawers until I found my bandanna handkerchiefs. I tied four of them together with tight little knots at the corners, pulling them as hard as I could. I had begun to cry, and by now I could barely see to work through my tears. I tried not to make any crying noises, so that anyone passing by in the hallway wouldn't think I was up to anything unusual.

The only object I could find that would support my weight was my closet rod. I threw all my clothes from their hangers to the floor to make room. Then I tied the handkerchiefs into a slipknot and anchored the free end of the noose on the rod.

There wasn't anything I wanted to do first, such as call Steve or take care of any personal matters. None of that would be important when I got to the Other Worlds. I would have to hurry before I missed the juxtaposition of the worlds.

Relief was on its way. I stopped crying. I stepped next to the clothes rod, put my head through the noose, and let my knees drop.

The slipknot caught on the knots holding the handkerchiefs together. I readjusted them and pulled the noose tighter, again dropping my knees to dangle myself from my neck. I felt my face gradually turning bright red with the blood return cut off from my head. I could still breathe, barely. I worked the noose tighter and tighter around my neck and lifted my feet off the floor. It hurt!

My legs tired, allowing my feet to drop back to the floor. Much as I wanted to let my legs hang loose, they stiffened, straightening out to provide enough resistance against the floor to reduce the tension of the noose around my neck. I bent my knees again, my body swaying forward as I hung from the noose. Still, I was getting enough air to live.

After trying unsuccessfully to hang myself for an hour, I finally stood up and attempted to free the cord from around my neck. I had managed to pull the knots so tight that it took me another full hour to untangle myself.

I changed into a turtleneck shirt to hide the abrasions from the noose on my neck, then sat down and reopened my chemistry book. How humiliating—I couldn't even do the simplest thing, killing myself. Many people find it a real struggle to keep alive in this world, and here I was not even able to stop living at will.

Despite my foiled attempt, things seemed to be back to their usual state, except now I felt more hopeless and trapped than ever. I couldn't study because I was so tired from my intense studying over the last several days. While the other dormitory students were celebrating the end of the week with Friday-night parties, I drifted off to an exhausted sleep. An hour or two later I was awakened by the sound of Steve knocking desperately on my door. The knocking sounded distant. If I ignored it, the whole world might go away, and I might be transported off to another dimension.

No such luck. Steve's pounding became so insistent that I got up and let him in.

"I was worried about you," he told me. "Why didn't you answer the door?"

"I was asleep. You know how heavily I sleep."

He wasn't satisfied with that. "You look like you've been crying."

I told him about the exams.

"Something must have gone wrong with the computer," he said. "Please, go talk to Dr. Sands first thing on Monday morning."

"That sounds like a reasonable thing to do," I said.

"Good, then it's solved. Let's go drinking." His breath smelled strongly of alcohol. He had already been drinking for several hours.

I drew away. "I'm tired. And I should be studying."

After much insisting, I got him to leave. He looked confused. I felt confused. We were growing apart. He was now a working man who wanted to party all of his free time; I was still a serious and dedicated student with lofty goals to pursue. He seemed lost in his own world, and I was absorbed in mine.

I tried to study during the weekend, but still found it difficult. On Monday I went to Dr. Sands's office to ask him about the exams. I was impressed that Dr. Sands remembered me—"Sure, you're the one who wanted to sign up for the first five units right off!"

While explaining my difficulties to him I couldn't hold back my tears. But I was careful not to admit I had been so upset about the exams that I'd tried to kill myself. Now, even more, I wished I had succeeded, because I wouldn't have to face this; Dr. Sands wouldn't have to be bothered with me, and I wouldn't have to go through the embarrassment of crying in front of him.

Dr. Sands went into his adjoining office to look at the exams. He came back wearing a sheepish grin. "My goof. The computer printed out questions to unit eight. No wonder you didn't do so well!"

He allowed me to retake the exams, this time promising me he would personally generate the questions so the mistake wouldn't recur to cause me more trauma. I liked Dr. Sands. I retook his exams and made perfect scores, then signed up for the next two units for the following week.

Each week I took the two maximum allowable unit exams, achieving A's on every one. After six weeks I'd finished the entire first semester's work.

"I wasn't prepared for anyone as ambitious as you," Dr. Sands confessed. "I've had to keep on my toes to get new exams prepared every week to keep ahead of you. The next person behind you is only a third of the way through, and he's making B's and C's."

Dr. Sands went on, "You've inspired me to go ahead and

design the second-semester self-paced program for you. I haven't done it yet." He proceeded to grind out exams for me every week until I'd finished the second semester's work with an A, three weeks before the end of the fall semester.

"The next person behind you is just about to finish the first semester's exams," Dr. Sands told me. "You've done phenomenally. You know, this means you've come out way ahead of over a thousand students."

Dr. Sands looked thoughtful for a moment. "How would you like to work in my lab and help me with my research, along with my graduate students? We don't usually let undergraduates do research, especially not students who aren't chemistry majors. But you've demonstrated your capability. I could offer you course credit for it."

I couldn't imagine anyone could be so nice. I was honored. I took him up on his offer, working in his lab for the next two years on a theoretical physical chemistry project. Together we published a paper on our work in a professional journal.

Besides doing the physical chemistry research, I managed to make straight A's in all my classes that year. I didn't have much time for anything but school, and Steve began to fade into the background.

I continued my struggle to remain functional in the face of constant distraction from the voices. The voices seemed to want me to flunk out of school. They weren't quite as scary now as they used to be, because I'd lived with them for so many years. I assumed I'd just keep living with them and surviving with them, even though it was often difficult and unpleasant. I'd stayed out of the hospital for almost a year now. I decided this was what "normal" was supposed to be like. I figured I had to put up with the voices and other phenomena only because I was more sensitive than other people—like the Princess and the Pea. I wished I could stop being the Princess.

I discovered that when I was physically fatigued and

stressed, particularly around exams, I was most susceptible to the tyranny of the voices. They took advantage of my vulnerability to influence my mind and disorganize my thinking with their continuous chatter. But in spite of them, I knew I had to keep my sights on my goals and keep studying, no matter what.

The summer after my junior year I moved out of the dorm and into a house with three other women students. In summer school I was signed up for the notorious organic chemistry course. I managed a B for the first semester.

Since organic chemistry was the most important class on the transcript for the admissions committees of postgraduate programs, I felt I had to push even harder in the second semester to get an A.

But the voices became more bothersome again. The Interference Patterns had returned to dance across the pages I was trying to study. Familiar chopping sounds began to filter faintly through the cracks in the walls, and before long I was hearing the helicopters roaring over campus again.

One hot, sticky midsummer day, as I searched the sky for a helicopter that was flapping overhead, the voices became excited.

"There go the helicopters!" they yelled.

"Where?" I wanted to know.

"There!"

I ran down the block to get a view past the edge of the tall chemistry building, but all I could see was the innocent blue sky, cloudless and helicopterless. I ran to my bike, unlocked it as fast as I could, and jumped on. "Let's go, Clepto," I whispered to the bike. "Follow them!"

"They've gone to Welmington," Hal said nonchalantly.

"Welmington? Why there?"

"I dunno. Ask them."

What were the helicopters doing going to Welmington? Was there some connection between Cedar City and Welmington? The only connection I could think of was me.

"It's okay," Hal reassured me. "You should go."

I hated to leave my organic chemistry work, since it was so crucial that I study hard to get my A. Still, locating the helicopters was of even more crucial importance, and they might help me understand more of the Parallel Dimensions. I would have to go. This was the perfect chance. If I ran into trouble in Welmington, Paul and Gilbert would be there to help me out. They understood.

I pedaled back to the apartment as fast as I could and threw a water bottle and a hunk of cheese into my backpack. No one else was there. Without thinking my plan through further, I jumped back onto Clepto and cycled as fast as I could to the nearest exit from town. The helicopters hummed away in the distance, and I felt desperate to keep them within range. Welmington was ninety-five miles away. It didn't occur to me that I might not make it before dark. My bike didn't have a light, and I didn't have a map. I would be depending on the helicopters to guide me.

The skinny road to Welmington wound around every little farm. It snaked over hills so big they would have given even Sisyphus a case of heart failure. Trailer trucks zoomed past me, brushing my blond forearm hairs as they passed, kicking up dust that blew into my eyes and made me weave in my blindness. Within the first half hour I had drenched my T-shirt and shorts with sweat. My rear end was already sore from taking the bumps on the cheap bicycle seat. I needed a break.

I'm gonna stop at this gas station and adjust my seat. The place looks plastic. I bet they zapped this whole place here in a hurry so I'd have a place to stop. Nice thinking. They've even got water. I'm sure thirsty. Hey, man, why are you looking at me so funny? Haven't you ever seen a lady on a bicycle before? Adios, turkey. I'll be in Scotland before ye. If the helicopters come by here, tell 'em I went thattaway.

My Guiding Pattern was there. Right in front of me. Now I wouldn't get lost.

I'd always considered the Guiding Pattern a curiosity of science, pondered what wondrous physiological processes could be producing it—now I knew. It was Other Worldly.

The helicopters or the voices had left the Guiding Pattern for me. They must have been feeling charitable to send me a Guiding Pattern for strength and encouragement. Not many people these days rated so high as to be sent signs like the ones Moses, Noah, Jacob, and Amos got. *This is a prayer, I'm living it.*

Damn. Crotch is wearing raw from chafing. Hey, crotch, you can't give in yet! I can't get to Welmington without sitting on you.

"She's stopping at another filling station," I heard the voices comment. "After only twenty miles, she's stopping again."

I needed that stop. Ready to go again. The attendant who helped me adjust my seat had a nice smile, didn't he? Let's go.

I followed the Guiding Pattern, my Star of Bethlehem, northward. My quadriceps ached. My mouth was sawdust. My brain was sandpaper.

"When can we stop, Mommy?" I heard one of the voices ask.

Maybe I was wearing them out too. Oh, well, at least I wasn't hurting for company.

My bike odometer said I'd been forty-five miles. My odometer wasn't like ordinary odometers: mine had a live voice. I wondered if dehydration was getting to me, making me weak-kneed and light-headed.

I stopped at a local grocery to escape the blazing sun, locking my bike outside. Inside, the store was cold from the air conditioning. I reached inside the refrigerated sections to get a can of soda pop and an ice-cream bar. After paying, I sat down outside the store on the shady cement, devouring my cold treasures.

Quaint little store—you guys have a great imagination when you go to zapping things around here. Thanks, guys, I needed this.

I'm exhausted. Let me just rest my head a minute.

After a while I became aware of people talking.

"What's she doing lying here on the cement? Kinda strange-looking, if you ask me. How come she's sleeping here?"

Hell, I dunno, what am I doing here? At first my mind was hazy, and for an instant I couldn't remember where I was.

"Tell them you're sleeping, fool," said one of the voices.

I pried apart my eyes, all the while feeling nauseated. I peered up at a crowd of women and children standing in a semicircle around me. The sun behind them nearly blinded me, dimming the sharpness of their outlines.

"I'm resting," I said. I couldn't think of what else to say.

"For rare species," said one of the voices.

"For rare species," I said, without thinking about it. There, didn't that take care of all the questions?

A woman in the crowd handed me a blanket, then helped me up and led me around back to a shade tree. "Rest here," she said. "You look tired. You look like you've had a long trip."

Wow, old-fashioned kindness. Wasn't that how they did it in the Bible? This was all a part of the prayer.

I dozed for about three quarters of an hour. The drone of nearby helicopters startled me awake.

The voices were yelling, "The plaster rafts! The plaster rafts!"

This didn't make sense, but I was sure the voices made perfect sense in some Other Dimension meaning-system.

I paused for a moment in my bewilderment, then I realized I'd have to hurry! The helicopters were still close—I couldn't lose them!

Wobbling, I mounted Clepto. I was stiff all over, and my crotch was painfully sore to the touch of the seat. I gritted my teeth and pedaled out on wooden thighs.

The hills steepened. Hours slipped away as the late afternoon sank down in the sky. There would be no more towns until Welmington. I was alone on a darkening highway. Soon I would be biking blindly into the night's blackness.

Hey, wait—where are the helicopters? I don't hear them. I don't see my Guiding Pattern anymore, either. Have they abandoned me? Hey, where are the voices?

The sun was gone, set for the day. Now I was in trouble. Wait—there were the lights of Welmington on the horizon! My oasis! I didn't know if I could pedal that far—my legs were shot.

I hadn't expected another steep hill. I could hardly turn the pedals fast enough to keep the bike from wobbling and falling over. I dismounted, walking my bike up the next two hills. It was all I could do to just walk the bike.

Please, Welmington lights, please be real. Don't be a blinkin' mirage.

Hey—the helicopters are gone. The voices are quiet. No advice from them now. Will they be back?

No.

Now what?

I was alone in Welmington with my bike, in the dark of the night, with ten dollars in my pocket. I was tired. I couldn't just lie down with Clepto on the street. I remembered my parents had once taken me to Gilbert's house for therapy. It was only a few miles away. Maybe he could help me decide what to do now.

I pulled up in his front yard just as he and his wife were returning from an after-dinner stroll down the block.

"My word, Carol!" he said when he saw me. "How did you get here?"

"On my bike," I said.

He looked down at Clepto. "All the way from Cedar City?"

"Yeah—I left at one o'clock. What time is it now?"

"Nine-thirty. Are you kidding? That's almost a hundred miles. You did it in eight hours? Why? And *how?* Do you know it was ninety-five degrees today?"

"It's hard to explain," I said. "It's got something to do with the voices and the helicopters. They're gone now, though."

"Don't tell me more," he said. "I understand. Where are you going to stay tonight?"

"I'm going back to Cedar City, I guess." I wasn't thinking too clearly.

"Nonsense," said Gilbert's wife. "We'll put you up here."

"Is that a good idea?" I said. "What if the helicopters come back? I don't want to bring my problems down on you."

"We insist," said Gilbert. "We can handle the helicopters."

As soon as the bed was made, I fell into it and dropped right off to sleep. I had insisted on parking Clepto right next to my bed, in case I needed to make a quick getaway.

The next morning I awoke to the smell of bacon cooking. The voices were still curiously absent. The sun's rays were beaming brightly through the window. Wow, I had to get up—I had a lot to do. I had to get back to Cedar City and get studying again. I jumped out of bed. When my feet hit the floor, my legs collapsed under me, and I slumped onto the carpet. I had forgotten all about my sore legs. I rubbed them a while, then slowly and stiffly rose to my feet. The ride back was going to be more difficult.

I thanked Gilbert and his wife for their very kind hospitality, and reassured Gilbert I would be okay. He insisted I box up my bike and take a bus back to Cedar City. I promised I would, then cycled off to a store to buy some food for the long trip. Of course I was going to cycle.

Outside the store I struck up a conversation with a traveling salesman who told me he was driving to Cedar City. I asked him for a ride. He agreed, saying he liked having company to keep from getting bored, then we bought some twine and tied Clepto into his trunk. He drove me all the way back to Cedar City and dropped me at my apartment. As I stiffly climbed the steps to my apartment, I wondered if I really would have had the strength to cycle back from Welmington in one day.

"Goodbye!" Hal shouted after the salesman's car as it drove off. I smiled, realizing the voices could never keep quiet for long anymore.

I entered my apartment to an uproar. My worried roommates informed me that my parents had been frantically phoning everywhere, trying to locate me. They'd finally called Welmington and heard I was there. Apparently, when I had disappeared without notice, Steve had panicked and called my parents. That was very unlike Steve. Usually he was calm and discreet. I wondered if he could be serving the Other Side's purposes. In a few days, the uproar blew over and I returned to being unobtrusively psychotic, listening to the voices and trying to locate the helicopters, between marathon studying sessions.

I managed to get my A in organic chemistry, then started making plans for the fall. During that summer I had begun to reconsider my career choice. I wanted to make full use of my abilities, to help people as much as I possibly could. I decided I could better realize this goal by becoming a medical doctor rather than an optometrist. But would a medical school accept someone who'd had as many mental problems as I appeared to have? Granted, I might have looked crazy to others, but I knew better. I had outgrown the label of schizophrenia. I believed I had merely been suffering from "adjustment problems" as Paul had described them; my mother had explained them as extensions of my "overactive imagination." I had managed to stay out of the hospital for about a year and a half now. I had held up under large stresses recently with only internal mental trauma, without collapsing completely. As I grew older, I was gaining more control over my symptoms. Yes, I could do it.

I phoned Paul in Welmington and talked the idea over

with him. "I think it's a terrific idea," he told me. "You'd make a wonderful doctor. Of course, I'd hope you would go into psychiatry. I think you'd make an outstanding psychiatrist. As far as your psychiatric history, I'll be glad to write the medical school a letter. I don't routinely diagnose people other than 'adjustment disorder' for the very reason that it might adversely affect their future, as in your case. I will tell them what I usually say in such situations—that you had an adjustment reaction and that you have grown beyond it, especially since you now seem to be functioning quite well. Carol, I'm excited for you! I think you can do it."

I phoned my parents to tell them of my decision. I expected they would be proud and thrilled. After I made the announcement, there was a long, uncomfortable silence on the line.

"What's the matter—don't you think it's great?" I said.

Dad cleared his throat. "Well, do you think you're up to that kind of pressure?"

Mom said, "You might be better off trying something not so difficult."

I was disappointed that they weren't as excited about it as I was. But at least they agreed to support whatever decision I made and help me in any way they could. I appreciated their support and love, yet I felt uneasy around the edges that they weren't one hundred percent enthusiastic, as I was. When Ed had gone to medical school they had been thrilled to have a doctor for a son. I couldn't understand why they weren't just as thrilled to have a doctor for a daughter.

"Look," I said to them, "I'm not likely to get accepted anyhow, because of my psychiatric history." No doubt my parents would agree with that.

When I saw Steve that night I said, "I'm going to apply to medical school."

I'd expected him to look thrilled. He didn't; he looked crushed. "Are you really serious about medical school?" he asked.

"You bet. I decided I'd rather be a doctor than an optometrist. I want to help others as much as I possibly can."

"Do you know what this means for us? Do you know how many years of education that will involve?"

"Four years of medical school, then three to five more years of training in a specialty."

"That's a long time."

"I'm sure it will be a grind, but I think I can endure it. I'm good at enduring."

"You're leaving me," Steve said. "You're fading away from me."

His reaction surprised me.

"Steve, you don't think my career will get in the way of our relationship, do you? Of course, I'll be busy, but that doesn't mean I can't love you." I felt frustrated at not being able to make him understand. Perhaps we had grown apart more than I had realized.

Steve seemed to sense it.

"It's what I want to do," I said firmly. "And I'm going to do it."

I sent off applications to six optometry schools—in case I couldn't get into med school—and five medical schools. It hurt to have to tell the truth on the application forms that asked about any history of mental problems, but I could never lie. Then I took the optometry entrance exam, scoring above the ninety-fifth percentile. I was thrilled—I knew this meant that with my solid 3.75 grade point average, I'd have no trouble getting into optometry. I didn't know about medical school. Next I took the medical-school entrance exam. It was a lot harder. My scores came back well above the seventy-fifth percentile, more than adequate for acceptance into medical school. I relaxed a little.

While awaiting responses to my applications, I received a letter from the admissions committee at State, my first-choice medical school. The committee wanted to interview me. I knew the school didn't routinely interview applicants. It was obvious what this was all about. Someone had once warned me that this would probably happen, because of my history of mental problems. I interpreted the request for an interview as a favorable sign indicating that after having reviewed my letters of recommendation and the letter from my psychiatrist, the admissions committee was still interested in me.

My interviewer turned out to be a kindly old family doctor who reminded me of Marcus Welby on TV. He immediately put me at ease by chatting about light subjects, hobbies, cross-country skiing. When he saw that I could converse like a normal person, he got down to business. "It says on your admission form that you have a psychiatric history."

I nodded. The voices remained in the background, not bothering me. I hoped they'd stay quiet till this was over.

"The letter from your psychiatrist says you had an 'adolescent adjustment reaction' and that you are doing well now."

"I haven't been hospitalized for the last year and a half." I honestly believed I had been functioning as well as any normal person.

"Have you ever been depressed?"

I didn't know at the time that his area of research was depression in family practice.

"Well, yes," I said, "I've felt depressed in the past—hasn't everybody?"

He didn't persist in asking further psychiatric questions. It didn't occur to him to ask me any questions about schizophrenic symptoms. After all, it was highly unusual for a schizophrenic to be applying to medical school. He knew that schizophrenia is a severely debilitating illness, generally leaving its victims so mentally crippled and deteriorated that the majority have trouble holding even the simplest jobs. He saw in my appearance nothing resembling a deteriorated schizophrenic, so he did not bother asking whether I heard voices or had strange ideas.

I was greatly relieved that he didn't ask me about voices or helicopters, because I would have felt obliged to answer his questions truthfully. If he had asked me those questions and heard my answers, he surely would not have recommended my admission.

He led the conversation back to lighter topics, and despite my nervousness I maintained a cheerful front, trying to come across like a normal twenty-one-year-old woman who wanted to become a doctor. I didn't want to slip up and give any indication that I might be distracted by voices or other phenomena.

At the end of the interview he said, "We'll see you in medical school next fall."

After I left his office I kept going over that last line in my mind, trying to impress on myself that he had really said it. If he meant it, then he was going to recommend my acceptance. He was probably the last word on the matter. Back at my apartment, I felt happy and glowing inside, but I didn't tell anyone what my interviewer had said to me.

I thanked the voices for being good, then I said a prayer of thanks to God for His help. What had just happened could have been no less than divine intervention.

The medical school sent out its letters of acceptance in three batches over three months. It notified the top-ranking people first. I knew I wouldn't hear the first month, because that was the month of my interview. But I wondered if I'd hear anything on the first day of the second month. I rushed home from class to my mailbox, and found a letter from the medical school waiting for me. Was it a letter of acceptance or a letter of rejection? I could barely stand the wait while I ripped the envelope apart. The letter began, "Congratulations on your acceptance . . ."

"WHOOOPPEEEEEEE!" I yelled at the top of my lungs. Nobody was around, nobody heard. I tore into my apartment and ran around the living-room coffee table about a dozen times before I could settle down and stop. Success!

I had been told that nobody flunks out of medical school, unless he really isn't trying or he screws up in a major way, like cheating or deliberately harming patients. Once you're in, you're in, and they're dedicated to helping you through. They want everybody to graduate. If that was really true, then the hard part was getting in.

Wow! I'd done the hard part! I was confident that now that I had gotten in, I would do very well, because I wanted it so badly. I wasn't at all afraid of hard work. If anything, hard work would be to my advantage, since I was used to it and accepted it. The future looked rosy.

"We're going to medical school!" I heard one of the voices say.

I smiled.

CHAPTER SEVEN

MED SCHOOL

I called everyone I could think of to tell my good news. My parents hadn't expected me to be accepted to medical school, and they couldn't hide their ambivalence when I told them I'd been accepted. I was surprised and again disappointed at their reaction. It subtly eroded my self-confidence.

I wanted to tell Steve, but over the past year we had been drifting farther apart. It wasn't Steve's fault; I blamed myself. For the past three years we had been growing into a state of mutual dependency. Most guys would have bailed out years before. But Steve derived personal satisfaction from needing to be needed. He had tolerated, even welcomed, the dependency that came with my illness. With true heroic spirit he had endured my symptoms with me, and he had helped me enormously. I felt indebted to Steve; I wanted to make amends. I hoped to stand independently now, giving him his chance to grow without having to carry the burden of my illness, being able to support *him* when he needed it. I didn't know if it would be possible to convert the relationship into healthier patterns without destroying it. But I knew I couldn't continue with it the way it was. I felt too guilty about it.

But what if our relationship didn't change? The idea of breaking up made me feel guilty too. I couldn't leave him now, after all he had done for me. I cared a lot about him; I still loved him.

One night Steve came by to see me after he had been drinking. His breath was particularly offensive. When he tried to kiss me, I drew away.

"Carol, what's the matter?" he asked. "Do you want to break up with me?"

"Do *you* want to break up?"

"I don't know. We're just not the same anymore."

I couldn't conceal my feelings any longer. I had hoped they would change, but they hadn't. "I know," I said. "Why don't we try getting some distance from each other? Maybe things will change. Whatever happens, I'll always feel close to you, because you're so very special."

I tried to point out the mutual overdependence in our relationship, but Steve either couldn't see it or didn't want to.

"I don't want to just be your friend," he said. "I don't think I can stand this."

At first I missed Steve so much that it would have been easier to forget about unhealthy relationships and go back to him. A few days later I ran into him on campus. He had just started graduate school in philosophy. He looked like a different Steve, disheveled, his gaze lowered. He said he didn't want to date other women. It really hurt me to see him suffering, but I couldn't think of a way to make it any easier for either of us.

I wasn't interested in dating anyone else either, but I couldn't continue our abnormal relationship during the strain of medical school—it might unbalance me completely. And it wasn't fair to Steve. Breaking up was something we had to do.

Several weeks later I saw Steve again. By then, he was dating other women. It hurt, but I knew it had to be. I could still see the pain in Steve's eyes, but he was going to make it.

The next thing I did was to terminate psychotherapy. My relationship with Rabbit was another abnormal relationship that had to go. I wouldn't have time for such foolishness as psychotherapy when I got into medical school, and I certainly didn't want any reminders of my sickness. I thought that getting rid of these "signs of sickness" would mean I was no longer sick. Although Rabbit thought I was making a big mistake, he quietly wished me well, and I thanked him for helping me. I didn't think I would need help ever again. I'd learned all the coping mechanisms, and now I would be able to make it on my own.

One of my roommates and I decided to move into a two-bedroom apartment. We rented a roomy townhouse apartment with wall-to-wall shag carpeting and air conditioning. Compared to our previous run-down college apartment, this modern apartment seemed posh. I decided we needed a parakeet chirping in a cage in the living room, so I bought a yellow parakeet and named it Banana. I worked hard to tame Banana, and before long the bird would sit for hours on my shoulder or poking around in my hair, while I busied myself around the apartment.

I wanted to earn as much money as I could over the summer before medical school, to gain as much independence as possible. I got a job waitressing full-time at a fancy restaurant, but that wasn't enough to satisfy me. I found a second full-time job doing the laundry for a hundred-bed nursing home. I liked the laundry job, but not the restaurant job. The voices were so distracting to my waitressing that I had difficulty keeping all the orders straight in my mind. While toiling over hot dryers folding endless laundry, it didn't matter whether or not I heard voices. The manual labor was so easy that even psychotic symptoms didn't prevent my accomplishing it.

I arrived at my laundry job at four in the morning daily and sweated in the hundred-degree heat till noon; then I went home and slept for two hours, and rushed off to my waitress job at four in the afternoon and worked till eleven or twelve. Then I rushed home for another two hours' sleep before hauling myself out of bed to go to the nursing home to repeat the whole cycle again the next day.

In a short time, I became chronically sleep-deprived. This is how doctors live, I told myself. I was trying to prove to myself that I could do what doctors do. I wasn't trying to prove anything to anyone else; I just needed to reassure myself that I was tough enough to be a doctor. I needed to be absolutely certain in advance that I could do it. Although I was incredibly fatigued, I was also happy to know that I could endure. And on top of all that, for the first time in my life I was paying my own rent and living expenses. I had graduated to being a responsible adult. My future looked bright, and I felt confident.

I thought of myself as a medical student first and as a person second. Accordingly, I designed myself a schedule consisting of attending classes all day, coming home and studying continuously until four in the morning, sleeping for two hours, arising at six, taking a brisk jog, and studying until time to leave for morning classes again. In the face of all the humanly impossible amount of work to be done, I saw that I had no choice but to work this hard if I was to survive.

During my undergraduate years I had managed to excel not because I was smarter than the other students, but because I was willing to work longer hours than anybody else. In medical school my major compensation factor, time at the books, would no longer be available to me, because there everybody worked to his or her maximum. There simply weren't more hours for me to work than my classmates were putting in.

Of my freshman medical class of about two hundred students, about eighty percent were male. Our first instruction on the first day was to divide ourselves into cadaver-dissection teams of four. Three guys approached me asking if I'd be on their team. I shared my side of the cadaver with Bruce Anderson. He was a tall, slender man with coal-black shoulder-length curls and a dark beard. When he put on his white coat and stethoscope, he looked so handsome that anyone could have mistaken him for a Hollywood doctor.

Bruce made the first incision across the cadaver's chest, exactly as in the dissection manual. I was surprised that watching someone cut up a human body didn't make me feel squeamish. The cadaver's skin looked unreal, like plastic, and it had the texture of rubber. It smelled so strongly of formaldehyde that no other odors could intrude. The incisions didn't bleed, and the whole process seemed as ordinary as cutting into a Barbie doll. After that first incision, there wasn't time for queasiness—we had too much to do.

From the first day of medical school, I felt left behind. I had made a serious blunder during my undergraduate years by placing my premedical emphasis on chemistry rather than on more relevant biology background courses. The official medical-school spokesman for premedical undergraduates had advised us to avoid excess biology courses, saying that we'd get all the biology we needed in medical school. He had also generally advised us to spend our undergraduate years becoming "well rounded" in disciplines not available to us in medical school. Having taken that advice to heart, I had established a terrific background in dance and physical chemistry, but I was somewhat handicapped by my ignorance of biology.

"Do you want to study anatomy together tonight?" Bruce asked me before our first anatomy quiz. "We could spread out our books at my place—it's pretty quiet where I live."

"Do you think I might hold you back?" I said. "You seem way ahead of me on the material."

"No, it'll be good review for me. Let's give it a try."

I ended up sitting up all night in his living room with the

anatomy books spread out around me; Bruce gave up and went to bed around midnight.

Despite cramming all night, I barely passed that first anatomy quiz. My score was near the bottom of the class. Fortunately, my medical school had discarded the old-fashioned letter grading system and adopted a pass-fail-honors system; otherwise I would have been making D's. This performance devastated me, since I was used to making A's in college. It was my first indication that maybe things weren't going to be all right.

After cramming all night, I wasn't able to stay awake through the next day's lectures. Before long, staying up most of the night was the rule, and my chronically sleep-deprived brain was unable to keep awake for more than the first five minutes of any lecture. The lectures were boring anyhow, mostly the product of uninterested M.D.s who had to take time from their valuable research to deliver their lectures, usually in thick, barely understandable foreign accents, on insignificant research advances like ion transport mechanisms of toad bladders. Bruce and I carried a huge thermos of strong coffee to class every day, and I supplemented the coffee with caffeine tablets. Others in the class were using amphetamines to stay awake.

The medical school considered itself progressive. Our class was divided into smaller "support groups," part of an experimental program devised by the school's administration to provide encouragement from our peers. Each group leader was a member of the medical school's faculty. Our leader turned out to be Dean Honeycut, the dean of students. He encouraged us to bring our problems to him. When I learned he was a serious long-distance runner and an avid bicycler, two of my favorite activities, I took it for granted that he was a genuinely good man.

Bruce and I found it convenient to spend all our time together. We divided up the homework assignments and pooled our efforts, but even with that arrangement, we still had trouble completing all the work. Before long, we were preparing and eating all our meals together, and also doing our laundry together, shopping together, and essentially living together, all wrapped up in trying to survive medical school.

Our classmates were poker-faces, too proud to admit worries about not being able to keep up. Bruce never complained, either. I had the impression that I was the only one who was feeling panicky about all the work to be done, and that thought only magnified my panic. I could never tell whether I was actually intellectually deficient or the course material was too overwhelming for anyone. Bruce was never good at discussing these things, so I never found out.

Having Bruce by my side in the crowded gross anatomy lab was reassuring. Anatomy overstimulated my senses, the dead bodies seeming to gravitate closer and closer to one another until I couldn't bend over to examine some aberrant little thread of a nerve on our cadaver without another student backing into me, or without bumping into someone else. The trouble began gradually, progressing so insidiously that I didn't notice when it started.

Our classmates' behavior intensified my confusion. They would yell to each other from opposite sides of the cadaver lab, making tasteless jokes about their cadavers, usually with related remarks about food or sex. In time, their voices came to assume an echoing quality. I was certain someone had set up an echo machine in the lab. I never knew whether the voices floating over the lab's roar were our instructors announcing changes in the dissection manual or whether they were messages to me from the Parallel Dimensions. I depended on Bruce for up-to-date information.

To avoid the sensory overstimulation of the daytime anatomy lab, I began stealing into the lab late at night to complete the dissection assignments. I accomplished more when free of distraction from the other students. Bruce eventually started joining me in my middle-of-the-night sessions in the lab, indicating to me that perhaps there was nothing unreasonable in my distaste for the daytime lab atmosphere. I assumed my confusion about the voices in the lab was simply an exaggerated normal response to a novel stress situation. I expected my panic would clear when I settled into the semester's routine more comfortably.

I needed Bruce. At first I needed his help to catch up on my basic biology; later I needed his emotional support and reality orientation. I depended on Bruce to help me sort out what was really going on.

I told Bruce a bit about my problems, explaining to him about the Parallel Dimensions, and even telling him that a psychiatrist had labeled me schizophrenic.

"Do you have to take medication for your problem?" Bruce asked me.

"No, I don't tolerate drugs very well. I try to get along without any."

Because I appeared to be functioning adequately, Bruce assumed that my illness, if I even had one, had retreated into dormancy. It seemed plausible that an atypically creative person like me might be called schizophrenic by an overenthusiastic psychiatrist. Although my ideas about a parallel existence seemed odd, Bruce didn't interpret them to be delusions; instead, he thought I was speaking figuratively, even poetically. He didn't ask me anything more.

Because he seldom expressed himself, Bruce had initially impressed me as dull. I couldn't understand how he repeatedly scored honors on exams I was nearly failing. But brief appearances of his keen sense of humor led me to observe him more closely. Slowly I came to appreciate his hidden brilliance and sharp wit, and I was privileged to see it blossom as our relationship deepened.

Bruce's phlegmatic style reflected his philosophy of maintaining external appearances. And so he ignored my subtle inappropriate actions, such as my occasional giggling at nothing; he hoped these merely represented fleeting vestiges of past misfortune to be forgotten.

By the time finals week started, I was exhausted; I would have to depend on Bruce to help me through.

Good grief, what's the matter with me? I can't concentrate anymore. It's all those Interference Patterns, beginning to spill over from the Other Side—I can't even read the words on the pages for all the colorful designs dancing over them. Somebody please tell me what this means.

No, ignore it: that's what Bruce would do. That's what Jesus Christ would do.

I refused to admit that the interference was bothering me, because admission of the distraction would automatically mean acceptance of it, and I certainly didn't accept it.

I wished I'd gotten more sleep that week.

"Bruce," I whispered in his ear, "I'm worried."

No response. He wanted me to ignore my concern. I was talking to the wall.

"Bruce, no matter how hard I study, I'm still flunking exams. I don't understand it. How can I possibly learn all this material by tomorrow afternoon?" (*Help me swim through this interference! Lead me out of it!*)

"Don't worry," he said flatly with two echoes.

Not very reassuring.

"You're going to pass this exam. I know you can do it. I've seen you pass plenty of other exams."

But this is different! You don't understand! You aren't lost in the fog of the interference. How come I can't sail through exams as you do? I work twice as hard as you! None of this makes sense.

The entire room felt SuperReal, imparting the words *things are not as they seem* that crept up the back of my brainstem into my conscious awareness.

"Look, babe, it's gonna be all right," he said, trying to reassure me as he rubbed the back of my neck with one hand, "and there is disdain in your brain."

What? Golly, did he really say that? Or am I just picking up on some stray wavelength? I thought his lips moved when he said that. Maybe not. It's hard to tell, with all those patterns dancing all over his face. I'm afraid to ask him if he really said it.

The room continued basking in the radiation of the Super-Real.

"Tell him the Ultimate Truth," Hal whispered in my ear.

"What Ultimate Truth?" I said.

"What did you say?" Bruce said.

"The voices know the Ultimate Truth. We need to know it to pass the exam."

"What are you talking about?"

"I wish I understood it better. I'll have to wait for them to tell me," I said.

"Oh my God," Bruce moaned, "tell me this isn't true."

"What?" I asked, perplexed, "what isn't true?"

"You. You're not making sense," he said. He looked scared, and he looked twice as bad with all those patterns crawling over him.

I answered, "Me? Of course I'm making sense. It's transcended sense. *You're* the one who's not making sense. I have an important Message to convey to you and you're not even pretending to listen."

"Listen, kissin', missin', pissin' . . ." I heard Hal say, now from behind the couch where I was sitting, mocking my words.

Bruce didn't say anything more. He just sat there, staring at me dumbly. His brain was distintegrating. *Don't worry, Bruce; I'll save you. Just hang on till I can get the rest of these Messages.*

Bruce still didn't realize what was happening to me. He just thought my illogical speech was an extreme but normal reaction to stress and sleep deprivation. He maintained cool reason and helped me study, then he directed me to final exams at the right time and place. By the end of finals week I had managed to garner enough points on the exams to pass every course—barely.

When I left school for Christmas vacation I hoped some rest would allow me to get my thought processes straightened out. I visited Bruce's family the first week of vacation. They had only recently moved to the Midwest from California, where Bruce had been brought up. Although they were a middle-class family, Bruce insisted on paying for medical school himself. This meant that he had taken out loans and held a part-time job in addition to a heavy course load. I was certain my parents would be impressed with Bruce's motivation and superior intellect, two things they'd criticized in Steve.

But when Bruce came to my house to visit during the second week of Christmas vacation, my mother criticized him to me endlessly, claiming he was eating everything in sight, saying he didn't have any personality. I decided she just hadn't gotten to know his less reserved side. Then my father drew me aside for a private talk: he wanted to discourage me from marrying Bruce.

Bruce and I had never discussed marriage, but after my father made the suggestion, we discussed it and decided to consider it. Over the next few days, Bruce, sensing my parents' disapproval, began to feel uncomfortable around my house, but he wouldn't discuss this with me. He finally became so uneasy that he cut his visit to my home short, and the two of us went back to school early.

Christmas break hadn't straightened out my thinking, but at least I had gotten some rest. When second semester rolled around, I felt ready to start.

As part of our second-semester physiology lab, Bruce and I had to attend dog surgery labs. We were supposed to learn cardiovascular physiology by performing heart surgery on anesthetized dogs and injecting them with various drugs to alter their blood pressures and blood-flow rates. At one time or another during the lab period, each of the sleeping dogs in the lab regained partial consciousness to fill the room intermittently with sorrowful sounds of whimpering and yap-

ping. Each time, the lab instructor came by to reanesthetize
the dogs, and they became still again.

After the lab, Bruce and I couldn't talk about it. But I
couldn't forget the sounds of those pathetic canine whimpers
and yelps.

We arrived late to the next physiology lecture. We had to
take the only remaining seats, in the middle of the back row
of the auditorium. As we settled in and opened our note-
books, a student in the class interrupted the lecturer to ask
him to clarify a point. Suddenly I noticed sounds of a dog
whimpering, filtering right through the cement wall at my
back. The whimpers were punctuated with painful-sounding
yelps, as if some animal were being tortured. The ruckus
grew louder and louder until it sounded like twenty canines
barking and whining right behind me, through the wall.

I glanced over at Bruce. He was busy scribbling away at
his lecture notes. He didn't appear to be hearing anything
but the lecture. Well, that was just like Bruce—he had such
a narrow attention span. I wouldn't expect him to notice the
sounds. I gazed around at the other class members. They
were all engrossed in listening to the lecture and getting it
down in their notes. They didn't seem to be at all concerned
about the noise. Was I imagining it?

I turned my attention back to the lecturer, and the yap-
ping faded somewhat. The lecturer was explaining the theory of laminar blood flow, drawing mazes of lines and arrows
on the blackboard with purple and green chalk. I stole a few
scanty notes from Bruce's page and tried to copy the professor's diagram.

Gradually the barking at my back intensified. Again I
looked around the auditorium, but still nobody else appeared to be noticing the sounds from behind the wall. Then
the other students all began to move as a unit to put away
their notes and slip into their coats. I guessed the lecture was
over—I wasn't really paying attention. The sound of the dogs
buried itself in the rustling of books and papers and the chat-

tering of my classmates as they filed out of the lecture room.

That semester Bruce and I divided up the work to enable us to get through it. Bruce attended the lectures I missed, and he took good notes. In return, I stayed home and took notes for us on the physiology readings we were supposed to be doing. As I read the physiology of the heart sounds, I took out my stethoscope and listened to my own heart sounds to help me understand what I was reading. Lup-dup, lup-dup, lup-crackle-scratch: I was hearing extraneous noise from my clothing brushing against the diaphragm of the instrument. I readjusted and listened again.

Lup-dup, lup-dup, crackle-scratch *GR-RUFF, ARF-ARF*. Not the dogs again! Somehow the dogs had gotten into my stethoscope!

A day or two later, the leader of our physiology discussion group invited a heart patient to class. I lined up in the front of the classroom with the other students to listen to the patient's heart murmur through the instructor's stethoscope. When it was my turn to listen, all I could hear was the dogs.

"Did you hear the heart murmur?" the instructor asked me.

"Sounds like he's got a dog in his chest," I said.

I don't know how my instructor took that remark. He didn't look surprised when I said it, but of course I didn't expect him to. I thought he could hear the dog, too. None of the other students seemed to notice. They were all absorbed in trying to learn every last detail to help them get that honors grade.

As medical students, we were supposed to have left cut-throat competition behind in our premed days; once we were accepted to medical school we should have adopted more mature, cooperative attitudes. But it didn't work that way: there were many savagely competitive, backstabbing medical students that the rest of us called "gunners." Although the term was derogatory, everyone harbored some secret gunner tendencies. I frequently heard gunners advising fellow students that they should take time out for their personal lives—"go play tennis"; "take a day off for your wife"; "take that ski trip over Thanksgiving"—then privately spend every minute of their weekends and Thanksgiving holiday cramming while their comrades took their advice and took a break. Then the gunner would blow away the next three exams. Although the class was full of gunners, no one would admit to being one. No one would acknowledge the competition pervading our class. Openly boastful students ("I went to Vegas last weekend and still managed to pull an honors on Monday's biochem exam") intensified my chagrin over my own poor scholastic performance. I wasn't playing tennis or going on ski trips. I was studying every minute of every weekend and holidays, but instead of enjoying honors grades, I lived in constant terror of slipping into academic deficiency. It didn't seem fair.

One night when Bruce and I went to a bar for a drink after studying hard all evening, I overheard a classmate sitting next to us.

"Med school is great," I heard him tell his date. "I don't hardly have to study at all. The material just comes natural to me." He looked so cool, so entirely self-confident, that his date couldn't doubt his words.

Later, on the street I passed several guys from my medical class on their way to the bars. I rarely went anywhere in Cedar City without running into classmates going in and out of places, apparently having lots of fun—at the fieldhouse, the recreation center, the bars, the movies, restaurants, parties— even the nights before exams. And if I was lucky enough to avoid them around town, I still overheard them in class talking about all their great parties and about their chief concerns: beer and women. Knowing all this only made me angrier at having to limit my own free activities. I had to study so hard that I could rarely attend movies or parties anymore, and there was precious little time for racquetball with Bruce, which had been our favorite form of recreation first semester.

One evening when my roommate, Megan, and I were with

Bruce, I began to complain that my classmates were talking about me behind my back. I told her, "They've even started talking about me right in front of me. But they've purposely started talking in cryptic phrases that they can understand but I can't, to keep me from knowing exactly what they're saying."

Bruce, Megan told me later, was standing behind me out of my view, shaking his head at her to let her know he thought my impression of my classmates was inaccurate.

"Can you give me an example?" Megan asked me, sounding dubious.

"Sure. Recently I overheard one of my classmates saying his coffee had grown cold. I didn't realize it at the time, but later when I thought about it, I knew he had really been referring to me. Because I was also drinking coffee, he was intimating that I was cold."

"That seems pretty obvious," said Megan sarcastically.

Bruce continued shaking his head, still out of my view.

"It *was* obvious," I said. "I don't know why I didn't pick up on it right away."

"Are you sure that's really what was going on?" she asked.

"Positive."

"It does sound a little farfetched, don't you think? After all, you've been under a lot of stress, not sleeping enough—"

"No." I cut her off. True, I had initially worried that maybe I was just being paranoid, breaking down under the stress. But when these incidents kept recurring in slightly different form I had decided I wasn't imagining them. My classmates really were talking about me. They were unscrupulous people.

Megan let the subject drop. She knew it was impossible to talk people out of paranoid delusions.

I continued feeling suspicious of my classmates. They seemed to have a conspiracy. They were going to make me flunk out, simply by pooling their mental powers and willing it into my brain. In my paranoid state of mind, I became hypervigilant, interpreting my classmates' normal conversational gestures as secret signs to each other about me. A casual glance at the ceiling by one of my classmates was really a disguised cue to someone else. I became preoccupied with trying to put together meaningful ideas from fragments of conversations I overheard, assuming they were part of the conspiracy. I felt so uncomfortable around my classmates that I quit attending almost all of my classes; I dreaded appearing for exams. When I did show up at lectures, people commented that they hadn't seen me in a long time; the comments made me more suspicious. I felt so conspicuous that I wished I could make myself invisible.

One day, sitting in the very back row of a physiology lecture that I couldn't follow, I felt an electric current pass from the top of the lecturer's head, over the class, and across the auditorium to where I was sitting. The lecturer seemed to be looking right at me and reciting his lecture to *me* personally. It was as if the rest of the class no longer existed. I had no doubts in my mind about what was happening; I didn't need to question whether it was possible that the lecturer was singling me out. I just accepted the idea. It was as if my mental censor for implausible ideas wasn't functioning. I even imagined I heard the lecturer say, "That, Ms. North, is the Message we will expect you to relay to the Other Side." With that concluding remark he picked up his briefcase and exited through the door on the edge of the stage.

After that I became obsessively interested in physiology. Every day I became this professor's private captive audience hoping to learn the content of the Message I thought I was supposed to relay to the Other Side, and every day he delivered a profound lecture intended only for me to understand. I couldn't comprehend all the deep Meanings I thought this man was conveying to me, but I had no doubt they were there.

During spring break, Bruce went home for vacation. I had to stay in Cedar City to continue my studying nonstop. We had a very important endocrinology exam coming up after spring break. It was the only exam in that class, and the score on that exam would determine the entire semester grade. I had to pass it.

I had plenty of outside help on the exam. A student in the row behind me kept whispering answers in my ear.

"The answer to the first question," the student behind me whispered, "is 'All of the above.' "

I circled E, "All of the above," with my No. 2 pencil and blackened in the corresponding fifth square in the first row of the computer answer sheet. Nice guy. That question would have been too difficult for me to answer by myself. Its meaning kept shifting. I would catch on to the second question more easily. I smiled as I read the second question. There was an important Message for me locked inside its structure. I felt grateful for being chosen to participate in the enlightening experience, and I sent the professor a thought-wave thank-you. As I considered the question's third foil and all of its attendant multiple meanings, the professor sneezed. Ah-hah! That was my cue! The answer had to be C. I blackened the middle square of the second line of boxes on the answer sheet. This was easy. I relaxed and let my pelvis slide forward in my seat.

The student behind me continued to whisper answers to me. "Number three is D, four is A, and five is E."

I darkened the appropriate squares on the answer sheet and then I decided to turn around and find out who belonged to the helpful voice. To my astonishment I discovered that I was sitting in the last row of the testing room! As I turned my head back around to the front of the room I noticed the professor had his eyes fixed on me. Not wanting to be accused of cheating, I once again absorbed myself in the exam.

The voice behind me continued whispering answers. But it couldn't be someone behind me. And it didn't sound like Bruce, so what I was hearing probably wasn't his thought

waves. It sounded like the voice on the TV show *Password*
that told the home audience the secret password. I concluded
that a voice from the Other Side was helping me out. All
right. I needed help. I darkened each answer on the computer sheet as the voice directed me, although I tried to answer as many of the questions as I could on my own.

Every question I read had a special significance that only I
could understand, I was sure. Each time I reread a question
it acquired a new Meaning which surpassed the profundity
of its previous Meaning. Several voices commented on a few
of the questions. They contradicted each other and argued
about the answers. At last my head was crammed so full of
voices and changing Meanings that I could no longer answer
the questions for myself. I allowed the voices to decide the
rest of the answers for me.

When I looked up at the end of two hours, I was, as usual,
the only student still left in the testing room.

"Grid in your name and ID number and hand it in," the
professor ordered.

Obediently I printed the digits of my ID number in the
nine allotted boxes and filled in the circles below with shiny
black marks. In the boxes intended for my name I spelled
out "A CAST OF THOUSANDS." Feeling confident of
passing the exam with all the expert help I had, I handed
him my computer answer sheet and dropped the "Property
of Evaluation and Examination Service" No. 2 pencil in the
return box. (I pilfered the pencil only if I thought I'd done
poorly on an exam—by now I had a whole box of these pen-
cils at home.) Then I headed off in search of the answers
posted in the hallway.

As I elbowed my way up to the front of the horde of students gathered around the posted answer sheet I pictured
their behavior in an entirely new light. I envisioned them as
horseflies swarming around a cowpie in the middle of a sunny
pasture. No, more accurately they were piranha fish driven to
the sight of fresh blood and tearing away little hunks of flesh

from live prey. I closed my eyes and I felt a piece of my left foot disappear.

I'm all right. Somebody just stepped on my foot. Just remember, I'm standing right in front of the answer sheet and all I have to do is compare my answers.

My answers didn't match up at all. I walked to the other end of the hall to calculate my score. Three points below passing. Ugh.

My classmates were feeling good. They had obviously liked the exam. As I looked around for Bruce I heard them boasting to each other about nearly perfect scores and planning post-exam celebration parties. Bruce was waiting by the door. Right away he saw the tears in my eyes.

"It was a bad test," Bruce said.

"Yeah, I know, but that doesn't help my score any. I didn't pass. What am I going to do?"

"Talk to Dr. Earls. After all, it was his test."

"You're absolutely right," I said as a tear dropped off my chin. I swiped a shirt sleeve across my salt-streaked face. Several students standing nearby had stopped their conversation to stare at me. What the hell were they gawking at? I turned and walked around the corner in search of privacy. Another group of students was standing there grinning at me. I walked right by them and their heads turned as a unit with their eyes stuck to the middle of my back.

"Assholes," I muttered through my teeth, enunciating each consonant. Then I bolted for the door as fast as I could. Bruce stepped into my path and grabbed my arms.

"Pull yourself together," he said, as he sent me off toward Dr. Earls's office.

"Sounds to me like you knew the information for the exam," Dr. Earls told me, "but your reasoning seems somewhat garbled. You have nothing to worry about, because I'll be lowering the curve and you will pass my course. But I would like to refer you to a counselor by the name of Suzanne Sellers in the dean's office. She offers programs to help medical students with their studying and test-taking techniques. I think you could use some help in this area."

"Thanks, Dr. Earls," I said. "I'll make an appointment to see Mrs. Sellers as soon as possible."

Mrs. Sellers administered several tests to me, and when I had finished them she said, "You already seem to have the correct studying and test-taking skills. I, too, am at a loss to explain your academic difficulties. Are you in good physical health?"

"As far as I know," I said.

"It might be a good idea to get a physical examination just to make sure we're not missing something medical that could be fouling you up."

After performing a physical on me and doing the appropriate laboratory tests, my doctor concluded that the only thing that was wrong with me was I wasn't getting enough sleep. That I hadn't needed to go to a doctor to find out.

The next day I found a note waiting for me in my student mailbox. It was from Mrs. Sellers. It said it was urgent that I see her. My doctor had called Mrs. Sellers to tell her that she was worried about my emotional health. I tried to think of what it was I had said to the doctor to make her think I was mentally unbalanced. I couldn't think of anything. I thought I had handled our meeting smoothly. I suspected that she must have been reading my thoughts and picked up on my spiritual unrest.

Mrs. Sellers looked pleased that I had returned to see her. "Have a chair," she said in a soapy voice. "We're worried about you."

I looked at her blankly.

"You're under a lot of tension," she said solemnly. She was leading up to something, it seemed. "Different people handle stress in different ways. Take me, for example. When I'm under a lot of stress I get blood in my urine. When it gets really bad my urine looks like tomato juice."

"Really?" I said, wide-eyed. I couldn't stop staring at the

huge black gap between her two front teeth and envisioning her drinking tomato juice through a straw poking through the gap.

"Yes," Mrs. Sellers continued, "that's how my system handles stress. You handle stress quite differently. I think the stress is getting you down."

I nodded. It was.

"I have a friend I'd like you to talk to," said Mrs. Sellers.

"A friend?" I asked, not yet realizing her intent. "What do you mean?"

"I have a very nice friend who is a psychiatrist across the street at the psychiatric hospital." She was trying to handle me delicately, as if I were a bomb liable to detonate at the slightest touch. This was silly.

"Oh, no, I don't think you understand," I protested. I had to stop this kind of idea right from the start. I was no loony. I was merely having spiritual conflicts. I stood up and slung my backpack over my shoulder. "You see, I've spent too much time over there already. I used to live there, several years back. I had to stay four long months. I can't go back there. It wasn't a pleasant experience." I took a backward step toward the door.

Mrs. Sellers was determined. "This psychiatrist is very different. I think you'd like him. He's not the typical psychiatrist. If you talked to him once and you didn't like him, you wouldn't have to go back." (I later found out that she didn't know this psychiatrist at all. He was the psychiatrist to whom the medical school referred any students with emotional problems.)

I sat back down. "What's his name?"

"Dr. Hemingway."

"That's a point in his favor. He's somebody I've never seen before." I paused a moment, thinking that it couldn't possibly do me any harm to talk to him, especially if I played it cool and avoided revealing much of my complicated psychiatric history to him. Besides, maybe he could help me with my sagging exam scores.

"He would be absolutely confidential," she added persuasively.

"All right," I said, sliding my pack off my shoulder and back onto the floor, "I'll do it."

She phoned Dr. Hemingway and set up an appointment for me to see him the next morning at eight-thirty. I didn't know that after I left her office she phoned him back to tell him privately that she thought I was "seriously disturbed."

As Bruce and I slogged across the medical campus through a dreary late-February rain, I vacillated as to whether or not I should cancel the appointment with the psychiatrist. He would have the wrong idea about me from the very beginning: Dr. Falmouth's records would indicate that he thought I was a hysterical female. I began to feel very guilty about whatever might be in my old records, and I didn't want anybody reading them. Those records probably weren't accurate.

I needed help, though. I would have to endure my guilt and keep the appointment with this Dr. Hemingway that Mrs. Sellers wanted me to see. I decided I couldn't tell him I had been admitted to a psychiatric hospital before, at least not until he knew me better.

As Bruce and I walked toward my car I sensed a sinister shading to the atmosphere on campus. I looked at Bruce walking along in a mental fog beside me. I wondered what he was thinking—probably something profoundly serendipitous like "It seems to be raining—well, how about that."

"Your time is coming," I heard Hal pronounce through the background whisper of the spattering rain. Little did Bruce know that he was not the only man in my life.

I wanted nothing more than to sleep. I didn't have time to sleep. I needed to grind through several more pathology units. I settled into my easy chair and thumbed through a chapter in my eight-pound pathology text. Right away I noticed the chapter had too few pictures. And its print was extra-fine. Crumb. The mere image of reading this chapter fatigued me. If I hadn't been feeling so run-down maybe I could have gotten interested in metastatic kidney disease.

I closed my eyes just for a second. I decided I'd better not. If I went to sleep now I'd be ruined for the rest of the evening. I stood up and stretched out my sleepy limbs and wandered to the kitchen to put some water in my hot pot for coffee. The steaming sounds of the water heating started Banana chirping. She hopped excitedly back and forth between the wooden perches in her cage and then she took a mighty leap onto the swing suspended from the top. I slid open the cage door and put my hand in. She lighted on my outstretched finger and I drew her out of the cage. I loved the warmth of her tiny feet grasping around my finger. She hopped to the top of my head and pulled up some strands of hair with her beak.

My coffee water was boiling, and I poured it into my cup as Banana continued to poke around on the top of my head. As I set the empty pot back down on the kitchen counter, a SuperReal feeling entered me through the top of my head and invaded my entire body. I became aware of a certain unity between Banana and myself. Never before had I experienced such a strong sense of RealBeing with the bird. Her feet began to radiate warm Message waves onto my scalp. The conception that I could control Banana mentally with my own thought impulses raced through my brain, pausing briefly in the heavier synapse areas. I had animal magnetism. This was not my own thought, it was a thought put there through Banana's feet by someone in the Spirit World.

I didn't question the thought. It seemed entirely natural that I could control the bird's actions with my thought impulses; it was self-evident. I mentally commanded Banana to fly to her cage. An electric surge squeezed itself out of the pores in my scalp and spread up into Banana's body via convection forces. Banana didn't move. I continued sending electric currents out of my scalp and finally Banana obediently flew over to her cage and climbed in. I'd done it!

I commanded the bird to shake her head and scratch her wing and climb to the bottom of the cage for a drink of water. She did each of those things exactly as I commanded! I expected that with practice, I would be able to make people work the same way.

I had forgotten all about my coffee. It was getting cold. I downed the entire cup at once. Bitter. I had used three heaping teaspoonfuls of instant-coffee crystals in hopes that it would make me feel more alert. It didn't. The day's caffeine high had succeeded only in making me jittery. I grabbed a stale saltine from the cupboard to soothe my "caffeine stomach" and then returned to my easy chair and picked up the pathology book again.

As I settled into the chapter's first page I began to notice my arms felt very different. They looked the same as usual, but they weren't mine anymore. They moved automatically: they had been programmed by the Spirit World. I didn't fight it. I stood up abruptly and the book on my lap dropped to the floor and slammed itself shut. My arms felt as if somebody had threaded stiff poles up them. A beam of raw energy shot down from the ceiling and hit upon the upper surfaces of my body. It surrounded me in a column formation. The top of my skull opened up and a tremendous weight pressed down on my naked brain.

Little buzzes shot out from my brain and down into my legs. As they traversed my joints they produced extra buzzes by cloning themselves. These sensations traveled down my shins and shot out my toes into the plane of the floor. These were the Messages. They were a complex mixture of Religion, the Supernatural, Ancient Philosophy, and Scientific Technology. They were going through me to get from one world to another. I had inadvertently stumbled onto a cosmic junctional point. I stood immobile to provide minimum resistance for the Messages to pass safely through my being without burning any holes in me or any of my circuits.

After some time I began to drain into the buzzes and my self slipped away from my brain. I dropped into the floor and far beyond.

"Welcome to the Parallel Dimension," said Hal.

His statement terrified me. I had only me, myself, and a finite bundle of past experiences to define identity for myself here. No matter what I thought, they could know what I was thinking and outthink me. It was a naked-ening experience.

I started to pray. I asked God to enclose me and protect me from Evil Forces I felt were lurking close by. I humbled myself and admitted to my human weakness and vulnerability.

The Beings inserted cognizance into my head, the realization that my own self had dissipated into God and dispersed as a drop of water into a rain puddle. Suddenly I hated God, I hated being God. I had to get back to being myself.

The Other Side placed instant knowledge into my head. I knew incredible Truths. I knew all about the real Laws of the Universe. The universe as I had known it up to this time was only a nearsighted fraction of the Ultimate Universe, and our petty laws of science were only a small part of a huge Macrosystem too great for the human mind to grasp.

On the Other Side I found that incompatible Truths could coexist without creating dissonance. Only God and certain enlightened Beings could absorb such contradictions without imploding in on themselves like a black hole. God could move the rock that was so heavy He couldn't move it. I was awestruck. This was Enlightenment. I didn't have to say it; it was unnecessary because it was beyond saying.

I sat back down in my chair and picked up the book again. My muscles ached as if I had been doing hard physical labor all day.

Ho-hum, what time does my watch say? Wow, it's one

o'clock in the morning! I must have stood here for six hours! Megan has probably gone to bed.

I decided to read pathology for two more hours and then go to bed myself. I made myself another cup of coffee and perched it on the arm of my easy chair as I began to read.

At first I tried to ignore the humming sounds coming from my house plants in front of the room's only window. When I looked up, the noise stopped. I swilled down more coffee and resumed my studying. I was determined to finish the section on metastatic kidney disease. The humming began to sound more like moaning. I read another paragraph before I looked up again. The plants looked sinister. I supposed it could be the lighting that made them look that way. I didn't want to jump to conclusions.

The plants stretched out their stems toward me as if they were grasping for me. I sat perfectly still, undecided as to whether I should go over and inspect them or run upstairs to my room. I couldn't judge if the crux of the decision was bravery versus cowardice, or foolishness versus caution. The indecision was paralyzing me. The plant stems grew in length, their leaf tips reaching closer and closer. Somehow I had been granted knowledge of the explanation for this: the plants had retained some vestiges of the earlier encounter with the Other Side. They were about to engulf me.

I pulled my feet close to myself in the chair, and as I did so I knocked my empty coffee cup onto the carpet. I stretched out my arm to retrieve it, but my arm had shrunk so much that I could not reach the cup. The cup had landed right side up, and it began to emit a cold force shield which wrapped itself around the front of my chair. The shield felt very powerful. The plants could not reach into the shield. This was a victory of Good over the Forces of Chaos. I would be safe.

I read the rest of the chapter, looking up after each paragraph to make sure the plants were staying far enough away. Finally I closed the book and carried my coffee cup back to the kitchen. As I set the cup in the sink I caught a view of

Banana asleep in her cage. She was standing on one foot with her head buried in her wing. I slipped the flannel cover over her cage, switched off the light, and tiptoed upstairs. The intensity of the evening had exhausted me.

The plants seemed to have calmed down. They looked so innocent, so harmless. Well, I knew better now. I knew what they're really like.

Every night before bed I had to set five alarm clocks. It was necessary to do this because I sometimes woke up totally spaced out in the middle of the night or in the early morning and shut them off. Many a time I had overslept in this manner. My body was trying to trick me into allowing it to sleep longer.

I set my five alarms for seven-thirty. Four hours of sleep would have to be enough. Tomorrow would be Friday, and I could plan to catch up on sleep over the weekend. If I hadn't had to go to the shrink at eight-thirty I could have slept another hour. It didn't seem worth getting up so early for, but I had an appointment, so I would go.

I pulled the covers up to my chin and zonked out immediately. I'd never had any problem falling asleep, at any time or any place. My problem was trying to stay *awake* during the day, because I was always so exhausted from my chronic state of sleep deprivation.

My head was predictably fuzzy when I came to. All five alarms went off. It didn't occur to me to shut them all off when the first one sounded. The second one caught me in the bathroom. I ran up the stairs from the kitchen to get the third, fourth, and fifth alarms all in one trip.

In the early-morning hours I had a tendency to slip into the Other Worlds. This morning was no exception.

"Love is blind," said the voices over my radio. "Have good hindsight."

The radio wasn't even on! I checked it twice. I even unplugged it, but that didn't help either. The stupid gadget was stubbornly intercepting bits of cosmic communications between the Spirits. I was irritated at the voices for bugging me before I had even had a chance to get fully awake. I hated being so easily confused when I was sleepy.

The voices accompanied me all the way to the psychiatrist's office, first over my car radio and then over hidden intercoms under the eaves of the hospital buildings. It was strange how the temperature outside had accidentally fixed the length of the resonance frequency of signposts to the exact frequency of the Messages being broadcast so that they picked up the Messages. Even my jawbone vibrated with the Message waves. Something was definitely going on this morning.

CHAPTER EIGHT

DR. HEMINGWAY

The psychiatrist was sitting behind his desk waiting for me to arrive. It was eight-thirty to the exact second. I thought that would make a good impression; my punctuality would demonstrate that I was sane and had things well under control.

He didn't seem to notice that I was on time.

"Carol?" he asked. "Are you Carol North?"

I nodded.

"Hi, I'm Dr. Hemingway."

"Hemingway, ocean spray. Love is blind, wined, and dined."

The voices were apparently still with me. I couldn't locate the speakers they were blaring from.

I took a closer look at Dr. Hemingway and wilted. This guy looked like a true Freud. He appeared to be in his fifties, and his beard and hair were pure white. He wore little round wire-rim spectacles which somehow seemed to complete the professorial effect of his tidy three-piece plaid wool suit. This guy did not look as if he would understand anything. I doubted he had ever had any metaphysical experiences like mine.

"What brought you here today?" he asked.

At first I thought he meant my car, but then he politely rephrased his query to ask what kind of problems I was having. I told him I had been treated for psychiatric problems in the past, but I didn't say that I had been in this hospital, or that I had been having psychiatric symptoms continuously ever since. I didn't want him to think I was a crazy, hopeless case.

He sat quietly while I described the disruptions in my concentration caused by the barking dogs in the lectures and in the stethoscopes. I told him I was having problems understanding exam questions and that they got me all mixed up, although I wasn't sure exactly how. Feeling guilty, I added that I'd been skipping too many classes. But, I explained, this was only because I couldn't make much sense out of the lectures and my time would be better spent at home studying or sleeping.

After a moment's pause to reflect over what I'd said and to think if there was anything I might have left out, I added, "I can't concentrate when I'm hearing the voices." (That was enough; I didn't want to have to tell him all about the Other Worlds' phenomena because it would have taken all day.)

Suddenly the voices turned on their Echo Machine, to get me to shut up about them, I supposed. My words didn't sound at all normal. They echoed. Next I heard Frank Zappa and the Mothers of Invention singing "Who Are the Brain Police" behind the wall, with more echoes. It all sounded increasingly sinister. So many things had seemed sinister lately. Yes, there was something going on today.

"Where do these voices come from?" The doctor's voice was echoing just as everything else was.

"I don't know, exactly. I think they're from somewhere else."

He looked puzzled. Twitching his eyebrows, he repeated, "From somewhere else?"

I nodded. "Yeah. Sometimes they come through speakers that are disguised in the walls. I can't ever find them."

"What do the voices say?"

His echo was starting to bother me.

"I can't always understand them," I tried to explain. "Sometimes they repeat snatches of conversation or make rhymes to it. How they sometimes sound is like they're having a cocktail party in the next room and I can make out only some of the words or phrases. It doesn't make a lot of sense."

I wished that frigging Echo Machine would quit. It made it hard to concentrate on the discussion.

I had to work hard to stay on the same subject. It took me a while to reconnect my thoughts. Finally, I resumed speaking, hoping I hadn't drifted too far. "Sometimes the voices talk about what I'm doing, like they're sports commentators, saying things like 'She is walking out of the Medical Sciences Building' or 'She doesn't know it but she's about to flunk this exam'—only they say things very calmly. Or they might tell me to do something ridiculous like walk across town and back in the middle of the night. A few times they've wakened me in the night by yelling in my ear, and I've been too scared to get back to sleep."

"You appear to be having some trouble concentrating on what you're saying today," said Dr. Hemingway. "Is there any particular problem?"

"Well, yes. They have sound-effect machines. Like now they are using an Echo Machine that makes both of our voices reverberate, and that bothers me so I can't think very well. There are other machines like the Barking Dogs Machine and the Helicopter Machine that they can use to produce sounds out of nowhere. Sometimes I can't tell whether noises are my neighbors or the sound-effect machines."

I felt creepy talking about the voices. It was like talking

about them behind their backs, except even worse because I knew they knew what I was saying about them. I hoped I hadn't gotten them irritated. The consequences could be severe. They could transform my next exam score from passing to failing at a whim.

"Do you ever hear your thoughts as if they had been spoken aloud?" Dr. Hemingway asked.

Wow, how does he know about that? Has he been reading my mind? I glared at him.

Finally I responded to his question: "Yes, I hear my thoughts out loud. In lecture. It bothers me." I wanted to cooperate yet not reveal too much now. I needed his help for my exams.

"Do you think other people can read your mind?" he probed.

Amazing how he knew about that too! Maybe he'd been listening to the same voices. "Yes," I said. "That's been a big problem for me."

He did seem to have good empathy. He was listening intently to everything I said. Nodding slowly, he muttered, "Mm-hmm," as if he was thinking hard. He didn't look totally convinced. "How do you know people are reading your thoughts?"

"My head's transparent. I can't protect my thoughts. Someone sucks all the thoughts out of my head and then I can't say anything because I don't have any thoughts left to say."

"Can you give me an example? When was the last time that happened?"

I felt my skin turning gray and starting to slide off my forearms right there in the psychiatrist's office. The sensation was so alarming that I couldn't possibly think to answer his question. It took all my concentration just to hold on to my skin. I was too embarrassed to tell him about my skin problem because I was sure it was a result of mental weakness.

"Is there some reason why you aren't saying anything?" he

asked, firing off multiple twitches from his eyebrows. "Has someone stolen your thoughts? Do you think I have stolen your thoughts?"

His twitches had to be an anxiety gauge or a puzzlement gauge. I didn't know which. I thought it would probably be better for me to tell him about my skin problem than for him to hear it from the voices or pick it up from my own thought waves. I explained to him that I had been quiet for a minute because I had been using all my concentration to keep my forearm skin from sliding off.

He offered up another "Mm-hmm."

"The shrink is pink," said Hal.

I started to smile, but stopped myself. Hal was right. That was funny.

Dr. Hemingway asked me various other questions about my life, including my medical and family history, educational background, and current living arrangements. Then he announced, "I'd like to prescribe you some medicine. If things get bad enough for you, you might have to quit school or go into the hospital."

Just as I'd suspected. If this guy was going to talk about my quitting school and hospitalization or other ruinous alternatives, he wasn't going to be any help at all. What I needed was someone to help me stay *in* school, not help me *out*. What I needed was a way to be strong against the Forces of Chaos. Couldn't he see my problem was essentially spiritual, even cosmic—and not really psychiatric at all? I refused even to think of hospitalization or quitting school.

To appease Dr. Hemingway I agreed to take small amounts of Navane, a major antipsychotic tranquilizer that he prescribed for me. That would make me seem cooperative and might help buy time until he could understand my problem in its broader sense and give me some real help. But I warned him that if the medicine made me groggy or sluggish or otherwise interfered with my schoolwork, I would have to discontinue it immediately. I needed my energy and my resources for medical school.

Dr. Hemingway wanted to see me again on Monday.

After I left he dictated a note which included the following statements about me:

> The patient looks rather quiet, answers questions with some degree of thought disorder, and has trouble such as reaching her goal. She appears somewhat confused about her thought processes and what is going on and about the meaning which she sees in many things. There is no push of speech, no flight of ideas. She seems to be on the concerned and sober side. Occasionally, answers are somewhat retarded. She appears to have some insight into her illness, but this is definitely impaired. Judgment also seems to be impaired. Impression: probable schizophreniform illness. The history of an acute episode a number of years ago with rather relatively good health in between would seem to support this, although the possibility of a manic-depressive illness cannot be ruled out.

The following Monday I returned to Dr. Hemingway's office for the follow-up appointment he had scheduled. I didn't know that in the interim he had found my old hospital record.

The first thing Dr. Hemingway wanted to know was whether I was having any problem with the Navane. As he studied my face, his bushy white eyebrows arched upward and then subtly furrowed into his wire-rim glasses. Simultaneously his nose twitched.

That is undoubtedly a signal. This is some kind of a test. He has somehow observed me all weekend and is now fully equipped to detect the inconsistency or lie that he is expecting me to blurt out.

The voices might have filled him in on the details. He couldn't be trusted.

I couldn't decide what to say. I wanted to accuse him outright. But I didn't know exactly what to accuse him of. I would have to pretend I didn't know anything until I had more evidence. The conflicting thoughts about what to say collided with each other in my brain and vaporized, leaving a vacuum where the thoughts were just a second before.

I felt pressured. He was sitting there twitching his eyebrows and nose and mustache, waiting for me to answer his question. I didn't have any thoughts, so how could I answer his question? I had to think of something to say quickly, something consistent. He was still twitching and waiting.

I was falling through space and time again, only he couldn't tell that. I was the only one who could tell.

He broke my fall by speaking. Instantly I had thoughts again.

"Did you take the Navane?" he asked.

"Yes," I answered him in the most normal voice I could summon. It didn't sound like my voice. The voices must have put in a substitute.

The doctor was grinning. He was frowning, too. His face was one huge grinfrown.

"Did you have any problem with the medicine?" he asked again.

With my substitute voice I projected the words "I'm a bit dizzy when I first wake up in the morning." I wondered what they'd done with my usual voice.

"That dizziness is just a side effect which should wear off in a few days," he told me. "Until then, don't stand up too fast first thing in the morning."

His facial expression began to alternate between grinning and frowning at a speed of about four times a second. That made it nearly impossible for me to be able to read his true facial expression. He didn't appear to be so intent on catching me in an inconsistency or a lie now. He looked more trustworthy. Maybe I had misjudged him.

"What did you do this weekend?" he asked.

That sounded like a reasonably innocent question. I relaxed a little.

"Well, you remember on Friday I told you I had to move to a different apartment last month?"

"Oh yes, after the spring rains when your roof leaked so bad?" His eyebrows and nose twitched noticeably as he spoke.

"Right. Yesterday just before dawn I sneaked back to see the old apartment," I continued, still trying to sound as normal as I could. "I got in because I kept a duplicate key." I was doing fine, I thought.

"Well, what did you see?" His twitches were becoming almost rhythmic.

Maybe his twitches meant he knew the answer to his question. I didn't even need to tell him, since he knew. I studied his grinfrown for a minute. The sentence "What did you see?" echoed around in my head several times until I didn't know whether I'd said it or he'd said it or maybe even the voices had said it. He looked as if he expected me to say something. I didn't know what we were talking about anymore.

It was up to me to fill the silence.

Dr. Hemingway's office was dusty. I was inhaling dust particles into my lungs. No telling where all those dust particles had come from. Some of the molecules in the air might have diffused from someone passing gas earlier and now I was breathing them in. Maybe one of the dust particles I was breathing had come from breaking off of King Tut's body and floating aimlessly on the wind for centuries, to finally wander into this room. This was a conceptual equivalent of the Interference Patterns. Maybe some plants had once incorporated a few atoms originally from Joan of Arc's body into their structure and then a cow had eaten the plants and defecated on the ground and some oats growing out of that soil had taken nourishment from the cow manure and had eventually been harvested and processed, and I had consumed the famous atoms in my Cheerios that morning! The idea became fixed in my head. This had happened, without a doubt.

"I am breathing King Tut and I have swallowed Joan of Arc," I told Dr. Hemingway. This was a very profound thought. It seemed intrinsically relevant to the discussion because of its profundity, although I was not quite sure how it related. The depth of its profundity seemed to far outweigh any qualms I had about saying it. It had been a good statement and would at least get the conversation moving again. The responsibility of making the next contribution to the discussion would be off my shoulders for the moment.

"Mm-hmmm." Dr. Hemingway was momentarily taken aback by the absurdity of my statement.

I was still marveling at the brilliance of my observation when Dr. Hemingway said, "But what do swallowing Joan of Arc and breathing King Tut have to do with how your apartment looked?"

I felt my cheeks burning hot from the inside out. He must have been simultaneously seeing my cheeks turn cherry-red from the outside in. I was embarrassed that I had gotten mixed up and forgotten that we were talking about my old apartment, and then said something completely off the wall. Was Dr. Hemingway trying to trick me?

Dr. Hemingway pretended I hadn't said anything crazy. "Tell me about your old apartment," he said.

I was relieved he chose not to embarrass me further by making a big deal out of my confusion. "Well," I said, "when I got up to Megan's old room I saw the ceiling bulging downward. The bulging was a Sign that the Other Worlds are impinging on this world, right? Pretty soon it will all come crashing in. Isn't that what it means?"

Dr. Hemingway didn't answer my question. He was twitching a lot. I couldn't tell for sure, but I thought he looked worried.

"I know it's true," I said soberly, "because I felt a touch of the SuperReal when I saw it." The SuperReal was such a profoundly significant concept that I couldn't convey its meaning to him in ordinary words. Instead I translated the concept into wordless thought waves which I transmitted to him through the air medium linking our minds. He didn't look at all receptive. I was finding communication with him difficult.

"Something else I saw over there upset me," I heard my substitute voice say.

That elicited a double-twitch response of his eyebrows.

"There were little green plants growing out of the carpet in Megan's old room. I didn't know what to make of them."

"Mm-hmm," he said along with his next facial twitch. It sounded like an mm-hmm of disbelief to me.

"But I *saw* them," I insisted. "They were really there. There were about five or six of them. They were about six inches tall, all single stalks. A couple of them even had little buds on their tips."

"Mm-hmm," he responded again. This doctor sure wasn't too quick with original responses. "Has Megan seen the little green plants?"

This was hopeless. Dr. Hemingway would never believe me, much less be able to offer an acceptable interpretation of these Signs. "No, I haven't shown them to her yet," I said, making a mental note to do just that.

He twitched again to signal a change of subject. He hadn't seemed satisfied with the last one. I hoped the next would be easier to discuss.

"Were you able to study over the weekend?" he asked.

I wished he'd quit twitching. It made me nervous. I still suspected it was some kind of signal. I answered his question: "I studied the whole weekend, but it was hard to concentrate because of the interference."

I anticipated another twitch from him at this point, but he just sat back in his chair grinfrowning.

I must have judged him right in the first place. I inter- preted his ambiguous grinfrown to mean that he already knew about the interference, most likely from the voices. He was carefully poised in readiness for a swift pounce on me with a shocking verbal assault as soon as I said the wrong thing. He had all the evidence he needed to incriminate me. I shouldn't have let him in on such a personal concept as the interference.

"Can you tell me a little bit about the interference?" he asked, looking sincerely interested now. He was starting to back off.

Now I felt a little safer. I answered, "The interference is like static on the radio. It—well, it interferes."

"Interferes?" he asked. "How?" His face appeared immensely friendlier than it had a minute before. I had never been able to judge faces.

"It impinges," I explained further. "Like the voices. Like the barking dogs."

"Can you be more specific—to help me understand a little better?" He looked as if he sincerely wanted to understand. Nobody had ever responded to me like this before. In the past, people had just dismissed me as some kind of nut, instead of showing interest in my ideas like the OtherWorldly phenomena. I knew the Other Worlds weren't a delusion I had cooked up out of a state of mental derangement. They couldn't be. Delusions were simpler than that, like when people thought the FBI was after them. The Other Worlds were far too sophisticated and intricate to be a delusion. And they stood up under too many kinds of logic. They had too much consistency and reliability over time to be false. I wanted Dr. Hemingway to understand that.

I explained, "The interference is other things besides voices, helicopters, and barking dogs. It's also patterns. The patterns jump around and flow in and out of each other and change colors. They march over walls, spaces, and people's faces—like radio static, but only in the visual sense. The interference spills into our perceptual grounds from leaks from other systems. *You* can see and hear it, I think. You have the capability within you now, but you have to learn how to perceive—just as the medical student must learn how to appreciate subtle clinical nuances that seem obvious to the seasoned physician."

I paused, but Dr. Hemingway was listening intently, expecting me to finish.

I continued, "I think everybody sees the interference—but they haven't learned to recognize what they're observing." That was what I meant to say, but I actually conveyed only about half of it, leaving Dr. Hemingway wondering what exactly I was trying to tell him.

He nodded thoughtfully. If I could get him to see that I had stumbled onto other dimensions, he might be my key to enlightening the world. People would be more likely to listen to a psychiatrist than to a former mental patient labeled schizophrenic.

"Have you ever discovered your phosphenes?" I asked him.

I could see I'd lost him there.

"Phosphenes," I explained, "are the brilliant colored patterns you see when you close your eyes and press on your eyeballs with your fingers. Try it."

"I know what those are," he said. "I've seen them."

"Good. The interference looks something like them."

I felt that I was starting to fall again. It was going to be difficult trying to explain things with this happening.

Dr. Hemingway persisted with his own questions: "Can you tell me about this SuperReal feeling you mentioned?"

"SuperReal, reel-to-reel banana peel," I heard one of the voices say playfully from a far-off world.

That was funny. I tried to subdue an uncontrollable smile.

Dr. Hemingway responded with the slightest hint of an involuntary grin and asked. "What about this SuperReal feeling? What's that like?" He was trying not to acknowledge my smile.

I managed to get my mouth straight again and explain, "The SuperReal is a feeling of reality that is stronger and harsher than the usual reality I know—it's like biting down on something cold when you have a cavity. It impinges, like the interference. It's a feeling that overwhelms me when we collide with the Parallel Worlds and part of their systems leak into this one."

Dr. Hemingway looked puzzled. He couldn't understand why I believed such absurd ideas. (What he didn't understand was that schizophrenic logic transcended ordinary logic.) I couldn't explain the SuperReal to him. He was in the wrong logic set. There weren't earth words to describe it. "SuperReal" was the closest I could come to describing it.

"What are these Other Worlds you keep telling me about?" he asked. "What's it like over there?"

I thought back to my last visit to the Other Side. Right then I was sitting on the wrong side of the SuperReal Barrier to be able to tell him about it. My mind over here couldn't grasp it. His probably couldn't either. I could only suggest vaguely that it was totally different from here. It was something you just had to experience for yourself.

Dr. Hemingway was still wearing his grinfrown. He hadn't stopped grinfrowning for more than a few seconds while I'd been talking to him. I wanted to ask him about it, but I thought maybe I was already supposed to know somehow, so I didn't ask. I didn't want to look stupid.

The unmistakable putter of a helicopter vibrated through the windowpane right behind Dr. Hemingway. He pretended not to notice it.

Why? Was he somehow involved in it? Had he informed them of my whereabouts? I tried to block my thoughts out completely in hopes that the helicopters couldn't locate me by homing in on my thought waves.

After an insufferably long minute the helicopter faded into the nondescript drone of the background interference, and I no longer heard it. I was aware that neither Dr. Hemingway nor I had said anything for quite a while. His twitch had quit. He was looking directly into my eyes. I thought he was trying to read my naked thoughts right through my pupils. He had me under some kind of a spell. It felt creepy. He was doing it with the power of his eyes. He was hypnotizing me. He could make me do weird things. He could make me do things I didn't want to do.

Well, stop staring at him, then!

But I couldn't.

"I'm going to increase your Navane from ten to fifteen milligrams a day," he said. "And I'd like you to come back and see me again in a week. Can you do that?" he said with another twitch.

I was under his spell. He could make me do that. I couldn't possibly fail.

He set me up another appointment for the following Monday. As Dr. Hemingway opened the door to his office, Hal announced, "You're leaving Dr. Hemingway's office now. You're about to step off the edge of the earth."

I gazed out the door in the direction of the voice. I looked back at Dr. Hemingway. He hadn't heard the voice. Well, then, I hadn't either.

"See you next Monday," he said as I stepped into the hallway with my book pack over my shoulder. I didn't glance back.

Dr. Hemingway dictated the following note:

> It turns out that Miss North has a very large record compiled here at the psychiatric hospital with at least one admission here, numerous outpatient visits. On the occasion of her admission to the hospital . . . she was diagnosed as catatonic schizophrenic. Apparently, when admitted to the hospital, she showed many of the present symptoms which she is complaining of. It is evident that this girl has had a serious and possibly chronic condition going back . . . at least [four years]

but has been able to function reasonably effectively in the school situation despite the chronicity of her complaints.

As I changed into my sweat clothes to prepare for my morning jog my breasts felt lumpy and tender. This had to be a side effect of the Navane. I'd also gained several pounds, thanks to the medicine. But the worst side effect was when I started finding wet spots on the front of my blouses, also from the Navane. I phoned Dr. Hemingway to complain that the medicine was making my breasts leak milk. Having previously experienced psychiatrists who were intolerant of "patient noncompliance," I thought Dr. Hemingway might get all huffy and demand that I either cooperate or terminate treatment. But at this point I didn't care; I couldn't tolerate these side effects.

To my surprise, he was sympathetic. He told me I was apparently very sensitive to side effects of drugs, and he elected to switch my medicine to small doses of a different antipsychotic tranquilizer, Haldol. I had had trouble with Haldol when I was being treated by Dr. Falmouth, but the doses had been large. Dr. Hemingway began my dose at a minimal half milligram at bedtime, and over the next week he gradually increased it to four milligrams. After a few days I began to notice that the voices were not bothering me quite as continuously, and that the interference was growing fainter and less disruptive.

I continued regular appointments with Dr. Hemingway. I began thinking it was time to be honest with him. He seemed trustworthy. I decided he knew me well enough by now that his opinions of me were already formed and he might not be so likely to be swayed by my old records if he read them now.

It wasn't easy telling him what I had to say when he was wearing that distracting grinfrown. I reached into my mental vacuum, grasping for words. "Dr. Hemingway," I began slowly and calculatingly, "I've got a confession to make."

Up went the eyebrows and then came the twitch. "A confession?"

"Yes, there's something you need to know about me. I didn't tell you sooner because I didn't want you to be biased against me."

Another twitch and an mm-hmmm. He was being most patient with me while I fumbled around for the right words.

"Well, I've been here before. In this hospital, I mean. I stayed here for four months back when I was a freshman in college. I know I should have told you sooner, but it was upsetting me to have to tell you about it. You probably won't believe anything I say now."

"Oh, I knew about that," he said. "But that's okay. It's perfectly understandable that you were embarrassed to tell me. I didn't tell you I found your old chart in the medical records department. I know old records aren't necessarily right. I always prefer to form my own impression. And I think the impression I have formed is correct."

"Then you believe everything I've told you?" I asked him. "You believe me when I tell you about the problems I've been reporting that I have with school and my exams and my classmates?" (After all, if he hadn't believed the problems I'd told him about, then what was the point in his trying to treat me?)

"Of course I believe you," he said. "I have no reason to doubt you."

I was still skeptical. He hadn't believed my story about the little green plants. No telling what else he didn't believe. But we spent more time going over the parts of my psychiatric history I had left out. He seemed satisfied with my confession, even though he did continue to make those queer facial expressions.

"Are you having any trouble with the Haldol?" he asked me. As I watched his face, the shadows and highlights reversed, like a negative photographic image, with the highlights turning black and the shadows glowing liquid gold and flowing into one another. This particular visual effect was no surprise to me. I'd seen it many times before.

I shook my head in answer to his question.

"Then keep taking the Haldol," he advised me. "It should help stop those confusing thoughts and the voices too. It will probably make it easier for you to study."

That's exactly what I wanted, to be able to study better. Maybe this guy really was trying to help me.

"I want you to know that I'm going out of town next week," he said with a twitch. It looked like a twitch of concern. "I've arranged to have you see Dr. Winterman while I'm gone. He's the chairman of the department of psychiatry. He'll also be the one you should get in touch with if you run into any problems while I'm gone."

I wasn't too crazy to be able to sense genuineness. Even through the heavy interference storm, I could detect Dr. Hemingway's caring attitude. He was unlike any other psychiatrist I'd seen. He seemed sincerely interested in my welfare and in the quality of my existence. I sensed this was how he could understand my inability to tolerate certain drug side effects, when former psychiatrists had not taken the same complaints seriously. What I really feared was being forced to take drugs that would prevent me from studying effectively. I would do everything possible to prevent another interruption of my education.

It didn't particularly alarm me that Dr. Hemingway was going to be out of town during finals week. I certainly wasn't anticipating any major crises.

The first thing I did after arriving back at the apartment was to take Megan over to our old place and show her the little green plants growing there. To my relief, the plants were indeed there.

"See?" I said. "I'm not crazy after all."

I could hardly wait to tell Dr. Hemingway.

CHAPTER NINE

FINALS

Almost finals time again, and I hadn't been to any microbiology labs for a month. I just couldn't go. The sensory overload in class stirred up new waves of Interference Patterns. It was more comfortable to stay home and study for other exams in other subjects. By now we were supposed to be able to recognize parasites under the microscope and know all the specific details of their life cycles and the diseases they cause. I was seriously behind.

I knew I would have to study like crazy to pass the test. I began to cram during every free minute. Had I not had so much to learn in so little time, I might have enjoyed studying this parasitology unit. But as it was, I was staggered.

With the approach of finals, our student support group was dwindling. None of us had time to attend the meetings, and eventually the group disintegrated completely. I missed seeing and talking with Dean Honeycut.

Since I was suffering from personal problems related to school, I wondered if perhaps Dean Honeycut might be able to suggest some strategies on how to improve my academic situation. If I didn't do something to change how things were going, I might not survive; I could conceivably flunk out. Dean Honeycut had a reputation for being able to chat on a personal level with students and to advise them. After all, Dean Honeycut had once been a medical student. When I ran into him again, I arranged a meeting with him. He suggested a brown-bag lunch.

We met out on the hospital lawn on one of those ideal sunny, seventy-degree spring days. To break the ice, we discussed our common passions, distance running and bicycling. I was always comfortable chatting with other exercise fanatics. Eventually the conversation got around to my academic difficulties.

"Mrs. Sellers told me about your academic problems this semester," Dean Honeycut said. "She said she referred you to Dr. Hemingway. I know him very well and I think it's a great idea you're seeing him. I think he can help you. Your present academic difficulties," the dean explained, "may predict that you might experience difficulty functioning in a clinical setting in the future. Perhaps you should instead consider directing your efforts into laboratory research after graduation." He scraped the last bit of yogurt from the bottom of the cup and licked it up. "Otherwise," he said, "I can't give you any other specific advice than to just keep plugging away as you've been doing." He appeared sincere. Even so, his advice distressed me and I didn't agree with him.

I finished my ham sandwich and poured myself another cup of coffee from my thermos. "But Dean Honeycut," I protested, "I *love* patient care, and I'd be deeply disappointed if I couldn't practice clinical medicine someday. I want to help people—that's why I came to medical school. Don't you understand?"

Dean Honeycut didn't respond.

After a minute's silence, I changed the subject. "Dean Honeycut, I want you to know I've made arrangements to spend the coming summer in my hometown of Riverside participating in the student externship program. I'm really excited about it. I'm expecting I'll perform well in a clinical situation, and I'm looking forward to my first experience with patients."

"I'm glad you feel so positive about your externship," Dean Honeycut said. "It should predict how you'll function in a clinical setting in the future. This experience could prove extremely valuable in that way."

That sounded reasonable to me. After our meeting, any apprehensions I harbored regarding difficulties in medical school were laid to rest.

My most immediate concern now was the impending case analysis final exam in pathology. Fortunately, I had scored sufficiently well on pathology exams all semester that all I had to do was *pass* the case analysis final in order to earn honors in the course. And all students would be allowed multiple tries at the exam. It wouldn't be as easy as it sounded, though, because it was rumored that the exam was extremely difficult and lots of students had already tried and failed, retaking it two or three times before passing. Rumor also had it that there was an easy form—form number three. I hoped I'd be lucky enough to get form number three the first time around. The chances of that happening weren't too great, though, because there were seven forms.

In between cramming for all my other finals I prepared carefully for the case analysis final. We were permitted to use any notes or books we wanted for the exam. I carefully went over all my class notes and the case histories from the semester's discussion group. I examined all the available microscopic slides of tissue and looked at all the pictures of tissue slides in my pathology book. I made detailed indexes of the entire semester's information. No other student could have prepared as carefully as I had. I felt I had no choice. I would even have to cut into my sleep. I *had* to pass.

Bruce failed the case analysis final on his first try. I took that as a bad omen. On his second try he received test number three and, consistent with the rumors that form number three was easier, he earned a grade of honors on the exam.

"Don't worry," he told me. "There *is* an easy form. You just have to be patient and keep taking the exam until you get lucky and get it." Bruce's solution to everything was always to tell me not to worry.

I practically needed a wheelbarrow to carry all my books and notes to the case analysis final. I lugged the materials in weary arms from my car to the pathology lab in two separate trips. I had signed up for the eight-to-noon time slot. I arrived at seven-thirty to make sure I could be the third person in line at the exam. That way, I hoped, I'd be given test number three. I was going to do everything I could to increase my chances of completing medical school.

I let two guys take their places in line in front of me and then I planted myself third in line with my two heaps of books and notes. No one objected; no one seemed aware of my plan.

The first student received number one, and the second, form number two. Expecting to get form number three, I was stunned to see that I was holding form number seven. I started to say that I didn't want that form or that there must be some mistake, but I cut myself off immediately, to avoid disclosing that I knew the secret about this exam.

The exam proved to be as difficult as was rumored. I flunked by two points.

I arranged to retake the exam the next day. As I stashed the load of textbooks and notes that had betrayed me back into my locker and headed toward my car, I heard Hal and several other voices laughing at me and repeating the word "dumb" over and over, right behind me. The voices followed me to my car. I locked myself into the car with them and curled up in the backseat in the fetal position and began to cry. I listened to the voices chatter away for two hours before

I could pull myself together enough to start my car and drive home.

Back at the apartment, Bruce told me he was sorry I hadn't passed. I thought I detected a note of satisfaction in his voice. What was happening to Bruce?

The following morning I dragged my stacks of books and notes back to the pathology lab. I was determined to pass the exam this time; this was nonsense. My skin prickled at the thought of having to waste five hours retaking the case analysis final when I desperately needed to be at home cramming for other upcoming finals, as Bruce was doing. When I saw that I had received exam number four, I felt the heaviness of fatigue settle onto my shoulders.

Five hours later the bright green letters of the computer screen registered me at three points below passing. To make matters worse, several students were standing behind me reading my score with me. I didn't know why they were still hanging around; they had passed. Why didn't they just go home and leave me alone? Why did they have to stare like that?

"Oh, hell," I said.

Another five hours down the tubes. I was beginning to think I was going to have to take this exam all seven times. Oh well, I would just sign up for another exam tomorrow. I couldn't stand to blow another five hours in the same day.

By the time I'd failed the case analysis final for the third time I became convinced the voices were somehow manipulating my exam scores to make me fail. It seemed they had it fixed so no easy form existed, at least not for me. And Bruce was helping them. I had that all figured out by myself without anybody even having to tell me.

It was true; Bruce had been behaving oddly of late. He was even more uncommunicative than usual. It didn't occur to me that I was becoming difficult to communicate with. I suspected he was hiding things from me. As I forced my locker door shut against the leaning tower of textbooks and clicked the combination lock closed, the explanation for his behavior seemed suddenly obvious. It took care of even little details such as why he had flunked the case analysis final on the first try (he wasn't yet cooperating with them).

I gave the combination lock my usual extra twirl and set off for Bruce's apartment. He was going to start explaining things to me.

I burst through the door without even knocking. Bruce was comfortably poised on his bed with a parasitology text. I took a running leap and pounced on him, yelling, "You told me there was an easy form! You lied! There's no easy form and you've known it all along!" Then I started shaking him.

He effortlessly rolled out from under me and pinned my flailing arms. "Settle down," he said. "What's got into you? There *is* an easy form, form number three. You will eventually get it. You've just got to keep trying. It's the only way."

He was so practical, so down-to-earth. I wanted to believe him.

Bruce didn't tell me that he thought I was grossly misintrepeting situations to the point of being delusional. There was no point. He couldn't have convinced me. It was slowly sinking in on him that I probably wasn't ever going to change. He was disappointed that Dr. Hemingway wasn't making me well. But he decided to give me the benefit of the doubt and put off any final decisions about our relationship till the end of the summer externship. Secretly he hoped I might recover from my illness when I was back in Riverside over the summer, away from the pressures of medical school. Besides, he wasn't certain of the wisdom of breaking off the relationship now when I was so obviously unstable and fragile and needed him more than ever. He didn't let me in on any of his thoughts or feelings then, and I unknowingly awaited their unveiling in the months ahead.

On the seventh and final try, I finally got number three.

It *was* easier. I finished it up, and passed it. I was ecstatic that I was now excused from having to take the comprehensive semester final in pathology, and I had indeed earned my honors grade. On the way back to my apartment, I was too exhausted to listen to the distant background chatter of voices. At home, I threw myself onto my couch and slept uninterrupted for several hours, the longest sleep I'd had in months.

There remained only two days to cram for three more finals. I told Bruce I was already exhausted, that I didn't see how I could make it.

Bruce got me started preparing for the rest of the finals. Even so, I found I couldn't do it. My brain was a sieve; the necessary information all slipped hopelessly through.

Bruce, by contrast, was tightly and efficiently storing away every pearl of information. I didn't know where he put it all. He was ruthless; he kept going and going. But that was exactly the support I needed.

"Aren't you pooped?" I asked him.

"Yes. Now, what will a complement-fixing reaction test show if the test antigen and antibody are specific for one another and form an antigen-antibody complex?"

"Oh, hell, I don't know, I'm too tired."

"There will be *no hemolysis*. Now look, I'm tired too. But we don't have time to be tired. We've gotta keep going."

Bruce was so tired he didn't want to deal with my symptoms. He continued to deny as much of my illness as he could. He was struggling to get himself through medical school, and he didn't have the energy to take on my struggle too.

We needed a study break. I went home to shower. As I stumbled across the apartment complex, I noticed a peculiar feeling deep inside my chest. It felt tight, almost as it felt when I was nervous, as I had been when I'd had to present case histories to my pathology class. But it wasn't quite like that. It was more as if my chest had a motor in it, and maybe it was idling too fast. I was becoming increasingly restless. To sit in one place for any length of time was unbearable. At first I thought I was having an anxiety attack. But it wasn't that. The restless feelings were from the Haldol I was taking. Since I was taking such small doses, I hadn't even considered the possibility that my motor-chest could be akathisia, the awful Walkies I'd experienced years before as a patient in the psychiatric hospital, when Dr. Falmouth had prescribed large doses of the drug.

Helluva time to get the Walkies, the night before a final exam. The initial signs of the restlessness had actually presented themselves at least a couple of days before, I realized as I reflected back. But I hadn't noticed because I wasn't used to noticing that sort of thing anymore, and because my mind had been totally absorbed with trying to pass finals.

I knew if my motor-chest got any worse I wouldn't be able to study at all, which could be a misfortune worse than any pain imaginable. I had originally been planning to study the entire night; otherwise I'd never be prepared for the final. This was crucial.

Unfortunately I'd already taken the full day's dose of Haldol, and it was already floating through my bloodstream. I went to my medicine cabinet and dumped everything out, looking for an old prescription of Cogentin I might have saved from years ago when I had taken it to counteract the akathisia that antipsychotics produced. It could slow down the motor chugging away mercilessly in my chest, perhaps enough to allow me to study tonight.

I didn't find any Cogentin. I was miserable. Trying to force myself to sit still and study for even one minute was unbelievable torture. Dr. Hemingway was out of town. I didn't know how to reach Dr. Winterman, and besides, he wouldn't want to be bothered with a mere patient. I had to have some Cogentin. I couldn't pull my all-nighter without it.

There was no choice: I would have to go to the emergency

room and ask a doctor to prescribe me some Cogentin. Since I knew exactly what my problem was and what to do for it, I reasoned it should be a relatively easy matter. I put a few books and notes into my backpack in case I felt calm enough to study during the long wait I anticipated in the emergency room, then I walked the mile to the hospital.

In the emergency room, I told the nurse that I had aka-thisia from the Haldol I was taking and that all I needed was a little Cogentin and then I could quickly be on my way to be studying for finals. She smiled, told me a doctor would be with me shortly, and whisked herself out of the examination room.

I sat on the examining table and swung my legs repeatedly back and forth off one side. I hoped I wouldn't have to wait too long. This waiting was awful, truly painful.

Finally, I couldn't sit still any longer. I got up and walked the three short steps to the other side of the room and back. The five minutes of wait had already seemed like hours. I poked my head out the door into the hallway. Two young men dressed in white were standing just inside another door-way conversing. They looked bored, as if they didn't have anything to do. I paced the floor several more times, climbed back onto the examining table and swung my feet a few more times, then paced around again. Next I walked to the far side of the room and opened up each silver drawer and peeked at all the stainless-steel instruments and white gauze, then shut each drawer again. All that effort had taken only five more minutes.

The motor in my chest was relentless. It motorized me around the exam room for another five minutes and yet an-other five minutes, and finally I caught a nurse flying by the door long enough to tell her I was extremely uncomfortable and truly needed to be seen by the doctor as soon as possible. She told me someone would be with me shortly and scooted off to another room.

"Your time is coming," I heard a falsely soothing voice

say from behind me with a smooth tone that made me uneasy.

I gazed around the room, noting that I appeared to be all alone. I was the sole contaminator of this isolated sterile cell. I reasoned that since I would only need to be seen for a minute, I didn't want to grub up the room's immaculate cleaning job. I pulled the neck of my T-shirt over my mouth and nose and breathed into it. There would be no need for them to have to scrub down this room again for the next patient.

Suddenly there was a commotion outside in the hallway. I looked up just in time to see a bloody hand wrapped loosely in bloody gauze, followed by a procession of worried-looking relatives parading by my door. The loud accompanying moans seemed to penetrate my chest, shaking up the motor inside. I suddenly felt silly. My reason for having come to the emergency room seemed so minor in comparison. How could the emergency-room staff know how disabling the akathisia was for me, how could they know how miserable I was feeling?

Finally a young man in white appeared with a clipboard and paper to talk to me. His nameplate identified him as a student in the physician's assistant program. I doubted he knew anything about Haldol, much less about akathisia. I pulled my T-shirt away from my face and asked him if he knew what Haldol was. He admitted that he didn't. Great start. I tried to explain to him as simply and succinctly as possible my problem and the facts about Haldol, akathisia, and Cogentin. That didn't satisfy him. He wanted my whole bloody life history. He seemed especially interested in getting all the details of my psychiatric history, a long and tedious story. By the time he was done interviewing me, he looked totally bewildered, though morbidly interested. He said he would have to step out for a moment but would return very soon, because, he said, he understood how uncomfortable I was with the motor-chest. Fat chance.

I knew very well that he was stepping out to talk to the resident on duty in the emergency room and find out what to do about my case.

Meanwhile, the voices fell silent. I imagined all those white coats made them nervous. I generally didn't have much use for the voices, except now I wished I could get them to hurry the doctors up. But I knew they didn't like to reveal themselves to other people, so they would never do that. I wondered why I was the only person in the world highly enough esteemed to receive the honor of their presence.

It seemed like hours before the physician's assistant student finally returned. He must have ordered up my hospital chart and pored hungrily over all the juiciest parts. Meanwhile, I was practically wearing a path in the linoleum floor from all my restless walking.

The student sat down and addressed me in a serious but condescending tone of voice. "What we would like to do," he said delicately, "is double your dose of Haldol. You're not taking a particularly large dose of the Haldol, and we think your restlessness is a sign that you need more medicine. Perhaps increasing your dose will help calm you down."

So they thought I was being crazy and delusional! I was *not* delusional! It was pointless to continue this conversation. I had already explained to him that I was unusually sensitive to side effects from major tranquilizers and that I could certainly recognize akathisia when I had it.

"Let me talk to the resident on duty," I insisted, purposely allowing a trace of irritation to creep into my voice. "I know what's going on with me. All I need is some Cogentin. I *don't* need more Haldol. Just send in the resident, *please*."

Five minutes later he returned with the resident, who appeared to be about as well informed as his physician's assistant student. "Look," the resident told me, "we've thoroughly discussed your case. We feel that what you need is a higher dose of the Haldol."

"You don't understand," I said, exasperated. "The side

effects are bothering me so much that I can't possibly study for finals. This is crucial. I've *got* to pass my finals, don't you see? Cogentin takes care of the akathisia pretty well for me—I know, because I've used it in the past for akathisia. Please, just prescribe me some Cogentin."

"I'm sorry, but that's our decision," the resident said firmly. I could see that he was going to remain adamant. He probably felt that he was the doctor here and his opinion was right because he knew far more pharmacology than any mere patient. How dare a patient tell the doctor how to prescribe?

I could be stubborn too: "This is ridiculous. I *know* what the problem is. Won't you please just believe me?"

The resident shook his head.

"All right," I said, "then let me talk to a psychiatric resident—is there one on duty?"

It took the psychiatric resident less time to come all the way from the psychiatric hospital across the street than it had taken for the emergency room doctor to step over from the very next room. I was glad I wasn't having a heart attack.

The psychiatric resident kept nodding his head as I explained my dilemma to him.

"What I'm going to do for you," he said, "is inject some Benadryl directly into your vein. It's a drug similar to Cogentin, but it should stop the akathisia even faster, because it will go into your bloodstream immediately."

He then injected the Benadryl into my arm. I felt total relief within a minute or two. He sent me off with a prescription for Cogentin to take for the akathisia at home. I was immensely grateful to the psychiatric resident for listening to me and helping me.

By the time I saw Dr. Winterman a few days later for my scheduled appointment, the side effects were under better control with the Cogentin. I had decided to quit taking the Haldol on my own, and I expected that in another day or two its effects would be worn off enough that I wouldn't need any more Cogentin.

Dr. Winterman didn't seem to understand or care the way Dr. Hemingway did. I appreciated Dr. Hemingway all over again.

I was so exhausted from the long weekend of studying that on the way home from Dr. Winterman's office I began to dream while I was awake. People I passed on the sidewalk seemed to be alien mutants.

I realized that my dreaming represented a serious signal of distress from my sleep-deprived brain. If I didn't get some rest soon, my delicate psychological balance could tip, toppling me over the edge of disaster at this crucial time.

Hang on, I pleaded with myself, just hang on, it's only a couple more days till the end of finals.

The dreams continued, and I couldn't sort out the chaos. Finals drifted into a never-ending nightmare. By the time I made it to my next appointment with Dr. Hemingway, I was totally confused.

"Finals week is over," Dr. Hemingway informed me. "Are you sure you haven't taken your physiology final?"

I sat perfectly still, like a statue. "No, I'm not sure," I said, moving just my lips. "I dreamed I went but I know I haven't really gone to the final yet."

Dr. Hemingway made a brief phone call to the physiology course director. While he talked, I observed the electrical outlet in the corner of his office blasting several volts of current across the room.

Above the crackling sounds I heard Hal say, "Do you want to get wired?" He was referring to the electronic connections to the machines inside me.

No, I didn't want to get wired. The flashing electrical display in the corner faded into the background Interference Patterns.

Dr. Hemingway hung up the phone and told me, "Dr.

Sherwood said you took the final. They have your answer sheet in with all the others."

So it hadn't been a dream, it had really happened. I must have actually gone to the physiology final.

"You look worried," Dr. Hemingway remarked.

"Worried" was an understatement. How could he look so casual when the Other Dimensions were leaking into his own office, when cosmic matters were climaxing in the world at this very moment?

He broke into his grinfrown. "Look," he said, "if you're starting to have a lot more problems again, we might need to think about hospitalizing you again."

"Hospitalize? Oh, no you don't." Not during these precarious times. I needed to stay free to protect myself from imminent hazards. In the hospital I would be exposed and vulnerable to unknown dangers. I would be like a bug in a glass jar—easily squished. No thanks, that wasn't for me.

"Well, then I'd like to see you again in my office on Friday," he said.

I was free to go. Dr. Hemingway waited until I was out of hearing to dictate:

> Today Carol came in looking confused, bewildered. She claims that she stopped taking her medicine two weeks ago. She can't even remember when her last examination was. I called the dean's office and found out that freshman final examinations were over as of yesterday. She is not sure that she took the final exam in physiology at that time. Accordingly, I have called Dr. Sherwood to check with him. She did. I suggested that in view of the fact that her medications had not been working and that she was experiencing increasing psychotic symptoms, she should consider hospitalization. She was opposed to this but agreed to return more frequently. Accordingly, we made arrangements to see her in two days.

She is not taking the Haldol because she had what sounds like an akathisia reaction last week. She went to the emergency room last Thursday evening and was seen by Dr. Miller, who recommended she continue her medication on a lower dose but also gave her Cogentin, which apparently alleviated her akathisia somewhat. She is not akathetic today.

I will urge her on Friday to again reconsider rehospitalization. It is apparent that her ability to function in the community is becoming lower and lower, and I do not see that in her current condition she will be able to take an externship program on the 23rd of this month when she is scheduled to start one.

"What about that physiology final?" was Dr. Hemingway's first question at my next appointment. "Did you find out how you did?"

"I'm not sure," my substitute voice said mechanically. "I think I passed and that's it." I felt as if my own face was grinfrowning. I tried to stop it.

Dr. Hemingway twitched his eyebrows a couple of times and adjusted his wire rims. "You're not sure? Would you like to come into the hospital now?" he asked.

He hadn't really said that. The words I had heard hadn't matched the movement of his lips. The voices were deceiving me into thinking he had actually said that. So I didn't reply.

"Hm," I heard Dr. Hemingway say. "Well, then, would you like to try some Haldol again? I really think you ought to be taking some medication."

My dead stare remained fixed on his eyebrows.

"We can start out more gradually and maybe that way you won't get the akathisia. Would you be opposed to giving it another try?"

I shook my head, gingerly. If I wasn't careful my head would spin clear around 360 degrees on its axis.

"I'd like to start you out with a half milligram every

night," he instructed me. "Do you need a new prescription?"

I shook my head again, being careful not to turn it too far to either side.

"Okay." A long pause ensued, and during that time it didn't occur to me to say anything. Dr. Hemingway interrupted the silence. "I'd like to see you next week."

I remained fixed in my position in the chair, locked into a stony gaze, staring across the room. It was too complicated to try to figure out how to do something different.

"Can you come back to see me next Wednesday?" he said, trying to stir me to respond.

I didn't answer his question or move from my position. I didn't want to lose the stability provided by my immobility.

"I'll see you on Wednesday then," he said with a final-sounding drop in his intonation.

I savored the steadiness of my rocklike position a moment longer. Finally I managed to activate myself, mechanically rising up out of the chair to slip one strap of my book pack over my shoulder and walk out of his office.

It was becoming clear to me that Dr. Hemingway was not like the other psychiatrists at the psychiatric hospital. None of them would have been willing to listen to my complaints about the medicine or to experiment with medications until we found one I could tolerate better. I felt grateful that Dr. Hemingway listened to me and took my ideas seriously. I could feel he sincerely wanted to help me become as functional as possible.

At last I had caught up on my sleep. Now it was going to be a luxury to be able to sleep as much as I wanted, all the time. I had to keep reminding myself that I'd truly finished my first year of medical school, because it didn't seem real. I was now a sophomore! I'd always heard the first year of medical school was the hardest. Now that I'd gotten through it I expected to have no problem getting through the next three.

The lease was up on our townhouse apartment. Megan and I agreed that though we had gotten along spendidly as roommates, it was finally time to get separate apartments; we both wanted more privacy. But we wanted to remain in close contact, and we accomplished this by renting apartments right next door to each other for the fall. Bruce applied at the same apartment complex and signed a lease for an apartment in the next building.

I had learned not to discuss my weird experiences with Bruce, but to save my discussions of the Other World phenomena for my psychiatrist. Bruce just didn't know how to handle the things I told him. Sometimes I couldn't think of a safe topic to discuss with Bruce, because I wasn't sure what was normal and what was weird. So we spent a lot of our time together in silence. Bruce seemed to be growing emotionally distant, and in the back of my mind I wondered if he might be thinking about breaking off our relationship. I tried not to think about this possibility because it scared me. I thought I needed him; he was my major contact with reality, and I sorely wanted to hang on to him. He had been the one who had supported me most and pulled me through the last semester of medical school; he had helped me study, he had encouraged me, he had loved me. I couldn't have gotten this far without him. Yes, I was emotionally dependent on him.

Bruce still hadn't told me he was planning to make his final decision about our relationship at the end of summer. By then I would have had three months away from the pressures of medical school. If I seemed better, he would know that my mental problems were a temporary and situational response to severe pressure, and if I did not, he could reasonably assume I was destined to remain permanently ill. He promised me he would write over the summer from his home town, where he would be in his own externship program.

I had mixed feelings about leaving him. Although I would miss him, I would also be relieved to have some distance from the strain I felt in the relationship.

I saw Dr. Hemingway one last time before I left town. He instructed me to phone him long distance every week from Riverside. His final note said:

> Today Carol is just about as confused as last time. She thinks it is three weeks since she last saw me. She has been taking, she claims, a half tablet of the Haldol, that is a half milligram, a day. She feels that there may be a slight restlessness and she is concerned about taking more. Therefore, we agreed to have her continue to take a half tablet, although I believe this is grossly ineffectual. She will call me this coming Tuesday from Riverside.

I decided that my parents needed to know I was seeing another psychiatrist at the psychiatric hospital. I described Dr. Hemingway as an old man with white hair, but I told my parents I thought maybe this psychiatrist was different from the rest, that maybe he was going to work out all right for a change. They were glad I was getting help again. They worried when I didn't have anybody looking after me. I was grateful to my parents for doing everything they could to help me, but there was only so much they could do. I couldn't possibly explain the profundity of my difficulties to them. There was no way anyone on earth could understand what I was going through, and particularly not my parents.

My mother believed that you shouldn't dwell on your problems and that other people didn't like to hear about your problems. With this in mind I thought it would be inappropriate to discuss mine within or outside the family. My family avoided communication on personal issues, and this increased my feelings of distance. My parents had an extreme sense of personal privacy, and thus they didn't relay much information about me to my brothers and my sister, who all remained quietly concerned about something they realized they knew nothing about.

At the end of the semester my parents arrived in Cedar City with a U-Haul, and we moved my furniture and other belongings back home for the summer. I admired their self-sacrifice for their children, even for me, their one child who had disappointed them, but I didn't know how to tell them so. We were never good at talking about feelings in my family.

I turned my thoughts to the externship program I would be starting. It would be my first experience in clinical medicine, and I knew I would like it a thousand times better than the tedium of academics. I was excited about my first opportunity to function in the role of a doctor, to actually help patients. My entire motivation for wanting to go to medical school in the first place had been a desire to help people in the most meaningful way I could, and now I was glad finally to be satisfying that need directly. I was certain I would perform well and enjoy it immensely.

"We'll see," I heard the voices echoing around in my head. "We'll see."

CHAPTER TEN

SUMMER EXTERNSHIP

The hospital director's voice was coming from his fingers, not his mouth. With each positional change of his hands he shot his words off to the far corners of the room.

"You see," he explained carefully, "we had decided not even to offer an externship program here this year until we found out you're a native of Riverside. Now we won't have to provide housing."

So he expected me to live with my parents.

"I can't live with my folks," I responded, not hiding my dejection. "Personal reasons."

"Well, wait a minute," he said. "We're lucky you're female. I think we could house you in the nursing dorm. But," he added, "it's no palace."

That sounded just fine to me. I would be paid eighty dollars a week by the hospital to work as an extern. It sounded like a fortune. All I would have to do would be to follow the doctors and nurses around and try to learn what I could, helping out whenever I could. I was thrilled to think of earning money working in the role of a doctor for the first time. The purpose of the externship programs offered at hospitals across the state was to provide an inspiring experience for young medical students, and perhaps to encourage them to return years later after the end of their medical training to set up their medical practice. Small towns sorely needed doctors, and this was one way local hospitals tried to attract them.

My first week as an extern at Riverside General Hospital was to be in the hospital kitchen, at the switchboard, in the business office, in the maintenance area, and in the supply room. All this was supposed to give me a broad view of the inner workings of the hospital. Even without the restlessness caused by my medication, I would have found this schedule boring at best. Dr. Hemingway had increased my Haldol to two milligrams a day, and consequently, I had the Walkies all over the hospital kitchen, the switchboard area, the business office, the maintenance area, and the supply room. I tried to look especially interested in everything so that the hospital staff wouldn't interpret my uncontrollable restlessness as boredom.

By the time I got to my surgery rotation weeks later, nobody had told me where the operating room was. I had no idea how to scrub in. The surgeons all looked so busy and important running around in their green scrub outfits and paper masks and booties that I dreaded even asking them a question for fear of somehow causing a patient's death by distracting them.

The Haldol Walkies were a major problem. Dr. Hemingway had prescribed me some Cogentin for the restlessness, but my case of akathisia was so stubborn that the Cogentin didn't completely eliminate it. Trying to keep my feet still during those long operations was an unbelievable strain.

In the daytime I worked long hours on the various hospital services; at night I was on call to the emergency room, and I was frequently called out of bed to see interesting cases. One night I had been in the ER sewing up a drunk's lacerated nose until four in the morning, and then at a quarter to seven I received a call to get back out of bed and get right down to surgery. I didn't have time to grab any breakfast, not even a quick cup of coffee, before scrubbing in. One kindly surgeon had warned me never to go to surgery without something in my stomach first, because the sight of all the gory blood and guts could make me really dizzy if I hadn't eaten. He told me that last year's extern had passed out cold during an operation and landed with his face right in the middle of the incision! It was comforting to hear that men, too, had trouble with dizziness at the sight of blood. I knew my own blood pressure tended to run low early in the morning, and the Haldol made it even lower. Sometimes I was dizzy before I even got near the operating room.

While gowning me up, the nurse explained that we were about to repair multiple facial fractures sustained by an eighteen-year-old who had been hit in the face with a baseball bat. My job was to assist with suction, keeping the wound dry to allow the surgeon to see what he was doing. It sounded like a simple task.

"More suction," the surgeon barked. "Keep it dry, will ya?"

I was trying. I wasn't tall enough to see sufficiently deep into the corners of the wound to slurp up all the blood.

"More suction. Like this." Roughly, the surgeon grabbed my gloved hand and shoved the suction tube around the corners of the wound, then he yanked the tube right out of my hand and did it himself.

"Dumb, dumb, dumb," the voices announced over the operating room intercom. Suddenly I felt I was going to cry.

"Here, you two switch," the surgeon growled at me. "You retract and the nurse can operate the suction."

For now I was out of immediate danger of crying. I

grabbed the retractors and squeezed hard until my fingers went numb.

When we had finished repairing that site, the surgeon started working on another area. First he peeled the upper gum away from the front teeth, then he made a hole through the underlying maxillary bone to the maxillary sinus. It was pretty gruesome, and seeing it made me feel sick. A roaring sound of water rushed in my ears, and my vision started to fade into shades of gray. The surgeon's and nurse's voices sounded distant. I was too proud to speak up and say I was getting light-headed. I wanted to try to outlast it and save myself the embarrassment. I wanted to be tough.

"Carol, I want you to hand me this ribbon in sections of about three feet apiece," said the surgeon. "Keep feeding it to me as fast as I use it."

There was blood everywhere, and the sickening odor of scorched bone dust from the surgical buzz saws filled the air. I dared for a quick instant to take my gaze off my own bloody gloved hands and peek through slitted eyes at the surgeon's work. He was stuffing all the ribbon I was handing him through the hole he'd made into the maxillary sinus. Immediately I fixed my eyes back on my hands again.

"Carol, a little more ribbon, please."

Wordlessly I fed him several extra feet and waited for it to disappear. Finally he took up no more slack in the line, and without thinking, I glanced over to see what he was doing. That was my mistake. With his right hand, the surgeon was tugging on the ribbon coming out of the hole under the gum, and with his left hand he was pulling the other end of the line out one nostril. He was sliding the entire line back and forth in a seesaw fashion. It was too late: I'd already looked and I wished I hadn't. The bright red blood covering the whole scene had burned its image onto my retinas in the flash of a second I had glanced at it. Closing my eyes didn't erase it.

A massive wave of dizziness crashed against my eardrums,

and my visual field faded into a fog. I could barely hear the surgeon asking his scrub nurse for a pair of hemostats over the roar. If only I had been able to get some coffee in me earlier this morning, or gotten some exercise to raise my blood pressure. Now I felt all hot and sweaty under my greens and I was becoming increasingly nauseated. I was fading.

I shook my rubbery legs and mentally begged them not to buckle under me. If I could just hang on a little longer the fog might clear. Mentally I coaxed my blood pressure to rise, meanwhile being careful to avoid looking at the mangled face again.

Oh, no, I felt myself going. In a matter of five seconds I would be out cold if I didn't do something. "Doctor," I said, "I hate to say this but I think I'm going to pass out."

"Well then, for God's sake, don't do it here," he bellowed. "Go lie down somewhere."

I broke scrub and found a stretcher right outside in the hallway to lie down on until I felt well enough to go for some breakfast.

While I participated in the externship program that summer, my delusions continued. I became convinced that the flesh of my hands covered shiny gears and colored wires inside. I took out my oils and painted my machine-filled hands on canvas. Then I painted pictures of the Interference Patterns and other special phenomena in an effort to record them on canvas and make them hold still while I examined them. I didn't have a lot of time for painting, though, since work was so demanding.

I felt an overpowering sense of duty to my job. I was working hundred-hour weeks. In order to do it, I had to gather my strength. I had to make a concentrated effort to keep the Other Worlds separate from this one long enough to allow me to complete all the work required of me at the hospital. When I wasn't working, back in the privacy of my own room, I withdrew from the world, allowing myself to drift with the interference, relaxing from the awful strain of trying to stay functional the rest of the time.

When I finally spoke with Dr. Hemingway by telephone again and told him about recent events, he urged me to return to Cedar City immediately to be admitted to the psychiatric hospital. I refused. I had work to complete here at the hospital in Riverside. Dr. Hemingway told me to double both my Haldol and Cogentin and call him again in a couple of days. He could reasonably have forced me to return to Cedar City and had me committed, but he decided that he could trust me to call him if I started to develop problems I couldn't handle. At the time I had no idea what a brave move this was on his part; all I knew was that I was growing to trust him immensely.

Following our telephone conversation, Dr. Hemingway dictated:

> Today Carol called from her hospital job in Riverside. I hadn't heard from her last week and we had missed each other in trying to call back and forth. She thinks things are going fairly well but is upset today because she is convinced that people in the cafeteria were able to look into her mind and see exactly what she was thinking. This made her very uncomfortable and she noted the same phenomenon in other contacts she has had with people this morning and I suspect this is the reason she called at this time when we were not scheduled to have a telephone call from her otherwise. We discussed the interpretation of this at some length and my final interpretation to her was that this is the sort of phenomenon that she has when she is under stress and the social tensions of the hospital lead her to this type of interpretation that people are reading her mind. I put this in the context of a type of sensitivity or of a special awareness of herself and embarrassment with others which manifests itself in this unusual way. She did not accept this wholly but is

willing to consider other interpretations. I also suggested that she try to take more Haldol to combat what she thought might be the effects of LSD placed in her food. She will call me back toward the end of the week.

Bruce took a weekend off from his own externship program and drove to Riverside to visit me. He seemed distant. I couldn't tell if this was a change or not, because he had always seemed somewhat distant, and I hadn't seen him in a while. Even through my psychotic haze, though, I could sense his withdrawal from me, and it made me ache inside.

When Bruce saw my most recent painting of my hands, he became concerned because it was so bizarre. It was obvious to him now that I hadn't gotten any less crazy, despite my current respite from the pressures of school. He was beginning to realize for the first time that I might never get well.

My next rotation at Riverside General was psychiatry. I observed that the ward psychiatrist invariably prescribed both an antipsychotic tranquilizer *and* an antidepressant medication for all of his patients, no matter what kind of psychiatric problem they had.

I listened closely to his psychiatric interviews, taking careful note of what symptoms in his patients suggested mental illness, then mentally rationalizing my own experiences as something entirely different: cosmic phenomena spilling over from the Parallel Dimensions. I decided that his patients' voices were hallucinations from their imaginations, but *my* voices were real entities from the Other Worlds. His patients' ideas were delusions, but *my* ideas were actually truths well grounded in supporting evidence.

Remembering that Dr. Hemingway had advised me to keep my own unusual experiences a secret, I was careful to avoid saying anything on the ward that might let on that weird things were happening inside my head. As a result, I projected a quiet, reserved outward appearance. On my

psychiatry rotation I was expected to sit in on all confer-
ences, activities, and therapy groups. At one particular group
session, when I was sitting in the circle along with two nurses
and several patients, the psychiatrist went around the group
and asked everyone to name something he liked about himself. This was supposed to be therapeutic, he had explained
to me; it helped patients learn how to feel good about themselves. When it came my turn to respond, I said that I liked
myself because I could fly. It seemed like a perfectly sensible
thing to say at the time, before I'd thought about it.

My answer raised a few eyebrows. The psychiatrist pur-
sued my response, asking me, "You mean, you know how
to fly airplanes?"

No, I was referring to flying across Dimensional barriers.
I told him, "No, *not* like fly in an airplane," but I couldn't
think of anything more to say, or a way to explain exactly
what I meant. He fortunately let the subject drop right
there. Only later did it dawn on me what a careless thing
I'd said. I could easily have blown my cover without realizing it.

Happily, the weeks passed without further incident, and
at the end of July I completed by externship at Riverside
General Hospital. The official evaluations of my work performance were favorable. It was time to return to Cedar City,
to prepare for the resumption of classes.

That night as I lay in bed trying to get to sleep after
moving to my new apartment in Cedar City, I heard the
voices singing the song "You'll Never Walk Alone." I knew
there was some kind of symbolic meaning intended in this
message, but I couldn't determine whether it was positive
or not. Finally I decided it meant they were planning on
staying with me permanently. I drifted off to sleep.

"Got to mow the car now."
I flew out of bed and dashed into the living room to the

bird cage. It appeared that Banana had finally learned how to talk.

"Bring on the bratricide."

The bratricide? I'd never taught Banana to say anything like that. I didn't even know what it meant. We were still trying to get down the basics of "pretty bird."

"Ha-ha-ha-ha-ha! Guess again, turkey!"

I had been mistaken; it wasn't Banana talking. It was a completely new voice, one that had initially sounded as if it came from Banana.

The voice flitted all around the room, each syllable landing in a different corner. "You're going on a trip," the voice said. "Soon."

I wasn't planning any trip. How could this be? I had to be here to start the fall semester soon.

"Don't bother packing any bags," the voice told me. "You won't need any. And don't try to hide. That won't help."

It sounded like a threat. I was scared. I went to see Dr. Hemingway, thinking perhaps he could help.

"You look stiff," Dr. Hemingway told me. "Do you feel kind of stiff?"

I couldn't bring myself to believe that he was actually talking to me. He was faking it. Neither could I overcome the feeling of inertia pressing on my brain to say anything at all back to him.

"Hm," he said with a twitch of his mustache, then a twitch of his eyebrows.

Poof, next I was back in my apartment, swimming through the patterns, drowning in screaming voices. Everything seemed so complete, so overly complete, that I didn't need to move at all.

Dr. Hemingway dictated after my visit to him:

> Today Carol sits and stares a lot without replying,
> and she reports she is spending a lot of time standing

or sitting and not particularly thinking but just indulging in "pure perception." She also complains of difficulty keeping her thoughts straightened and in order. We talked a great deal about events in the last few days but because of Carol's vagueness it is very difficult to note just what is going on. However, she states that she might be "ready to go on a trip in a few days." We talked about the advisability of coming into the hospital since the possibility of what might happen seems to be frightening her; however, she was quite adamant against coming into the hospital. I did, however, reach an agreement with her whereby she would call me before going on any kind of trip. She will return in one week.

I lay around in my nearly motionless state for the entire next week. At my next appointment, Dr. Hemingway decided I was no longer able to care for myself at home, and he phoned my father to have him take me for admission to the Welmington psychiatric ward.

The helicopters followed us the whole way, their blades flapping right outside the back window. At the hospital, my father had to coax me to get me out of the car. Moving slowly, like putty, I had to be led by the hand into the emergency room. Once there, my father stepped out of the examining room, leaving me alone briefly while he talked to the admitting doctor privately in the hall. A moment later, my father peeked back into the room to check on me. I had vanished. Apparently I'd escaped through the other door on the opposite side of the room.

Golly—time for work. I can't be late. Here's a rack of lab coats. I guess I'm supposed to find mine. I wonder where it is. This one looks like it might fit. I'll try it on. Sure enough, it fits. Off I go, looking for my station at Riverside General Hospital.

"You're gonna be late," said one of the voices.

I had to hurry. I wandered around a maze of hallways, not finding any familiar territory. I ended up in a strange lab, wondering what to do now. I was tired. I decided to look at a magazine on a rack while I rested and figured out what to do next.

A nurse popped her head in the door. Seeing me sitting there in a white lab coat and reading a magazine as though I belonged there, she asked me, "Have you seen an escaped psych patient around here?"

I didn't remember seeing anyone like that. I shook my head.

"Call the ER if you see her," she said before departing.

I continued thumbing through the magazine and pondering my situation.

"You're too late now," the voice informed me. I felt bad about being late.

After combing the hospital, the psychiatric staff finally located me in the lab, where I was babbling incoherently about a person named Hal and insisting I had to get to work. To everyone's relief I was captured and safely admitted to the psychiatric unit.

Poof—the next thing I knew I was spread-eagled across white sheets, my ankles tightly strapped in leather restraints that looked like leftovers from a horror movie. I didn't know how I had stumbled into this Dimension but I had to find a way out fast. I had once read that Houdini dislocated his thumbs to escape from bonds. Maybe I could do that too.

It didn't hurt at all; I slipped off both wrist and ankle cuffs with ease, then I threaded my body back out of the snug waist cinch. If I could let a ray of sunlight from the window fall upon even a few of my skin cells I would be normalized back into a form that traveled effectively, and then I could be transported back to my apartment in a flash. I leaped up onto the windowsill to bathe my body in the morning light, or afternoon light, I didn't know which. I didn't even know if morning and afternoon existed in this Dimension I'd slipped into.

The words "Oh, no!" rang from the hallway. Then more distantly, "Hey, you guys, come here and look at this! You won't believe this! She's gotten out of her restraints!"

I was busy transforming. I balanced myself perfectly on one stork-leg, grasping the opposite leg behind my back and over my head with one free hand. With the other hand I was shooting "help" messages out my fingertips to the sun.

Three men dressed in white lifted me down from the window and molded my arms and legs back into their former positions inside the leather straps tied to the bed. I watched them pull each strap a notch or two tighter, securing each one with a special key. "Do you know where you are?" one of them asked me.

I was afraid to ask where.

"You're back in the hospital in Welmington," he said in soft soothing tones that made me wonder if he was in some way related to Hal. "You've been in this hospital before, remember? Your father brought you here last night."

Now all the weird things that had happened were beginning to make sense.

One of the voices interrupted the conversation, whispering in my ear, "Let's go on that trip now."

Frightened, I pulled hard on my left hand, and it popped right out of the leather restraint like a cork from a wine bottle.

I heard a few murmurs of "How the hell . . ." and then they leaped on my wrist and tightened the leather cinch so snugly that I could barely extend my fingers. I watched the key disappear back into a pocket.

I heard another soothing voice call my name. "Don't you recognize me?" the voice said. "I'm Dr. Black, remember me?"

Of course. He was smiling down at me from beside my

bed. I was glad to see his familiar face. My eyes glued themselves to his salt-and-pepper beard.

Dr. Black explained, "We had to put you in restraints like this, Carol, because we were afraid you could get hurt. We'll take them off when you're feeling better, I promise."

I believed him.

"Now," he told me, "I've got to do something you won't like, and I'm sorry. I've got to give you an IV."

He gathered together all the necessary equipment, then scrubbed my arm with alcohol and thrust the needle far up a vein. Finally he hooked up the plastic tubing, adjusting the drip rate of the clear solution sliding down the tubes into my arm.

"Now," said Dr. Black, "do you know why I had to do this?"

I looked at him blankly.

"Because you weren't eating."

Of course I wasn't eating. The voices had put LSD in my food.

"You've lost weight," Dr. Black continued to explain. "You need your strength. When you get around to eating again we can take out the IV. Now why don't you try and rest."

Dr. Black and the others disappeared, and the lights went out. I was tired. I fell right to sleep.

"Good morning," said a cheerful lady in a white lab coat as she clanked a wire tray of glass tubes full of blood against my bedrail. "I only need a little bit today." She tied a rubber tourniquet around my left arm and scrubbed it vigorously with an alcohol pad.

As she felt around for a good vein, I said slowly and clearly, "You might try my median cubital vein, over here. It's a good one."

She straightened up, snapped off the tourniquet, and whipped herself and her tray out of the room. From down the hallway I heard her screeching, "What is that girl, a psychic or something? How does she know about median cubital veins?"

Before long, Dr. Black arrived and removed my IV, then he called an aide to unlock the restraints. I insisted that I had to get back to Cedar City to go to class. Dr. Black told me it would be a while before I'd be able to leave the the hospital.

As my head cleared over the next few days, the voices grew distant. Vague almost-images floated past my memory, just outside my mental grasp—something about looking for Riverside General Hospital in a strange lab coat, something about leather bands squeezing my wrists, something about sun in the window—fugitive dreams I didn't care to chase. Examining my wrists, I found bruises that were tender to the touch and turning from black to purple and yellow. Trying to figure out what was real was so confusing that I gave up. I had more important things to think about, such as how I was going to get back to school in time.

By the end of the week Dr. Black decided I was coherent enough to be discharged from the hospital. I was in a hurry to get back to Cedar City. Classes would be starting in two days, and I wondered how I would ever be ready.

The last night before class I dropped by Bruce's apartment to let him know I was back in town and to make plans to walk to class in the morning, just as we always did last year.

He looked uncomfortable or unfriendly, I couldn't tell which. "Are you doing better now?" he asked.

"Yeah, I'm all right."

He didn't say anything for a long time. It seemed he was looking at me almost with disgust, as if I were a dead fish in his living room. I wondered if I had done something to hurt him or insult him. No, I was just imagining this. I I knew I tended to get paranoid and imagine things about other people, and I realized I was probably even more likely to do that since I had just gotten out of the hospital and was in a delicate state. I told myself to ignore my perceptions and try not to worry.

Still, he looked more uncomfortable than I had ever seen him. His silence persisted. I decided not to interrupt it, because he probably needed it to think. He had always been a slow thinker.

Finally he started a conversation, beginning by announcing, "I won't be walking to class with you tomorrow."

"Oh. Then maybe Tuesday? Have you got something else planned tomorrow?" I didn't want to interfere if he wanted to go with someone else.

"No. And I think you should find your own seat in class. Don't plan on sitting with me."

"Bruce, what are you telling me?" If he truly wanted to break up with me, I was crushed. I hadn't expected such an abrupt loss. "For God's sake, Bruce, please tell me what's going on." I felt sick.

He couldn't explain. He seemed defensive, though I wasn't sure. I felt that I couldn't be sure of anything anymore. My world seemed to be falling apart all around me, at a time when I most needed its stability.

"Bruce, *please,* can't you explain anything to me?"

He paused for a long time, thinking. Finally he said, "I just need some distance for a while. That's all."

"Do you want to quit seeing me altogether?" I would cooperate and leave him alone entirely, if that's what he wanted.

"No," he said, "that's not it."

"What, then?" I persisted. I had to know.

"Well, we can still study together sometimes—but not all the time like last year."

"Okay. Let me know if you ever want me to put extra coffee in my thermos for you."

He said nothing more. I was left hanging. I would have to

learn to be comfortable living in limbo. This was only the beginning of the breakdown of all the different areas of my life. I saw it coming and I dreaded it.

"But you've got us," Hal said in his familiar soothing tones. I couldn't imagine the voices could get me through what I had yet to face. In fact, I had no idea of all that I would be facing.

R.T.C. LIBRARY, LETTERKENNY

CHAPTER ELEVEN

SOPHOMORE MEDICAL YEAR

In class I purposely sat as far away from Bruce as possible, to maintain as much distance as I could from my pain. I was still feeling devastated and profoundly empty without Bruce. How could I survive without him?

In my self-absorption I hadn't noticed that one of our female classmates had failed to return for the fall semester. I first noticed her absence when I heard two women in the row behind me gossiping about her mysterious disappearance. I tried to remember what Bobbi Blakemore looked like, but I couldn't conjure up an image of her face in my mind. Later I overheard her best friend saying that she had failed pathology last year, and that one day near the end of last year when she had gone into the student mailroom to pick up her mail, she discovered her *mailbox had disappeared*. Her name had been pulled off her mail slot, and all the other names had been moved to the next slot, so that hers simply no longer existed. Zip, just like that. In the next day's mail at home she received an official letter from the dean's office informing her that she wouldn't be allowed to continue in medical school.

Wow, as simple as that—no warning, nothing. This piece of news hit me hard in my already fragile state. I had nearly failed microbiology last spring. Could I have been thrown out of school? I recognized that sooner or later I could easily flunk something. I needed to know if I could be kicked out. I decided to go ask the dean about school policy.

"Dean Honeycut," I said hesitantly, fixing my gaze behind him on an abstract painting barely recognizable as a nude on his office wall, "do students ever get kicked out of med school here?"

He offered up a welcome smile, and a reassuring "No, of course not."

Still, I wasn't entirely satisfied. "You mean nobody has ever gotten kicked out of this school?"

"Look, Carol, it's not the policy of this school to try to flunk people out. Our initial selection process is thorough enough that people who won't be able to handle the work never get in. We don't admit more students than we have room for and then flunk out people till the class is the right size. We have a special place in the class reserved for each student we admit, and we like to keep every spot filled. It's a terrible waste of a position if there is attrition, so, you see, we do everything we can to help each student get through. We want to graduate every student we admit."

I didn't have the nerve to ask about Bobbi, as I wanted to do.

"Is there something else on your mind?" he asked.

"Yes." Suddenly I felt bold. "What happened to Bobbi Blakemore? Did she get kicked out?"

"People who leave our school always want to. It's a mutual thing. Bobbi wasn't motivated, and she knew it; we did too. A couple of years ago we had an engineer who started med school, and he didn't do well in his classes, so we called him in and talked to him. As it turned out, he wasn't really interested. He had started med school here because of family pressure—his father wanted him to be a doctor. His true love was engineering, so he went back to it. It was the same kind of situation with Bobbi."

I thanked Dean Honeycut, and then departed. My fears vanished and I quit worrying for a while. Now with my mind free of heavier concerns, I could concentrate more on my studies. But I was still feeling lonely without Bruce. To keep Banana from suffering with me, I bought a second parakeet for companionship, and named it Ananab (Banana spelled backwards).

Unfortunately, the sophomore year of med school was proving to be even tougher than freshman year. There were more exams, and I was studying every extra second, cutting into my sleep to a serious degree. As a result, I was chronically exhausted. And worse yet, I was barely passing exams.

Taking advantage of my discouragement, the voices chose this time to start telling me I could improve my situation by drastic means, by escaping to a higher form of existence. I wasn't ready for any drastic changes yet, because I was hoping I could continue to get through school by ordinary means, as I had been doing. I didn't know exactly what the voices meant, but I did listen to them.

At my next appointment with Dr. Hemingway I told him what the voices were saying to me. I was feeling discouraged enough to start considering their advice, even if it was drastic.

"Do you know specifically what the voices have in mind?" he asked me.

I just shrugged my shoulders and gazed hopelessly into the distance.

"I can't let you do anything drastic," he said. "The voices may suggest something really harmful that could prevent you from ever finishing school. Did you ever think of that?"

"I wouldn't want that," I said. "But I do need help."

"Would you consider coming into the hospital now?" he asked.

Slowly, I shook my head. The hospital wasn't a viable alternative. Bouncing in and out of the hospital could ruin my medical career.

Not a question this time: "I want you to come into the hospital."

No. No hospital. As I shook my head again, molten blobs of thoughts slipped off my skin and splatted onto the carpet in neat little paths.

"There's a bed open on Ward One. Won't you come in?"

God no.

"If you come into the hospital we might be able to get your next exam delayed. You're in no shape to take exams right now, don't you agree?"

He was right. Hospitalization might actually aid my cause.

Dr. Hemingway continued, "The school's officials would see good and sufficient reason to give you extra time if they realized the seriousness of your problem, if they knew you were getting intensive medical care. After all, they're physicians, and they if anybody should understand about a student having a health problem."

That sounded reasonable, even though deep down I didn't believe my problem was medical; it was spiritual. But I couldn't possibly handle any more exams right then, and there were several coming up soon. My coming into the hospital should demonstrate that I was trying to get my problem under control, and buy me some time to pull myself together.

"Okay," I said at last.

Without even a knock on the door, the nurse burst into my hospital room. She held out a Dixie cup containing a little green pill and a little white pill.

"Military pellets?" I asked.

"No, this is Haldol. Dr. Hemingway wants you to take it."

I swallowed the pills. The nurse, satisfied with the completion of her mission, turned on her heel and exited.

Next, a man in a long white coat and a tie burst in.

"Is there no privacy?" Hal protested.

"No!" said another voice. "It's the day of the eagle."

"Hi, I'm Dr. Dolby," said the man in the white coat. "Can we talk for a little while?"

Not filtering out my irrelevant ideas, I asked him, "Are you wearing white because this is the Day of the Eagle?"

He looked at me strangely, then repeated, "No, I'm Dr. Dolby," in a louder-than-normal voice, as if I were hard-of-hearing. Positioning his yellow legal tablet squarely on his clipboard, he said, "Can you name the last five presidents?"

It sounded like some kind of trick question to me. Too bad he didn't realize I had the power to diffuse my molecules and slip right through the brick wall to the outside. He could never keep me here. In the meantime, I decided to answer his question: "Ford, Nixon, Johnson, Hal . . ."

"Mm-hmm."

My eye caught on somebody outside my window climbing up the elm tree to look inside at us. I leaped to the top of a desk right under the window to peer out through the heavy institutional screen.

"And now," the doctor continued as if nothing at all had happened, "can you tell me what this means: 'Don't cry over spilled milk.'"

Flat. That phrase was flat. *It must mean the milk is flat.* "Milk sours when it spills," I told him. Was there a hidden meaning locked into that phrase?

Before I had time to uncover the deeper significance of his words, he shot off another proverb: "'A bird in the hand is worth two in the bush.' What does that mean to you?"

I thought he must be referring to my parakeets, Banana and Ananab. Those were the only birds I knew. I told him, "It means parakeets sit on your hand in pairs because their feet are warm." I hoped he'd understand that without further interrogation, because I didn't think I could explain it any further.

The ceiling light was making noises. I stared up at it.

"Is there something up there that's bothering you?" the doctor asked.

I kept staring. I spied a small microphone cleverly hidden in one side of the light fixture. "I didn't want to be recorded," I said. I felt my body beginning to stiffen from paralyzer beams shooting out from the walls and focusing on me. I stared right at the doctor, then through his chest and past him, out to the Other Side. Meanwhile, the paralyzer beams levitated my hands over my head and held them there.

"What are you doing?" the doctor asked. "What does that mean?"

Too late: I'd left him way behind in a place that no longer mattered. As I hovered up in the room's far corner looking down on him, he stood up, opened the door, and walked out.

"See you tomorrow," he said as he closed the door behind him.

His dictated admission note read:

> Identification: Carol North is a second-year medical student who was admitted by Dr. Hemingway with continuing problems of psychosis. Currently she is floridly psychotic with a variety of Schneiderian first rank symptoms including thought broadcasting, thought insertion, auditory hallucinations and virtually the entire 11 symptoms. The patient has had a history of psychosis which appears to be increasing and her symptoms are currently interfering with her functioning in medical school.
>
> Diagnostic impression: Hebephrenic-catatonic schizophrenia. I feel she probably represents a process schizophrenia which seems to involve a lot of first rank symptomatology.
>
> Therapeutic recommendation: It seems imperative to get Carol on reasonable doses of antipsychotic medication in order to have her deal more realistically with her vocational options.

Dr. Hemingway knew I was dependable, even while I was psychotic. If he asked me to be at a certain place at a certain time, he could trust me to be there. He gave me more freedom on the ward than he gave his other patients. I got gate passes to leave the ward for everything I needed. Dr. Hemingway viewed the hospital not as a place to lock me up, but as a facility to provide for my basic needs like meals and medications, which I grossly neglected at home. But—I later found out—the hospital staff criticized Dr. Hemingway for allowing a patient as disturbed as I was to have so much freedom.

Dr. Hemingway granted me a pass to go visit Dr. Lance, the pharmacology course director, to request a late exam. I was in no shape to take the exam that was coming up in two days. I explained my situation to him, and through his big smile he told me he would write a makeup exam for me if I brought him a doctor's excuse. Mission accomplished.

By now it was apparent to Dr. Hemingway that conventional treatments weren't helping me much, if at all. Time was growing short; it was crucial to get me functioning better soon, or I would probably lose my opportunity to continue in school. Dr. Hemingway had heard of some new forms of treatment that weren't well established scientifically but had achieved good results according to the claims of scattered enthusiasts. New treatment methods have to get their start somewhere, he thought, and perhaps he could find something different to help me. But realistically he knew the chances of success were minimal.

First, following the new treatment directives, he ran some blood tests to determine my blood levels of trace metals. To his surprise he discovered that my blood zinc level was abnormally high and my blood manganese level was too low. He didn't know what these results meant. Proponents of megavitamin therapy claimed these abnormalities suggested a vitamin deficiency as the cause of the schizophrenia, and they recommended replacement of multiple vitamins in extraordinary doses. Although I had taken megavitamins once before without success, Dr. Hemingway decided it was worth another try, to thoroughly exhaust every last treatment possibility.

In addition to the Haldol, I now had to take seventy vitamin pills a day, to get all those vitamins into me. Once in my stomach, the vitamin pills nauseated me and made my face flush. But since they didn't interfere with my studying, I was willing to take them.

After about ten days in the hospital, my psychotic symptoms had quieted down some, and Dr. Hemingway was able to discharge me.

The nurses told Dr. Hemingway they were amazed at my unwavering motivation and dedication to my studies despite the severity of my symptoms. They kept asking him how I was managing to stay in school at all with such severe illness. I knew I was hanging on only because studying medicine was more important to me than anything else, more important even than the Other Worlds. If I couldn't pursue my dream of medical school, then I didn't care to live at all. The Other Worlds were important only in that I believed they might be able to help me in school: if I could crack through the barriers to see the Other Side clearly, I might experience Enlightenment as no one had ever experienced it. No one had ever been granted a glimpse into the Other Worlds in the way I had, and I felt Enlightenment awaited me there. If I could just get over there and view its magical secrets in detail, I could absorb enough knowledge to whip right through the rest of medical school like Superwoman. But I feared the unknown. As long as I could, I preferred to be tough and try to make it on my own, by ordinary earthly means, as I had been doing. Using transcendent powers would be like cheating, and I didn't want to resort to that unless there was no other way. That would be a big step, and it would mean I would have to give up ordinary life on earth as I knew it. I wasn't sure I was ready for that yet.

I disciplined myself to study twenty hours a day, using No-

Doz to keep awake. Pushing myself as hard as I did seemed not the best thing to do, but it was the only way I could possibly succeed. I didn't consider my work schedule insane. I persisted, thinking I couldn't let up my efforts at all, fearing that slacking up even a little would mean certain ruin. I kept seeing Dr. Hemingway for treatment, hoping he could help me survive.

At my first appointment after my discharge from the hospital, Dr. Hemingway asked me, "How are you getting along at home now?" He was leaning far back in his office chair, blowing purple smoke out one nostril. I wondered why he was doing that.

Getting any words out of my mouth took herculean effort. "Well, I'm still taking the megavitamins and Haldol," I managed to say.

"Oh, good. Are they giving you any problems?" he asked.

No. No problems.

I heard a distant flapping of helicopter blades coming from outside. *I don't like this,* I told the voices telepathically.

"Is there some reason why you aren't answering my question?" Dr. Hemingway prodded gently.

I did! Can't you hear my brain waves?

He was waiting. He wasn't hearing me. Opening my mouth was too much work; trying to utter words seemed an absurd effort.

Still he waited.

Finally I managed to tell him, "I'm sending you the message through the air."

"But don't you realize I can't hear messages through the air?" he asked.

Tune in, buddy! This is the core of reality!

After a few more minutes of patient waiting, he said, "Hm. Well, how is pathology going?"

I was falling through interdimensional space. I gripped the arms of the black leather chair I was sitting in to steady myself. Straining to get more words out, I said, "I'm studying as hard as I can, but I still don't think I can get all the units done in time for the next exam."

"You seem to be having more trouble with school all the time," he said. "Do you think maybe you ought to drop out for the rest of the semester and then start back to school again next year if you're feeling better?"

I told Dr. Hemingway emphatically that I would never quit school, no matter what, not even for a while.

Dr. Hemingway sensed my distress and backed off. He suggested I talk to Dean Honeycut about perhaps getting an extension to finish up the pathology course over Christmas vacation. I worried about exhausting myself over the vacation and not getting the rest I urgently needed before the start of the next semester, but I recognized that this was probably the only way I could pass. I would have to worry about the next semester when it arrived.

Dr. Hemingway wrote me the excuse I needed for the makeup exam in pharmacology, then he reminded me to see Dean Honeycut about the extension in pathology. We set up another appointment, and I thanked him and left. Dr. Hemingway dictated:

> Today Carol looks much worse—two days after discharge—than I have seen her in some time. She is retarded in movements, stiff, spends a good deal of time today staring off into space or staring at me, saying she is sending me messages. She is preoccupied with hallucinations and the possibility that she might have to drop out of school. She has arranged to postpone a pharmacology test for one week. She plans to see Dr. Honeycut tomorrow at 3:00 p.m. and then we will talk again at 4:30 regarding her plans for school.

Time to hit the books. I arranged myself in my easy chair with my books and papers all around me, my cup of coffee balanced on the arm of the chair, in preparation for a serious study marathon. A weird calm settled over me. Something was decidedly different, though I didn't know what.

I didn't pay the feeling any attention. After all the years of coping with strange occurrences I had learned to keep right on studying in spite of them; otherwise I'd never get anything done. So I didn't interrupt my reading on account of the weird calm.

"Carol." The sound of a new and different voice filled my living room. Super-calm. Not suspicion-raising calm, like Hal, but genuinely comforting. "Carol, I am with you."

"God, is that you?" I ventured.

"No, but you're close." The voice had an unearthly quality, coming across in unnatural tones and sound-wave frequencies. I'd never heard anything like it before.

I waited patiently for the voice to make its identity known to me. I was surprised that I was unafraid.

"I am a messenger from the Holy Spirit," it said.

"Oh, wow, an angel?" I asked.

"If that's how your pea-brain needs to understand it, yes."

I didn't say anything more for fear of further insulting the Messenger of God.

Then I very distinctly heard the angel say, "We want you to know—there is a place for you in medical school. You will succeed, therefore do not question the Lord your God. But you must keep on studying. I will get you through. Remember, I am with you."

I was totally awed.

Poof—the angel was gone and the room cleared of the strange calm. I was left with a vestigial inner peace that lasted for days. Remembering the angel's instructions, I delved right back into my studies, now with improved concentration. I kept pinching my cheeks to make sure I was really awake and it was all real.

I never woke up from a dream. It was all real—as real as the rest of my life, anyway.

The Good Angel Vision had given me strength. When I visited Dean Honeycut I was able to face him calmly. He assisted me in arranging to get an extension in pathology over the Christmas vacation. He seemed genuinely helpful, genuinely understanding.

Dean Honeycut seemed to be such a good person that I wondered if he was also religious. "Are you religious?" I asked him. "I mean, do you go to church?"

"Oh, yes, I go to church," he said.

"Well, then," I told him, "I think you'll understand. I want to tell you about something, something personal."

He raised an interested eyebrow.

"I had a vision," I said. "I was visited by an Angel of God." His facial expression didn't change at all.

I continued, "The Angel told me I was going to get through school. God is helping me. I'm going to make it now, I'm positive."

He didn't smile, but he didn't look at me with disbelief, either. For a moment he didn't say anything. His face remained emotionless.

"Isn't that wonderful?" I asked, trying to get him to respond. I couldn't understand why he wasn't receiving my good news with the same ecstatic feelings I had about it, but then it wasn't as important to him as it was to me.

Finally he said, "I'm truly happy for you. I'm glad you feel you're going to do fine."

"I knew you'd understand," I said. "Only religious people can understand these things."

My next chore was to pass the makeup pharmacology exam. The exam was in two parts, an essay and an oral exam, to be given on successive days. I took the essay part in Dr. Lance's office in the morning. It was horribly difficult, and I was very depressed about how badly I thought I had done. I even dropped in on Bruce to tell him how awful it was. He seemed concerned. I spent the rest of that day cramming for the oral part of the exam. Having to take an oral exam frightened me, because I'd never had one before. When I got there I found that the professor who had been selected to test me was a kind person who tried to make me feel comfortable right away. He didn't start the questioning until he saw that I had relaxed.

During the exam I felt the presence of the Good Angel standing right behind me. I thought I saw the professor acknowledge the Angel by smiling past me. It wasn't necessary to ask the professor if he was aware of the Angel's presence; I could tell that he knew, and I knew that he could tell that I knew. I thought all this cross-exchange of knowledge was taking place very knowingly on a transcendent nonverbal level, and it made me feel good that my examiner was another individual who had special awareness like mine.

At the end of the questioning the professor told me I'd scored one hundred percent. After I left he phoned Dr. Hemingway to tell him he was amazed and thought I had a photographic memory, because I had answered the questions verbatim from long passages of his lectures that semester.

My composite grade on the makeup pharmacology exam was honors. I didn't think that was possible, since I'd performed so poorly on the essay part. I suspected Dr. Lance had felt bad about making his part of the exam so difficult and arbitrarily raised my grade to honors. But however it had happened, I was encouraged. The Good Angel was being true to his word.

I hoped the upcoming pathology exams would turn out as well, despite my having to finish them late. I sat in Dr. Hemingway's office waiting for him to finish writing my medical excuse for completing pathology over Christmas.

I took the note directly to Dean Honeycut.

"Things are looking up," I told him, then added, "And exams are starting to go better. I even got honors on the makeup pharmacology exam."

"What do you mean, things are going better?" he said.

Suddenly something seemed all wrong.

"What was this I heard about how terribly you did on the pharmacology exam?" he demanded.

How did he know about that? I thought the only person who knew was Bruce. Had the voices been talking to Dean Honeycut?

The dean went on, "Dr. Lance told me you wanted to kill yourself."

Oh, no. I had said that to Bruce after I took the essay part of the pharmacology exam. But how could Dr. Lance have known that?

"But Dean Honeycut," I protested, "Dr. Lance's test was so difficult it was ridiculous. It made me horribly discouraged . . ." My face was growing hot.

"I got a very distressing call from Dr. Lance. He wanted me to know you were talking about killing yourself."

Now it all made sense. The voices had undoubtedly talked to Dr. Lance.

"I happen to know you've been in the hospital again, too."

Wow, how did he know that?

I felt the Other Worlds closing in. I had to get out of this office. My words were now coming only slowly. I bid the dean an abrupt goodbye and left his office.

When I arrived home I was still feeling confused. The Dean Honeycut I had just talked to wasn't the same Dean Honeycut who was my friend. This Dean Honeycut made me uncomfortable. Maybe he was under control of the voices.

I talked to Bruce about my confusion over the abrupt change in Dean Honeycut's demeanor and the mystery surrounding Dr. Lance's knowledge of my suicide threat. Bruce confessed that after my pharmacology exam he was afraid I might kill myself. Because he was so upset and didn't know what else to do, he had called Dr. Lance. Dr. Lance admitted that he had purposely made my makeup exam especially difficult because somewhere he had gotten the idea that I had a habit of screwing off and skipping the scheduled exams, then requesting makeup exams. Bruce had later informed him that

I'd never taken a makeup exam before, that I wasn't screwing off, that I was genuinely ill and now so upset that I was seriously suicidal. When Dr. Lance heard that, he told Bruce he felt sorry, even guilty, about what he had done. Dr. Lance had felt it was his responsibility to inform the school administration of my suicide threat, which accounted for how Dean Honeycut knew everything.

The whole episode had been blown to huge proportions without my knowledge of any of it, which explained why Dean Honeycut had changed so drastically the last time I'd seen him.

After my meeting with Dean Honeycut, I felt increasingly distraught and my psychotic symptoms intensified. By the time I saw Dr. Hemingway the next day, the voices were carrying on a constant running commentary in my head and interjecting nonsense comments, making it nearly impossible for me to follow even simple conversations.

I tried to tell Dr. Hemingway about my meeting with Dean Honeycut. "He's changed," I said. "They're hypnotizing him."

Dr. Hemingway didn't try to argue with me. "I think it might not be wise to talk with Dean Honeycut when you're feeling like this," he told me.

"Do you think maybe he wants to throw me out of medical school?" I asked.

Dr. Hemingway looked surprised that I had suggested that. "Look, Carol, I don't think he's got the power to throw you out. And I don't think he'd want to, either. You know, a while back he told me he really likes you."

After Dr. Hemingway told me that, I felt less worried for the time being.

Dr. Hemingway interpreted my worry about being thrown out of school as a paranoid symptom. He had seen no evidence to suggest the possibility of my being thrown out.

The voices were rumbling off meaningless words in the

background. "Hydroxide particles. Calculate. Hibernate. Incinerate." They had always liked to rhyme.

Dr. Hemingway's eyebrows twitched. He was thinking. "Hmm. How are you eating? You look like you've lost some weight."

I had. I could slip my jeans off without even unzipping them.

"How about the medication?" he wanted to know. "Are you still taking the Haldol?"

"*Foul wall.*" Hal had joined the conversation.

I nodded. This conversation was getting confusing.

"What about the vitamins?"

"*Seven sins. Has-beens.*"

I nodded.

"Good."

I ran my fingers lightly across one thigh and then the other. "Has-beens?" I repeated. Who had said that? Me? Dr. Hemingway? Maybe it was an amplification of his thought waves.

Dr. Hemingway's bushy eyebrows furrowed contemplatively into his wire rims. "Carol, why don't you come back into the hospital." It was more a statement than a question.

"*Endofiddle.*"

"You could get regular meals there," he continued, "and we could make sure you get in all your doses of your medication. I don't think you're taking all your meds."

"*Pencil leads.*"

Dr. Hemingway's words didn't seem to be his. I wondered who was really saying them.

"I'm doing okay," I said firmly. "No more hospitals."

"For example, what are you going to do over the Thanksgiving vacation this week? Are any of your friends going to be around?"

"*Ground round.*"

No, Bruce was going home to his family. Everybody I knew was leaving town for the holiday. I shook my head.

"Are you planning on having Thanksgiving dinner with anybody? You know, you don't do well all alone for extended periods of time without talking to anyone. The hospital could provide that."

"I don't want to come into the hospital," I insisted.

"All right." He straightened up in his chair. "You don't have to decide right now. If you have any problems over the holiday you can call me."

"Trolley."

He added, "Will you do that?"

"Splat."

I nodded, then got up to leave. He gave me an appointment for the following Monday.

Dr. Hemingway had no idea of the high activity level of the voices as we talked, and he didn't know that the voices were heavily influencing me. To him I looked flat, vacant, catatonic. I moved slowly and left giant gaps between my words. I talked very little as far as he could tell, but *I* felt I was talking a lot. After all, I was carrying on simultaneous conversations with him and the voices.

In his dictated note he said:

> . . . Yesterday she saw Bob Honeycut and misread a lot of the social and verbal signals there, was very tense, got very paranoid, and evidently confused Dean Honeycut. I have talked to him today and he indicated that he thought she was confused, didn't make sense all the time and was quite upset. As an upshot of this, Carol began hearing more voices yesterday. . . .

I couldn't concentrate on my studies. I was supposed to be using these four vacation days to prepare for a pathology exam. This was only the second day and already the voices were wild. They kept yelling, distracting me from my work.

I couldn't take it anymore. I sat up and stared at my telephone for an hour and then tried to call Dr. Hemingway. I finally reached him at home. I asked him if there was something else he could possibly prescribe for me to quiet the voices and allow me to study.

"What are the voices telling you?" he asked.

"Lots of things," I said.

"Well, tell me the most important thing, then."

"They're telling me about a big crack in the bottom of the river. They told me to go swim down there and look into the crack. I don't know what they want me to see in the crack, but if I don't do it, they say they'll arrange to have me flunked out of school."

"Carol, don't you realize if you swim to the bottom of the river you'll probably be killed? It's freezing out. That river's damn cold."

"But I'm scared," I said. "I don't want to flunk out."

"Now look, Carol," he told me, "I want you to come into the hospital—today, right now. You'll be safe in the hospital, I promise. I won't let anything bad happen."

I trusted Dr. Hemingway. I agreed to come into the hospital, but only because I was scared and needed his protection. But I refused to be put on a different ward from the one I had stayed on last time, because I didn't think I could be as safe anywhere else. Dr. Hemingway promised to arrange to have me admitted back on Ward One when I arrived.

I told him I would pack up my things and walk right over to the hospital. I hoped I had the strength to accomplish that.

From my vantage point on the ceiling I could look down on Carol packing up her pathology notes into a bundle. She slipped them into her backpack with her notebook. I watched her wad up an extra sweatshirt and stuff it into her pack. She looked so small, so vulnerable.

Carol reached under her sink and tore off two scraps of aluminum foil. Carefully she wrapped one of the pieces around several NoDoz tablets and the other around some Cogentins. Logical, this kid. She knew she might need these. The bits of foil fitted inconspicuously into the corner of her wallet.

I was impressed by how efficiently she closed up her wind-up clock and slipped it into the pocket of her pack along with her toothbrush and toothpaste. She seemed to move in quanta, like a wind-up toy. If she ran down, the doctors would call her "catatonic." I would know differently.

Finally, looking down from my vantage point, I saw Carol hoist her full pack over her parka and fit her eight-pound pathology book and her seven-pound internal medicine text both into the angle of her right arm.

She turned to slip the protective flannel cover over the bird cage. As she disappeared through her apartment door she pulled her scarf across her nostrils to protect her lungs from the twenty-below wind chill factor outside.

CHAPTER TWELVE

HOSPITALIZED AGAIN

As I walked straight into a strong north wind that stung my face with blowing ice and snow, I didn't turn around to see who was following me. I didn't have to, because I could hear the voices jabbering away behind me. It seemed I would never get to the hospital. My right arm felt as if it had rigor mortis from the weight of the books.

At last, I arrived at the hospital waiting room. I thought I'd never thaw. I was too stiff from catatonia and cold air to unzip my coat or take off my scarf. I sat down in a chair without removing my pack or putting down my books. I wasn't about to move any part of me I didn't have to.

"Hi, I'm Dr. Allen." A pudgy, dark-haired man wearing a baseball cap that said DODGERS across the front sat down in the chair next to me. "You must be Carol. Dr. Hemingway said you would be coming to the hospital here to be admitted."

I was so relieved to be safe there in the waiting room that I couldn't speak.

Two ladies seated on the other side of the room had both stopped smoking their cigarettes to watch the crazy person who was going to be admitted.

The doctor lifted a hand to my scarf and pulled it away from my face. "Gee, what a pretty scarf. Did you knit it?"

He was twenty worlds away. There was no point in answering him.

"Will you come onto the ward with me?" he asked gently. "We have a bed all ready for you."

My words tumbled out in crystal chunks of ice. "Okay, I'll come."

Meekly I followed the doctor down the hall and around the corner. But he turned to go into Ward *Two*. Dr. Hemingway had promised me a bed on Ward One. They had deceived me.

Abruptly I spun around and walked back out the hospital door. I had nearly reached the street when I heard the doctor calling to me.

"I don't want you to leave." I heard his voice floating past my ears. "Where are you going?"

North. I was going north. Better than that, I *was* the North. I turned around and said, "I am the North."

"Please come back and stay here," he begged. "Dr. Hemingway is expecting you."

He was absolutely right. I couldn't disappoint Dr. Hemingway. I had given Dr. Hemingway my word that I would come into the hospital. I had to go back.

After looking over my old records and talking to Dr. Hemingway, Dr. Allen wrote my admission note:

> . . . Carol is very difficult to talk to, as she gets into statements like "Someone is trying to kill me. I am not in this world, I'm in another world." Facies [facial expressions] are flat except for a look of fear and rigidity occasionally. . . . Appearance: neatly dressed, well groomed, ectomorphic. Orientation: variable. Affect: restrained, approach dullness. . . . Im-

pression: chronic schizophrenia, exacerbated. This
woman has the potential to be a very fine and com-
petent physician; however, she will have much difficulty with school if she continues in her present state.
I hope she is willing and able to allow her healing.

No walls could protect me from the voices, not even thick
hospital walls. The voices kept chattering away, sometimes
with nonsense words, sometimes with threats. Through the
rambunctious activity in my room I clearly heard one of
them teasing, "How many voices can dance on the head of
a pin? How about on the head of the bed?"

Finally I couldn't stand to stay locked up with the voices
any longer. I went to the nurses' station and announced that
I had to sign out of the hospital AMA (against medical
advice).

The nurses called Dr. Allen. When he arrived, he told me,
"I think you're playing games. I talked to Dr. Hemingway
this afternoon for over half an hour. He told me he likes
you. I think you're pulling the wool over his eyes."

I pictured Dr. Hemingway wearing a wool baseball cap
with the edge that said DODGERS pulled down over his
eyes.

Dr. Allen continued, "What's wrong with you is that you
have a scared little girl inside you. You have a badly beaten
child ego state."

Immediately I recognized the vocabulary of transactional
analysis. At that time TA was a relatively new and popular
brand of psychotherapy best known through such books as
Games People Play and *I'm O.K., You're O.K.* In TA, everything was explained by duplex transactions of parent, adult,
and child ego states. All abnormal behavior was a result of
people playing games in their different ego states.

Dr. Allen continued, "Your parents taught you how to
feel not-okay and disrupted your ability to think for the rest
of your life. They did this as part of their own chaotic transactions and games, by putting you into double-bind situa-

tions. They hooked your not-okay child and rejected it, and your response was to go crazy. Now, Carol, it's up to you to take responsibility for getting well. You can help me help you if you decide to let me."

Then Dr. Allen pulled an old photograph of himself out of his wallet. In the photo he wore long scraggly hair and looked like a hippie. "I was once sick like you," he said, "but I got better by taking megavitamins and stopping all my games."

By the time Dr. Allen had finished his soliloquy, the voices had gotten bored and disappeared. My room was so quiet that I could now tolerate staying here. I told Dr. Allen I didn't need to sign out of the hospital anymore.

He walked out of my room with a victorious smile on his face.

During my stay at the hospital, Dr. Allen would often return to the ward late in the day and change Dr. Hemingway's orders. One night when the nurses brought me my bedtime medication I saw that my four Haldol pills were blue-green instead of yellow. Immediately I knew something was up. Someone was dosing me up with enough Haldol to drop my blood pressure to nothing and to give me severe muscle spasms.

I protested that someone had made a mistake or was messing around with the orders, but by that time of night all the doctors were asleep in bed and couldn't be bothered. I refused to take any medicine Dr. Hemingway hadn't told me about. I couldn't believe he had ordered me such huge doses of Haldol without telling me.

When Dr. Hemingway arrived on the ward the next day, he was outraged to discover that Dr. Allen had increased my bedtime dose of Haldol by a factor of ten. He didn't scold me for refusing to take my medicine.

I sat in my hospital room studying for an entire weekend. Finally, I laid aside my books. I was groggy. A good run might make me more alert. I slipped on my sweatpants, sweatshirt, and running shorts, then tied a warm scarf around my neck.

"I'll be back in forty-five minutes," I told the aide as he unlocked the heavy outer door to let me out.

I took off sprinting through a freezing mist. I always liked running in light rain or snow; it made me feel more connected with the world.

After about a mile I came to a busy street I wanted to cross. The cars and trucks were zooming back and forth across four lanes, and I couldn't tell how fast they were moving or even which way they were going. I looked around behind me and saw two men in trench coats walking toward me. I couldn't tell for sure, but they looked like two men from the dean's office. I took off across the busy street and raced down the block to the corner, turned it, and disappeared. Then I turned another corner—and there were the two men in trench coats again!

Quickly I changed my course and ran down the muddy half-frozen shoulder on a winding lane. Every car passing by left a trail of red-blue-and-green jagged and curly lines that shimmered and dissipated in the mist.

I heard the voices breathing heavily behind me, saying, "She's running, faster now . . ."

I wrenched my head around to see that there were now three men in trench coats trailing me. One of them looked like Dean Honeycut. His lower jaw looked tight, as if it was working hard against his upper.

The sky was closing in. Grayness was eating up the landscape. Now most of the cars had their headlights on.

I removed my mittens. My sweat was running into them. Within a few minutes my fingers grew numb in the cold and I put my mittens back on. I looked around and saw that the trench coats were gone.

Faster and faster and faster my machine-legs carried me,

until the road flashing past me was a big blur. As I ran I shed my rain-and-sweat-soaked sweatshirt, tying it around my waist. The icy mist hitting my face and bare arms felt good.

Every way I turned to go back to the hospital the men in trench coats were always there, sometimes two of them, sometimes three. By now I had run at least seven miles.

"Get her before she runs away," I heard one of the trench coats say. "She'll never come back to school." The muscles in Dean Honeycut's cheek were pulsing.

Changing direction, I shot across a viaduct. I darted behind a tree and escaped down into the slushy road below. I ran down the street a while, crossed it, and puffed up the hill to the back of the hospital. The outside back door was unlocked; I opened it and stepped in. I looked back once more, and to my relief I had lost the trench coats.

I climbed the flight of stairs up to the ward, my thighs like cement blocks. I let myself collapse on a middle stair to catch my breath and rub out a cramp in my side.

I didn't know how long I had been sitting in the same stonelike position on the stair when one of the aides from the ward came traipsing down the steps and discovered me.

"Carol . . . ? What in heaven's name are you doing sitting here?" she asked.

I could only stare vacantly.

"Oh, boy," she sighed. "What's happened to you?"

After a short struggle to speak I said, "I never ran so fast."

"Why? Why did you run fast?"

"They were chasing me."

"Who?"

I told her, "They will bury me in front of the psych hospital."

"Carol, let's go back onto the ward now," she coaxed. "You'll be safe there. Nobody's going to bury you."

Gratefully I let her escort me to the safety of the ward through the Interference Patterns swirling over the hallway floors and ward door. The voices were laughing heartily, though I didn't know what about. I wasn't feeling like laughing with them.

"Why don't you take off those wet things and go shower now," the nurse suggested.

Good idea. I hadn't thought of that.

Dr. Hemingway was aware that my mental condition was not improving significantly. He discontinued my megavitamins. He had tried me on almost every antipsychotic medication ever invented, but I couldn't tolerate any of them in therapeutic doses because of the severe side effects. He even tried me on lithium, an antimanic medication, on the chance it might help; I was able to tolerate the side effects, but it didn't improve my condition at all. Dr. Hemingway had exhausted his therapeutic options. He didn't know any other ways to treat my illness. He had conceded that it was chronic, with a poor prognosis for future improvement, typical of schizophrenia.

Dr. Hemingway continued encouraging me to take time off from school, but I absolutely refused to consider it. I was afraid dropping out would mean a permanent loss of my opportunity to continue in school. It was now obvious to everybody but me that I was too sick to stay in medical school any longer.

I managed to pull myself together enough to get through finals week. I was relieved to have successfully passed pharmacology and my other courses, and I was astounded to learn that I'd received an honors in neurophysiology. However, I still had the two unit exams in pathology to complete after the end of the semester, which I'd arranged by special permission.

Although I had made it through finals intact, I wasn't by any means well. Since I was past the major stresses, Dr. Hemingway was now willing to discharge me from the hospital before Christmas.

His discharge summary read:

> The patient showed her usual fluctuating course with periods of relative lucidity followed fairly quickly by other periods of severe thought disorder and delusions and acting upon some of these delusions. . . . She was allowed gate passes to attend classes and to take her examinations and she managed to pass all of her courses during this period of time. As the stress of her examinations grew less and less, the patient became more oriented and rational for longer periods of time and during the few days prior to being discharged showed generally fairly well goal-oriented speech and was planning rational future activities. Her discharge diagnosis is chronic schizophrenia.

Christmas vacation was tough. Because I had just been discharged from the psychiatric ward, my parents presumed I was in a delicate state and consequently tried their hardest to make everything go well for me during my time at home. They overdid it, and it was embarrassingly obvious to me how hard they were trying to maintain an ultracalm atmosphere at home.

The voices proved to be too disruptive at home, making it impossible for me to concentrate. I decided to head back to school and try studying there through the rest of the semester break. I detested having to finish up pathology while all the other students were still home on vacation.

I wasn't able to study at school either, and I began to despair of ever passing pathology. When I finally took the last two pathology exams the next week, I passed, but I didn't do well enough to maintain an honors average. That meant I would be required to take the comprehensive pathology exam. I didn't think I could pass a comprehensive exam. Pathology was a required course, and if I didn't pass it, I wouldn't get through med school.

"Time for a change," the voices told me. "If you will die now you will emerge into the Other Worlds where help will be waiting. You will be enlightened and be able to come back and succeed. Do it."

I didn't want to die, but I wanted to succeed more than anything else. Death appeared to be the only way.

"It's the only way," the voices said, echoing my thoughts.

"All right," I told them. If achieving success meant I had to die to do it, then I would die. Maybe there was something better than this life, as the voices had suggested.

On my way home from the medical library, I passed by a five-story parking ramp. It seemed to beckon to me.

"Time for the change," the voices kept repeating. "Now, now, now, now, now . . ."

I climbed up to the top of the five-story structure. Off in the distance, I could hear the helicopters, verifying that what I was about to do was right. A cold January wind swept through my long hair, nudging me closer to the edge.

"Don't worry," the voices told me. "We'll take care of pathology for you. When you return everything will be okay."

That was all I needed to hear. "I'll be back with reinforcements," I whispered to no one in particular. I felt relieved that I was about to make everything better in my life. I slipped my pack off and set it down on the cold concrete of the parking ramp. I wouldn't be needing it where I was going. Without hesitation I threw my right foot over the ledge and peered down at the sidewalk from my straddle position. Taking a big breath, I smiled and closed my eyes.

A voice boomed from below. "Go ahead, jump!" It sounded like somebody teasing, as though he thought I was someone merely resting on the edge with no intention of jumping. I looked down and saw a janitor who had spotted me from the doorway of a nearby building.

"G'wan, jump!" he yelled. "See what I care! Hurry up!"

"We don't need an audience," the voices advised me. "You'll have to wait. The time's not right."

"G'wan, jump!" the janitor persisted. "I wanna see ya splat on the pavement!"

The voices were absolutely right. I didn't want to take any chances of ruining my effort by making my attempt at an inopportune time. I would have to wait and try again. I climbed down from the ledge and ducked down where the man couldn't see me. I descended from the parking ramp in a hurry in case somebody had called the police. I rushed home to study for the next pathology exam and wait for the voices to advise me about the right time to try again. Until that time, I would have to keep up my efforts to succeed here in the regular world.

The voices advised me what to do next. Following their instructions, I went to a grocery store and got a cardboard box, then I cut two holes in it with a kitchen knife. I threw the box into the trunk of my car and filled up my tank with gas. I felt peaceful, hopeful, relieved. Soon I would be able to study and perform well in school. I felt destiny smiling upon me. Perhaps this was the Right Moment, after all.

The voices directed me toward a deserted park on the north side of town. "Please, God," I prayed, "don't let me make any mistakes."

Leaving the motor running, I jumped out of the car. A strong wind blew through the treetops and across the side of my face as I lifted the box from the trunk. Several inches of snow already covered the ground. I shivered. The wind grew even wilder, and I began to hear intermingled with it the chopping noises of a helicopter force approaching over the tops of the trees.

I had to hurry. I didn't want to miss the critical segment in time and space where the Dimensions coincided. I set the box down under the back bumper of my car, positioning it so that the exhaust pipe would empty directly into the hole I had cut in the top of the box. I lay down in the snow and, supporting myself on my elbows, propped my face up to the second hole, the one I'd made in the side of the box. The flapping wind chased cold air up my pantlegs.

"Relax and breathe," Hal said, in his super-calm, reassuring voice. "Go to sleep."

The exhaust fumes inside the box were hot and gaseous, with little particles that stung my nose and seared my breathing passages all the way down. I had to concentrate to suppress the urge to cough it out.

After a while my head started to throb, and my stomach got queasy. The muscles in my upper arms began to shake, allowing my head to sag weakly away from its breathing hole. I fought to keep my face up to the vapors, but I didn't have the strength. I sank to the ground, landing facedown in the snow. Yes, I was finally on my way. . . .

I awoke, still in that same awful park, feeling sick to my stomach, my head hurting, and cold to the bone. The landscape all around was silent.

"Hey, where are you?" I demanded of the voices.

Silence. Snowflakes fell, but not a trace of a helicopter anywhere. It appeared that I'd missed the critical moment again. I wondered if I'd ever have another chance.

I returned home to try to study once again.

I was so discouraged about my failure with the box that I told Dr. Hemingway about it at my next appointment.

He looked alarmed. "You did *what* with a box?"

"Don't worry," I reassured him, "I'm going to get help. All I have to do is get to the Other Side. Then I'll be okay."

He fidgeted in his chair. "Carol, I think you ought to come into the hospital again. Now."

"But why?"

"Do you realize you almost killed yourself?"

"No, I didn't. You've got to believe me. Please. Have I ever lied to you? You know I always keep my word. I know what I'm doing. Please, just believe me."

He fidgeted in his chair again. "I don't think your judgment is very good right now. I think the voices are misleading you."

"I can't come into the hospital," I insisted. "I could miss my next chance while I'm in there. Besides, the hospital wouldn't help me any. It didn't help those other times."

I'd never seen Dr. Hemingway so upset. Usually he was calm and unflappable. "If you don't come into the hospital, I'll have to call the police and have them bring you in," he told me.

This wasn't the Dr. Hemingway I knew and trusted. He had never threatened me like this before. What was going on? Had the voices finally gotten to him? Were they hypnotizing him and controlling his mind?

"I'll give you an hour to go home and get your things," he told me firmly. "If you're not back by then, I'll have to call the police."

I could see I had no other choice. The Right Moment was going to have to be put on hold. "Okay," I conceded.

"Can I have your word?"

"All right. I'll be back in an hour."

I raced home and phoned one of the nurses I knew from Ward Two. I told her about my situation in an incoherent manner and asked her to help me escape. She agreed to help me, telling me she had to pick up something on the ward first before she could go anywhere. She picked me up at my apartment, and I accompanied her to the ward. She told me to wait right inside for just one minute while she went to get what she needed. Then she tricked me. Just as soon as the ward door slammed shut she said, "Ha! Now you're inside and it's locked! I'm not letting you back out!"

I was officially admitted.

The dayroom ceiling was bulging downward. The Other Worlds were weighing it down, making it sag that way.

They would collapse through on our heads if I didn't do something about it. I raised my arms and locked the gears in my elbows against the weight of the ceiling. It was all up to me, Atlas, to prevent this disaster.

A nurse was suddenly standing right in front of me. For a minute she watched me standing there with my arms over my head, then, in all innocence, she asked, "Hi, Carol, what's up?"

Wow, what's *up!* I looked upward, fixing a glazed stare at the ceiling.

The nurse looked up too. "Carol, whatever are you doing?" she asked in an accusatory tone, as if she thought she was talking to a totally demented person. When I didn't answer her, she said, "Carol, there's no need to do that. Now come on, put your arms down." She grabbed my wrists and forced them to my sides. "I need to conduct an admission interview on you," she said. "Let's go back to your room."

I had been given my old room back.

"Now, Carol, can you tell me why you're in the hospital?"

"I'm not sick," I told her. "It may look that way, but the real reason I'm here is because I'm having trouble in school and my doctor is going to help me pass my exams."

The nurse was busy scribbling down every word.

I continued, "You're in psych hospital but I'm not in this world, I'm in that world." I was managing to say only occasional fragments of my thoughts.

She wrote down my last statement too.

"Are you presently taking medications?" she asked.

"Like I said, I'm not sick," I repeated. "So why should I need to take pills? All I need to do is get to the Other Worlds and then I can pass my exams."

The nurse noted that I had little insight into my illness. Under the category "motor activity" she wrote: "Agitated, moving papers, standing up on chair, moving about room."

And under "physical appearance": "Nice-appearing, thin, complexion pale." Under "affect and mood": "Flat affect." For "thought content": "Disoriented."

She slipped off her glasses to ask me with great intended frankness, "Carol, what is your goal for hospitalization? What do you want from us here?"

"I want to leave. I want to study. It's too loud to study here." I was referring to all the noise the voices were making in the background.

And so my "goal for hospitalization" was officially listed as "I want to leave. I want to study. It's too loud to study here."

The nurse's final comment on the admission form was: "Her outpatient doctor thinks she should be taking drugs because he does not accept the fact that she receives messages and communicates with other power systems. She knows there is a reason for things that are happening to her and knows that others will come to accept her reality sometime in the future."

The door to my room opened, sweeping Interference Patterns in shades of yellow and gray across the room. An overweight doctor in white peeked his head in the door and said, "Hi, Carol, I'm Dr. Kopetti."

"Where's Dr. Hemingway?" I asked.

"He'll be here later. I need to interview you first."

The nurse stepped out and the doctor sat down in her place. He asked me essentially the same questions. "Do you know where you are?"

"It looks like I'm in the psych hospital, but really I'm in another world."

"Oriented times two," he wrote. "Disoriented to place."

Normal people were supposed to be oriented times three: to person, place, and time. If he had only known—I was oriented times at least seven. I was oriented in Dimensions we didn't even have here in the regular world.

The doctor said in his admission note:

> On admission her mental status was that of an alert
> twenty-three-year-old white female who was suspicious,
> somewhat jumpy. She answered questions directly but
> would not answer all questions. . . . she was in a cata-
> tonic state of waxy flexibility and posturing. . . . her
> affect was flat. . . . She has been having a lot of con-
> flict about whether or not she should stay in school.
> She says she very much wants to be a physician. . . . I
> suggested she take a leave of absence for a year to de-
> cide if medicine is really what she wants to do. She
> will think about it.

I had no intentions of taking a leave of absence. I had no
doubts that medicine was what I wanted to do. Whenever
anyone suggested I quit school I got upset.

In the hospital I continued my studying routine. It an-
noyed me to think that since my cumulative score in pathology was two points below honors, I would have to take
the cumulative final. It was becoming increasingly difficult
to study. The voices would give me no peace and quiet, and
they talked incessantly during my pathology final. The questions made no sense to my distracted mind. I failed the exam.
The professor allowed me to retake the final the following
day, advising me to study the material again overnight. I
studied half the night and all morning up to the time of the
exam.

*Walk. Walk in the door. Go into the pathology lab. Take
out your ID. Pick up the test. Go on, do it. Stew it. Chew
it. Screw it.*

I was exhausted. My thoughts were disconnected, beyond
my control, flowing in and out with the voices.

"Speaking of wasted lives . . ." Hal whispered in my ear.

Okay. First question: What does "bloody rusty sputum"
suggest?

"Your car."

*Put the pencil in your hand and blacken a square, any
square. Just get it done. Keep moving. Keep ahead of the*

stiffness. Turn down that radio, will ya? Awful desk edge hitting me in the nipples . . .

Second question: Assuming that the patient's white count is over fifteen thousand, does he have . . . *Start over, I can't remember what I'm reading.* Assuming that the patient's white count is over fifteen thousand, does he have . . . *Ivory soap. Damm it, stop that! . . .* Does he have . . . *Ivory soap.*

"Wasting away, cachexia . . ."

What?

"Your mind. Cachexia."

Repeat: Assuming that the patient's white count is over fifteen thousand, does he have . . .

"Ivory soap."

Stop that, you guys.

. . . is over fifteen thousand, does he have . . .

I'll come back to that one later. Next question.

You are a meatball. *It says it right there. You are a meatball. Ivory soap, banana legs.*

. . . is over fifteen thousand, does he have . . . *Any answer, fine. Blacken another square. That's progress. Getting stiff. In the nether zone. Can hardly move. Am insulated. I may never move again.*

Sweating, profusely.

The end. *Give it up. Give it away. To the lady, the receptionist-mannequin.*

"I don't think I passed this time either," I told the receptionist as I handed her the computer answer card, moving slowly and stiffly.

When I looked at her again she was grinning, showing all her teeth. Or was she snarling? "Congratulations!" she said.

"What?"

"You passed! By two points!" She looked honestly happy for me. She had felt sorry for me, seeing me struggle all year, and she wanted to see me pass. So she had feelings. And I had thought all year that she didn't care at all.

Passed . . . ? You mean I'm done . . . ? Walk through the door, across the street, back to the psych unit. Do it. This is real.

"Hi, Carol," said the nurse who let me in. "Did you pass your exam?"

Nod to the nurse. Smile. Step through the door. Let it slam behind you. Don't wince. Even though it sounds like my middle-ear bones slamming into my eardrums. Yow. Step into the hospital's energy force field. Feel it glowing on my skin, feel it penetrating into my head. Feel the waves ricocheting back and forth against the insides of my skull. My thoughts are sliding away, I'll never catch them now, just have to slide with them.

"Carol, what are you doi-oi-oi-oi-ng-ng-ng-ng?" The nurse's voice waves echoed across Dimensions. "Can't you mo-oo-oo-ov-ov-ove?"

Oh. I forgot to move.

"Ca-aa-aa-aa-aan you ta-aa-al-al-to-oo-alk-ooo me-ee-ee?"

Garble. Okay. You want me to move. I will try. The inertia is planetary centrifugal. Impossible to lift the force of the universe.

The helicopters. Oh no, not the helicopters. Have come to tear the feathers out of my frontal lobes. Help me, nurse, help me, can't you hear them? Gotta get back into my body to save it. Am so far away. Out of reach of the neural connections. The doctor is thinking I would make good glue. He is a witch doctor. He is sending radio messages to the helicopters to help them find me.

Dr. Kopetti observed:

> . . . still catatonic at this time. Totally unresponsive. . . . I would wonder if she'll be able to cope with the pressures of school again. . . . she apparently does not respond to antipsychotic agents and has a low threshold for extrapyramidal symptoms [muscular side effects].

Dr. Hemingway sauntered briefly into my room, then hurried back out, shaking his head.

Big pieces are cracking off the edge of my consciousness. I will never be back. The universe disappears with one slight wave of my hand.

A nurse observed in my chart:

> Data: patient acting out in response to voices, i.e., posturing, crying out. States she's frightened, refused to undress for sleep for fear of needing to get out of room quickly. . . . was found standing in one place for long periods of time, eyes wide open, staring. . . . patient standing in room facing wall, arms outstretched to wall. . . . was not responsive to verbalization, responded with blank stare. . . . frequently pacing around room suspiciously, jumps when others approach her. Several times said, "Am I dead?" Seemed out of touch with her body at times, holding her hands in angular positions.

The pendulum has swung to the far side where everything dissipates into everything. It can't swing back. I am scared of the change. I am scared to move.

"Would you like to be made into hotdog meat?" *Ah, the voices. Where have they been? I must be on track again.*

"Hotdogs for lunch!"

My head splits down the middle, brains falling out all over the floor, and I put out an awkward hand to catch them. They slip right through my metal fingers. Do they put brain meat in hotdogs?

"You can put down your hand, Carol. You don't have to hold it there." *Had the nurse said that or had I said it? Or had the voices said it? Or was it a slice from another Dimension?*

Hand back to my side. Try to think straight. There is

a logical way out of this maze. Just don't forget your thoughts. Don't forget.

. . . Patient talked about having difficulty telling "where the voices ended and her thoughts begin." Thought that her skull was split in half and asked me to examine it—was reassured that I didn't see or feel a split. Also said she feels like she's going to "fall out of her body," but didn't know where she'd fall to. At one time, patient put her hands over her ears and said, "I don't want hotdogs for lunch" when it had nothing to do with the conversation.

My thoughts, hanging on the ceiling. Gotta get up to them. Can't let them escape. Magnetize your fingers by rubbing them on the wall, like balloons. Reach, magnetic thoughts with negative charges will shoot into your fingers and slide down to your brain where they belong. Then staple them down.

. . . standing on bed with arm outstretched toward ceiling. Firm directioning and assistance required to get patient to lie down. . . . patient sitting on bed with left arm raised, staring at door. Patient was unresponsive. . . . maintains position when arm raised by me.

The nurse's eyes turn all white. Her pupils and irises have been bleached out by lasers. Either you're weird or I am, lady.

. . . frightened and cowered in corner and refused supper tray. Patient was sitting on bed posturing with hands outstretched around her until spoken to. Patient was reminded she could control the voices.

Horrible. Why am I doing this? She says I can stop it. Well, stop it, then. I must want this to be happening to me, otherwise I'd make it quit. It means I'm evil because I can't stop it. It's ugly, I'm ugly, the demons have taken me over and I have become rotted flesh of devils, bastards, barons. I hate myself because I am creating this.

> Data: patient seems suspicious of others and of her sur-
> roundings—looks around with quick jerks with her
> eyes narrowed or open very wide. Told me she's afraid
> of me because I'm "controlled." Stated that she thinks
> everyone hears voices. When I told her I didn't, she
> didn't seem to believe me.

The chair wanted me. It was breathing. *Get away, chair.*

"Carol, sit down, relax. You'll be okay."

If I held very still they couldn't touch me.

"Carol, what's the matter? Are you hearing voices again?"

"That chair there," I managed to say with maximum effort. Those words stood for the breathing chair, the thoughts
on the ceiling, and the bathroom tiles. She would understand. It was verbal shorthand.

"What, Carol? What about the chair?" The nurse's words
were coming from the chair.

I raised both arms into the air to meet the oncoming force
waves. *Push them back with my mental energy, shove, concentrate, don't let them any closer. Don't back off. Hold my
ground.*

"Carol, try and control the voices. I know you can do it."
The nurse returned my arms to my sides.

They were about to attack from behind. My force shield
was weak there. I jumped up, whirled around, and delivered
a well-placed karate chop into the center of the attack waves.
I was starting to disintegrate. My cells were crumbling off
and falling to the passing Dimensions.

And all because I wanted this. I didn't feel myself wanting
this. They only said I wanted it.

The nurse grabbed my arms. The nurse was with them!
Now they were coming from all sides, tossing comets and

meteoroids past my head, nicking pieces off my ears! She was calling in reinforcements.

Concentrate on astral travel. Hurry up, motate my energy. Think in thought-concepts, not words, to keep them from stealing my thoughts. It's the only way to hang on.

They attacked with whips and chains and pain devices from the far realms. Eight Spartans charged from six sides with magic shields and glinting swords and suddenly we were all immersed in a dark swimming pool, struggling and twisting and squirming. I called on my cosmic strength. The machines in my limbs vibrated with motion and as I watched my attackers all grew third eyes. I must have reached hell.

I panicked. Fear exploded in my chest and I caught my breath on the vapors. We emerged into a second waiting room, tile green. I was deposited onto a cement floor. They unzipped my pants. *No, you can't do this!* I jumped to my feet; they could not hold me. They ripped at my hair; reflex tears filled my eyes. Arms pinned me down. They sat on my legs.

"Carol, we have to undress you. Please cooperate."

They tossed me into a flimsy cotton gown and disappeared through the three-inch-thick door, their arms stuffed with my clothes. I was left to shiver on the cold cement.

> Data: patient posturing, nonverbal, appears to be hallucinating and frightened, too restless to remain sitting in dayroom, was taken with physical force by staff to the Quiet Room to decrease stimulation. . . .

The Other Side had won. Alone in the Quiet Room over the next few hours I calmed down and the voices retreated. I was able to think my thoughts more completely before they disintegrated. I had to figure out what was going on. It was so complicated.

By the time Dr. Hemingway came to see me later I was coherent enough to be able to tell him that I knew I was finished. I knew I couldn't continue in school like this. I had tried to my maximum ability and beyond, and here was where it had left me. I still had not succeeded.

Dr. Hemingway's checkered suit pants seemed to have great depth and contrast. The checkers jiggled around and blinked before my eyes.

I told him what I was thinking about my difficulties in school.

"Okay," he said, "we'll get you a leave of absence for the next year, and then we'll see how you are at the end of that time."

My head lowered in humiliation, I let Dr. Hemingway lead me out of the Quiet Room.

CHAPTER THIRTEEN

THE CHANGE

I had no idea who I was anymore. I had previously thought of myself as a medical student. But I was no longer in school. I had identified myself as Bruce's girl. Now Bruce had gone on without me. I was living in limbo.

How could I survive this?

I had to do something besides just sitting around listening to the voices and staring at the walls. I had to find work.

After hunting unsuccessfully for a job for a month, I became discouraged. Dr. Hemingway informed me that he had obtained government funds and could hire me to do his research on a half-time basis. Soon after that, my sophomore medical class hired me to type its semester's lecture notes for its lecture note service. Painful as that was, it would help me keep in touch with medical school and help me to continue learning while I was away.

Bruce talked me into studying the assignments he was reading for his sophomore spring-semester classes. Every day he faithfully brought me handouts and reading assignments from class. I hoped to have a head start on the material when I started back to school in a year.

The thought of taking exams and being in school again next year panicked me. How could I ever do it? My self-confidence had taken a terrible beating. Every time I sat down with the books my palms sweated, my heart pounded, and I trembled.

Since Cedar City was so small, every time I went out I unfortunately saw at least one old classmate, my "token class-mate for the outing." It was painful for me to see them out having a good time when I felt so miserable. I never failed to run into old classmates when I went to a movie, went out to eat, or went shopping. I ducked around corners and walked down blocks I hadn't planned to go down, just to avoid them. Overwhelmed by humiliation, I couldn't face them. I assumed they considered me a failure just as I con-sidered myself a failure.

One evening when I was home typing lecture notes, Bruce phoned me, and right after that my parents called. They all told me about a TV show they'd just seen independently of each other. The show was a news documentary that showed a segment on treatment of schizophrenics with ordi-nary kidney dialysis. The doctors in Kentucky who were using this new treatment were claiming about a two-thirds cure rate. It sounded too good to be true.

Like me, my parents had been getting discouraged. They had spent a fortune on hospitals, medications, doctors, and psychotherapy. In spite of everything, my condition was gradually deteriorating. It appeared that if something didn't happen to help me, I was going to end up permanently com-mitted to a state institution just as the doctor had predicted to Steve five years before. Why wasn't Dr. Hemingway up on the latest treatments, my parents wanted to know. Why wasn't he treating me with dialysis if the cure rate was so high?

The following day my parents called Dr. Hemingway. He told them he knew about the dialysis treatments, but he was cautious about trying such a new and untested method, especially because dialysis is not a simple procedure and involves considerable risks. He hadn't wanted to instill false hopes in me and my family until more definite results came out of the dialysis research. The theory was that the dialysis removed some unidentified substance from the blood, presumably a chemical responsible for producing schizophrenic symptoms. Scientists thought this chemical might be a beta-endorphin, a substance which when injected into rats made them catatonic.

Biochemists who studied the dialysate, the material filtered out of the schizophrenic patients' blood during dialysis, found that it contained a much higher concentration of endorphins than expected. In samples taken after several dialysis treatments, however, the concentration of endorphins was lower. This suggested that the dialysis was removing it. Other patients were found to have abnormal amounts of other related chemicals, called leu-endorphin and met-enkephalin, in their dialysates.

This chemical analysis strongly suggested that the dialysis treatments were removing a toxic chemical from the schizophrenic bloodstream, a chemical that was seeping into the brain through the bloodstream to create havoc, manifested by psychotic symptoms. Some of these chemicals were not present in normal individuals; others were present but in much smaller concentrations than those found in schizophrenics. Where do these chemicals come from? One theory is that schizophrenics have inherited a defective gene that is programmed to "turn on" at a specific age, producing these abnormal chemicals that ravage the brain. Whether or not that is the case, today most experts agree that schizophrenia is a brain disease, and its cause is biochemical. The exact biochemistry of the illness is still a mystery. So even though no one understood exactly how dialysis worked in schizophrenics, these early reports of its success were exciting. At last, there might be new hope for schizophrenics.

My parents were desperate. They wanted Dr. Hemingway to try the dialysis on me. This would not be so simple as they imagined. First Dr. Hemingway would have to propose a dialysis research project and obtain federal grant money to run the project—about fifty thousand dollars. He would have to hire a kidney specialist and a highly trained dialysis nurse, get access to a spare dialysis machine, and find a surgeon to put a specialized access site called a fistula into me to provide a place to insert the dialysis needles. Dr. Hemingway said he would read more about the dialysis treatment and think about it.

Dr. Hemingway buried himself in the psychiatric journals in the medical library, hoping to discover how to help me. Although dialysis had been used for years as a life-saving treatment for patients with kidney failure, it had only very recently been used to treat schizophrenia, and the scientific literature revealed only a few scattered reports on dialysis as a treatment for schizophrenia. The methods were similar to those used to treat kidney patients, the main difference being that the pores of filtering membrane that removed the toxic molecules were much smaller for treating schizophrenia, because the molecules that are thought to cause schizophrenia are much smaller than those in kidney failure. Only about fifty schizophrenic patients had ever been treated in this way. Approximately two-thirds were considered "improved," and the majority of these were described as "cured."

A cautious and scrupulous scientist, Dr. Hemingway noted that none of the medical reports about treating schizophrenia with dialysis were conducted in a scientifically rigorous manner. The treatment was so new that there just hadn't been time to do this. But since the ratio of success was so high, the researchers had gone ahead and published what they had observed, rather than waiting five to ten years to complete the necessary studies and attend to all the tedious details of the confirming research.

Dr. Hemingway thought seriously about what he must do, weighing the risks against the benefits. It would have been easy for him to conclude that it was too risky since there wasn't enough evidence yet, or that it would be impossible to obtain a research grant and maneuver around all the obstacles of setting up such a project. But every time he wavered, he was haunted by the image of me struggling desperately to succeed. He felt I had it in me to succeed, if I could have a chance. He realized that I was suicidal and that if I continued to deteriorate, I was almost certain to die. Faced with that, he thought the risks of dialysis were worth taking.

Meanwhile, I kept working at my jobs. Every day I had to pick up the handwritten lecture notes the medical students had placed in my student mailbox for me to type that night. One day at the end of the afternoon I made my usual stop by my student mailbox to pick up the day's lecture notes I was supposed to type that night.

My mailbox was gone.

I knew I couldn't trust my perceptions. It had to be there. I looked again.

It was still gone. The name "Ostendorf" stood where mine used to be.

As I left the mailroom I thought about the other two students in my class who had taken leaves of absence at the same time I had, and I wondered if their mailboxes were still there. I turned around and went back to the mailroom.

Yes, their names were still on their boxes. I checked for mine again. No, it was still gone. I had to get away from there quickly; I couldn't stand to have other students see me at the moment I was recoiling from the ultimate insult. All I could think about was Bobbi Blakemore and how her mailbox had disappeared just before she had been thrown out of school.

I ran to Dr. Hemingway's office and told him my mailbox

had just disappeared. Dr. Hemingway advised me not to jump to conclusions. He reasoned that my mailbox had been removed simply because the administration didn't think I needed it anymore, and the incident didn't mean any more than that.

That night I told Bruce about my mailbox disappearing, and he offered the same explanation as Dr. Hemingway. He promised me he would go to the dean's office on Monday and arrange to get my mailbox back for me, since I needed it to receive the lecture notes. It was simply a misunderstanding, he reassured me, and he would get it cleared up.

As Bruce had promised, he went to the dean's office to get my mailbox back. He wasn't successful. The best he could do was to get them to give me a box labeled "Sophomore Lecture Note Service."

"That's just as good," Bruce told me.

But it wasn't. Now I couldn't keep in touch with events, since I would no longer be receiving routine medical-school mailings. But even more important, my mailbox had been a symbol of my place in the medical school, and losing it was a painful blow to my identity. I had been reduced to a sophomore lecture note service.

I hoped the year would pass quickly, so that I could get back into school and regain my official medical-student status. Until then I would continue to feel incomplete as a person. I continued to work for Dr. Hemingway. My job entailed transferring research interview information into numbered codes on code sheets in preparation for computer data analysis. Even though I heard voices continuously and had to fight my inertia, I was a conscientious employee. In fact, I was so efficient that Dr. Hemingway would walk into my office to observe me as I coded interviews, then he would walk out shaking his head because he couldn't believe how fast I was. After I had left for the day he would send in another research assistant to check my work. "It's perfectly accurate," the research assistant told him. I became the talk of the department. How was it, everybody wondered, that I could do such fast and accurate work when I was so obviously disabled by a severe psychosis?

Every day after work I went home to type another day's lecture notes, which often amounted to twenty pages or more that had to be done by the next morning. After that, I tried to study the day's class assignments and then turned into a statue, staying rigid until the next day, when I forced myself to go to work again to code interviews.

Dr. Hemingway had predicted that my condition would get considerably better when I got out from under the immediate stresses of school. To his chagrin, I didn't show significant improvement. It was unrealistic to be very hopeful about my future, but like my parents, Dr. Hemingway never lost hope. Other psychiatrists at the hospital told him he was out of his mind to think I might ever improve enough to go back and finish medical school, much less ever function as a physician.

I continued to see Dr. Hemingway for psychiatric treatment. He insisted that I try Mellaril again. I'd had significant side effects on it in the past, but he thought he could prevent a recurrence of these problems by starting me out on a low dose and building it up slowly.

That night I took the two hundred milligrams of Mellaril Dr. Hemingway had prescribed and went to bed.

Wow, what time is it? It's light already. Good grief, I feel drugged. Can't focus my eyes on the clock. Keep staring, it should slide into view; it slides right back out. Can maybe catch it in transit next time around. Double clock. Double vision. Keep straining, pull the two clocks together. So fuzzy. Too blurry to see. Eyelids feel like shoe leather.

I slumped back, let my eyes seal shut again. Too much effort.

Now what time is it? Can't make the two clocks merge yet. Full bladder.

I raised myself on my elbows in an effort to get to the bathroom, then passed out again.

Phone is ringing. Sounds like my neighbor's phone, distant. No, it keeps on ringing. All right, all right, I'm coming.

I swung my feet to the floor and stood up.

All right, I'm coming!

I started to black out, then remembered to bend over to try to maintain consciousness. I hung on to my desk to keep from staggering while reaching for the phone. I was reeling. I swooped up the receiver on my way to the floor. "Helyo." Thick tongue. I tried to get up.

"Carol, are you okay? You don't sound so good." It was Bruce. I could barely hear him over the roaring in my ears.

"Uh-h, I'm dizzye." I lurched toward the couch, dragging the phone on the end of the cord.

"Hang on, Carol, I'll come right over."

No sooner had I got the receiver back on the hook, it seemed, than I heard my apartment door open, in some far-away dream.

"Where's your blood-pressure cuff?" I saw two Bruces ask as they whirled through my viewspace.

"On the sheyylf." Tongue so fat. Mouth like cardboard.

I didn't even struggle to keep my eyes open while he fooled with the cuff. Inflate, deflate, inflate, deflate, I didn't care. *Do whatever you want. I just have to lie here passively with my eyes shut.*

He seemed to be having trouble getting a pressure. More inflating and deflating.

"I can't believe this," I heard him say.

"Whayyyat?"

"I get sixty over zero. I didn't know such a low blood pressure was possible."

"I'll cawwwl Dr. Hemingway whe' I cayyn," I mumbled. I didn't care; I just wanted to keep lying there with my eyes shut.

"Did you take more Mellaril than he prescribed?" Bruce asked.

"No."

Bruce went back to the hospital, and later I called Dr. Hemingway. He advised me to discontinue the Mellaril.

By the next day I felt well enough to return to work. I refused to try any more medications for a long time, and I managed to get my work done in spite of continuing severe symptoms. By the end of the semester I had typed eight hundred pages for the lecture note service. When that job was over, I spent more of my time sitting and staring into space, listening to the voices.

Now that Bruce would no longer be bringing me daily reading assignments from the sophomore spring semester, I would be seeing him less frequently. Just a week after the end of the semester, Bruce began his junior-year clinical rotations, the part of medical school everybody can't wait to get to, when you get to put on your white coat and start playing doctor for real, with real patients. It seemed that Bruce and I had little in common anymore. His new schedule was stressful in a new way for him. The rotations were more time-consuming than the basic sciences, and in addition to having to cram for exams, there were now the pressures of caring for sick patients on the wards and keeping up with clinical duties and library assignments on a daily basis. There was no way I could share in his new clinical experience, which was completely foreign to me. Our time together was limited, and I could no longer be convenient to him. We saw each other only occasionally when he called me up to play a quick game of racquetball. I began to feel ambivalent toward him, still loving him yet at the same time hating him for having the thing I wanted more than anything else: a career in medicine.

The following year Bruce became engaged to a nurse at the hospital. He was gone and I had other things to worry about.

The Message came over my radio: "You have to make your own changes."

My own changes?

"Yes."

Such a profound statement could only have come from the Other Side. I took it as a personal message with significant impact on my own life. I interpreted it to mean that if I wanted things to change, I would have to take an active part in shaping my own destiny. The words from the radio had the ring of such profound truth that I didn't question them.

The voices informed me that now was the time to put my affairs on hold to wait for "the Change." They explained that the Change would require me to perform certain specified acts according to their exact directions. I would need to wait for their announcement of the Right Moment, at which time I would climb up to the top floor of the Physics Building, one of the tallest buildings on campus. Then I was supposed to throw myself off, making sure I landed in the perfect position on my head. If I did it correctly, the ground would open up and swallow me, and I would be taken up to the Other Side for a period of three to four days and would be enlightened. After that I would be returned to my body to come back and enlighten mankind. Back on earth I would have more than enough enlightenment to be able to finish medical school easily. I began to look forward to the Change with mixed feelings of eagerness and apprehension. I imagined it couldn't be any worse than the way things were now.

True to my character of not wanting to inconvenience other people by failing to keep my scheduled appointments, I informed Dr. Hemingway that I might not be able to keep my next appointment with him. Making an appointment and then not showing up for it would be just plain rude. I thought I might be away doing the Change at the time of my next appointment.

"Why do you think you won't make it to your next appointment?" he demanded to know, suddenly looking grave. "What do you mean?"

I didn't want to tell Dr. Hemingway about the Change. I was afraid he might be able to prevent it somehow, and I felt the Change was crucial. I couldn't afford to miss it. My whole future hinged on its success.

But Dr. Hemingway persisted in wanting to know. He looked worried. Since he was so insistent, I had to tell him something about the Change. He sat silently, looking uncomfortable the entire time I talked about it. The patterns were rippling across his face.

At the end I told him, "I'm scared."

He said, "I am too, Carol." His voice was tense. "I think if you jump off the Physics Building you'll be killed, and that'll be the end of you."

"Please don't prevent me from doing the Change," I pleaded with him. "I've got to do it to make things right. This is my big chance. Don't spoil it."

He straightened up in his chair and leaned forward. "Be logical about this, Carol. There are certain laws of physics that even voices and Other Worlds have to obey. Carol, I think if you do this thing you'll be killed and you won't ever come back to your body. It's a big chance to be taking, with big consequences. The voices have lied to you before, haven't they—like on exams? Remember?"

He had me worried. I would have to think this over some more.

"Carol," he said, "I want you to make me a promise. If you get any Messages that it's time for the Change, will you call me first? You know, I care about what happens to you, and I'm worried now."

I understood that he cared, but he just didn't understand the situation the way I did. "No promises," I told him. "I can't make promises I might not be able to keep." That wouldn't be fair.

"Then I'm going to have to put you in the hospital again."

"All right, you win. I promise." I knew I would have to keep my promise to Dr. Hemingway.

He set up another appointment and I left. He dictated:

> Last week was not a good one for Carol. About Wednesday she was fairly catatonic, quite delusional, was not eating. . . . she still feels tired and washed out and continues to be preoccupied with "the Change." This is something that has been developing over the last year or so which is now present in a more stable and elaborated form. The Change involves a belief that she will be told a time and place when she is to jump off a building, land in a certain fashion, and "free her spirit." We have been combating this by questioning the validity of the advice of the voices by pointing out that she has had other signs which meant nothing and other messages which were not reliable or valid. We furthermore discussed the chance that if she did something like this she would probably end up killing herself. However, she seems convinced this will not happen. She states that the Change is not due to occur for another week or so. In the meantime, we will discuss this at greater length with her and this may require hospitalization if it seems that she remains convinced, in which case I think she will be a fairly serious risk of self-injury if left to her own devices.

After my talk with Dr. Hemingway, I was sick with worry that the Change might not work. Dr. Hemingway was sick with worry that the Change *would* work.

Two days later the voices told me to hurry up and get ready for the Change. The Right Moment was to occur at sunrise. I went to the Physics Building and ran up all seven flights of stairs to check out the building's roof. The door at the top of the stairs was locked. Maybe Dr. Hemingway was right. Maybe the voices were lying.

As I'd promised, I phoned Dr. Hemingway to fill him in on what was happening. I told him I was confused because I didn't know how I was supposed to get past the unlocked door to the roof of the Physics Building.

"Look," he said, "I think that's a very strong clue that your plan isn't going to work. The voices are really leading you on this time. Now, if you can't promise me you'll resist the voices and forget the Change at sunrise, I'll have to put you in the hospital right now."

"Don't do that," I said.

"Carol, I'm sorry, but I don't have any choice, and neither do you. I'll make a deal with you. If you'll agree to call me first thing in the morning to tell me you're safe, then I won't put you in the hospital."

I didn't want to miss the Change, because I didn't know if or when there would be another opportunity. But then again, Dr. Hemingway was beginning to sound pretty convincing in his arguments. There were too many details about the Change that didn't fit right. Perhaps this wasn't the best time after all. The risks were too great. I didn't want to die. I promised I would call him in the morning. He knew I would keep my word.

I couldn't sleep that night. The voices kept calling my name, waking me with a start just as soon as I got to sleep, then yelling, "The Change!" over and over. Their offer was beginning to seem more inviting, but then I remembered my promise to Dr. Hemingway. I could never let him down. At dawn a violent thunderstorm blew out of the west, swept through the city, and lashed against my apartment as if it had a personal vendetta against me. I was certain this storm was evidence that the voices were angry with me for passing up the perfect opportunity that they had designed specifically for me. I wondered what awful thing they would do to me now.

First thing the next morning I phoned Dr. Hemingway at his office to reassure him I was all right. He sounded relieved to hear from me.

Dr. Hemingway sensed that the risk of my imminent self-destruction was high, and was still increasing. Not even hospitalization could provide a definitive solution. He knew he would have to do something fast. He decided to pursue the dialysis project more actively. Two months previously he had sent off a protocol for his proposed dialysis research project, requesting grant funds from the federal government. Now he was notified that his protocol had been approved, and he received enough grant money to run ten schizophrenic patients through a trial of dialysis. I was to be that medical school's first experimental patient to try dialysis for the treatment of schizophrenia. I was to be the guinea pig.

"That's very courageous of you," Dr. Hemingway told me.

I thought *he* was the courageous one, not me. He was the one taking the risk. I was merely going along for the ride. If it failed, I could still pursue the option of the Other Worlds.

Dr. Hemingway located an interested kidney specialist, Dr. Roberts, to perform the actual dialysis treatments. Dr. Hemingway would supervise the project and handle the psychiatric aspects of treatment. The three of us met in late August to discuss the plan. Dr. Roberts informed me I would need to have an operation to have an arteriovenous fistula put in me. This entailed hooking up one of my major arteries to a major vein to create a spot where the large-bore needles could be inserted into me to draw off the blood for the dialysis treatments. He explained that during the treatments I would be physically hooked up to the machine. A needle would be inserted into one of my arteries to remove blood from my body. The blood would then be pumped through plastic tubing into the machine and through the filter that was supposed to remove the toxic chemicals from my blood. Finally, the blood would be sent back through other tubes and returned to my body through a second needle in another vein. The whole process would take place all at once, so that there would be blood running continuously throughout all the tubes and the filter back to my body. At any one time, only a small amount of blood would be outside my body.

I decided if I was really going to undergo the dialysis, I'd have to get going on it quickly in order to have it completed in time to return to classes in January. Dr. Hemingway agreed. He understood how anxious I was to get back to classes at the scheduled time.

Dr. Roberts told Dr. Hemingway that first they would have to get the fistula implanted in me. Next they would need to find a dialysis nurse and arrange access to a kidney machine. He thought it would be late November before all this was accomplished, and then they could start dialyzing me.

Dr. Hemingway asked Dr. Roberts, "How soon do you think we could arrange that operation for the fistula?"

"Not before October," Dr. Roberts said. But he added, "You must understand, though, that there's a small chance the fistula could clot off and then we'd have to put in another one. We've never tried to put a fistula in anybody with healthy kidneys before, so we don't know exactly how it's going to work. I don't anticipate any problems, though."

The operation lasted about two hours. When I woke up in the recovery room, Dr. Hemingway was standing over my stretcher.

"Did it work?" I said through the thick halothane fog in my head.

"Yes, I think so," Dr. Hemingway told me in an encouraging tone of voice. "The surgeon said your artery went into spasm, contracting down to the size of a small piece of spaghetti. But after he got it sewed to the vein and closed you back up, he was able to hear the whoosh of blood flowing through it with his stethoscope."

Unfortunately the fistula clotted off an hour after surgery. The surgeon would have to try again, but next time he would put an eighteen-inch segment of a cow's artery into my groin, hooking it up to the big vessels traveling deep inside my thigh. The next operation would be far more complicated and extensive. The worst part was that nobody knew if this second operation would work either.

The surgeon wasn't kidding when he said the operation was going to be more involved this time. He had to tear up a large portion of my thigh to put in the cow's artery. I emerged from surgery with four ugly scars and a tender, swollen, and multicolored bruised leg.

My dialysis treatment was scheduled for three weeks after surgery. The pulse in the fistula was strong. I could feel the blood rushing through it all the way up my leg to my waist on that side. It was reassuring to be able to put my hand over the fistula site and feel it buzzing away. It felt like a kitten purring.

The dialysis protocol required that all patients be medication-free before the first treatment and throughout the entire dialysis phase. Two weeks before my first dialysis Dr. Hemingway took me off the small doses of Haldol I was then taking.

Consequently, the Interference Patterns began to break through more heavily and the voices intensified. They kept insisting it was wrong for me to go through with the dialysis, because I would be missing the Change. I knew they were right, but at the same time I knew it was also wrong for me not to go through with the dialysis. Dr. Hemingway and my parents were counting on it. I couldn't stand to disappoint them. I couldn't think of any way to satisfy both sides. No matter which option I chose, I would still be doing the wrong thing. I wanted to do everything I could to help myself be in the best possible shape. Dr. Hemingway promised me that if the dialysis didn't make the voices go away, he would help protect me from them. I trusted him. Besides, everyone told me that my own judgment was impaired, so it seemed sensible to rely on Dr. Hemingway.

Finally the day of the dialysis treatment arrived. I felt dead inside, too dead to be afraid. It all seemed to be happening to me without me. My brain was vacant, without thoughts, as I stared at the scene. The dialysis machine stood before me, a robot four feet tall by three feet wide. It emitted high-pitched beep, beep, beeps while blinking its red, green and yellow lights. I could hear Hal muttering in the background, but I couldn't hear enough to make out what he was saying. The dialysis nurse ordered me to lie down on the bed by the machine. Dr. Hemingway took my arm to assist me. The nurse prepped my leg with antiseptic. Ouch! The pain of the pipe-cleaner-sized needles piercing my thigh flashed triangular patterns of turquoise and burnt orange in front of my eyes. The triangles changed color and shape and location with every painful adjustment the nurse made in the angles of the needles in my leg.

The plastic tubing sucked up my blood and ran it around in tubular mazes, through the pumps, and into the fibers in the artificial kidney. My own body's machinery had been plugged into the dialysis equipment, a perfectly natural connection, I thought.

"You're on," the dialysis technician told me. Then he taped the needles to my skin to prevent me from accidentally pulling them out. "I'm doing this because I don't want to have to wash your blood off the ceiling," he explained. "The blood flow through your fistula is powerful."

I lay back and tried to pass the time for the next eight hours. The voices chattered away, making comments on everything that happened. At the end of the treatment the nurse ripped all the tape off my still-swollen thigh, taking numerous hairs with it. I decided I would shave there before next week's treatment. Next he yanked out the needles. Ow! A new pain triangle pierced my left eye.

"Well?" the nurse asked me, looking at me intently as if I might have some marvelous revelation to tell him about how the treatment had affected me.

"Well what?" I stared past him vacantly.

"Well, how do you feel?" he asked, sounding as if he expected some kind of metamorphosis already.

"Exhausted," I said flatly. "And nauseated. I've got a headache." I didn't feel any different, really. I was disappointed. This dialysis wasn't going to work. How could such a medical treatment alter my cosmic experiences?

The chairman of the department of psychiatry, Dr. Winterman, had been running independent psychological tests on me to determine whether my psychiatric condition was improving. After the first dialysis treatment he told Dr. Hemingway he thought I looked maybe slightly improved, though not enough to be clinically significant. Any changes in my condition could be considered within the limits of usual variability.

Dr. Hemingway thought I looked better, though he admitted he might have been overly anxious to see a change.

I noticed the voices weren't bothering me quite as much as before, but I wasn't convinced that meant anything. Other than that, I didn't notice anything different. I didn't like the dialysis. The needles hurt far worse than I'd expected, and the whole experience had been uncomfortable and unpleasant. Already dreading the next week's treatment, I went home exhausted and fell into bed.

That night I had a terrible nightmare in which I dreamed that I had died. I woke up suddenly. Over the next hour I was able to convince myself that I was still alive, that I hadn't really died. I was afraid to go back to sleep.

The next day I told Dr. Hemingway about my nightmare.

"I'm not much into symbolism," he told me, "but if I were, I'd interpret your dream to mean that you are undergoing a significant change, like dying to your old self and being reborn into a new self. Maybe it means the Other Worlds are dying and you're about to start a new life without the voices and helicopters and Interference Patterns." He didn't tell me that he took my dream as an indication that I might be starting to experience significant changes in my psychiatric condition on account of the dialysis.

By the time Dr. Hemingway dragged me to the second dialysis I felt absolutely certain that nothing had changed for me. I didn't want to go. I was hoping the Change would come and swoop me up before we got there.

When we arrived, the kidney machine was beeping insistently, as if hungry for blood.

"Hello, Carol," Dr. Roberts said. "How are you feeling today?"

"The same," I said, not trying to hide my disenchantment with the dialysis.

"Oh, okay. It may take time before we start seeing any improvement in you. We'll just have to be patient. Why don't you weigh in and hop up on the bed here so we can get started."

The second treatment was even more unpleasant. Maintaining the correct fluid volume in my bloodstream was no easy task, and in the middle of the treatment, I became dizzy from insufficient blood volume. The nurses responded to the problem by tilting my bed to raise my feet and lower my head to allow blood to circulate better to my brain. Then they adjusted the kidney machine to return additional fluid to my body. When my bloodstream became overloaded, my kidneys filtered the extra fluid into my bladder, and before long I needed the bedpan. It was no easy task to use a bedpan while lying in bed tilted upside down, with two needles sticking into my groin, and in the presence of male technicians and doctors.

"It's not easy peeing uphill," I told them.

Everyone laughed, and I did too. Dr. Hemingway mentally noted that I was looking slightly better, but he still wasn't convinced the improvement was enough to be significant.

Eight hours later the dialysis nurse pulled out the needles and said, "Now that wasn't so bad, was it?"

Yes, it was. I hated it. I had the headache again, and I felt weak and shaky.

That night I drifted off to sleep feeling fearful that something awful was about to happen. The voices were unusually quiet. I was in the eye of a hurricane. They were gathering their forces for a huge maelstrom. If only the Right Moment for the Change would arrive before then. It could save me. It was my only hope.

CHAPTER FOURTEEN

THE SILENCE
IS DEAFENING

My telephone was ringing insistently. I jumped out of bed, tripped over the covers that were twisted around my ankle, and picked up the receiver.

"Hello?" I said groggily.

"Hi, Carol." It was Dr. Hemingway. "Did I wake you up? I was wondering if you might be able to come to work a little early today. I've got a rush project I'd like you to help me with." His voice flowing out of the receiver sounded unusually clear, like the chop of a hatchet in the woods after a heavy snowfall.

I listened with awe. My apartment was deathly still.

"Carol, are you okay?" he asked.

Clarity such as I'd never heard before. Everything seemed sharp and crisp, unmuddled by interference. Strange.

"Carol, what's going on there? Are you feeling all right?"

"Something's different, really different."

"What's different, Carol?"

"The silence."

"The silence?"

"Yeah—it's, well, like, it's—deafening. The voices are gone. It's never been this quiet before. And the interference has left me."

"Are you kidding me? Carol, *are you kidding?*"

"No, I'm not. This is weird. It's—wow, I don't know what this is."

"This I have to see," he said. He sounded really excited. "Can you come into the office right away? I'd like to see what's going on with you."

"All right. See you soon." I hung up the phone.

My apartment was emptier than it had ever been. For the first time it felt all mine, for the first time I felt truly alone. On my way to Dr. Hemingway's office I studied my surroundings, noticing things in a way I'd never seen them before. Everything looked so bland and ordinary, beautifully ordinary. A tree was a tree and that was all; there were no faces hiding in the leaves for me to discover. The sky was crystal blue, undisturbed by Interference Patterns. There were no Messages or special Meanings to decipher. My mind felt unbelievably clear, as never before. Walking to work was easy today.

This was it, the big Change! I was convinced. Nothing had ever seemed so cosmic to me as this clarity I was experiencing for the first time. It was so simple, so perfect. The dialysis had chased away the voices and the helicopters, the interference and the Other Worlds. I wondered if they would ever come back.

It was truly wonderful to be able to control all my own thoughts, and to have privacy about what I was thinking. My head was bursting with questions. What would this new reality be like? Would I really like it? Although this new experience was pleasant and exciting, it was so different that I was still afraid of the unknown that lay before me.

When I got to Dr. Hemingway's office I found him anxiously awaiting my arrival. Immediately he saw that I looked very different today. It was obvious that something big had happened to me during the night while I had slept. "This is truly incredible," he said. "I've never seen you like this, totally coherent, not immersed in the patterns or distracted by the voices."

I couldn't stop smiling. It felt great.

Dr. Hemingway was so excited he didn't know what to do. "Wait here," he told me. "I've got to tell Dr. Winterman about this. He's never going to believe it." Then he rushed off to Dr. Winterman's office, bursting with his good news.

Dr. Hemingway was right: Dr. Winterman didn't believe him. "That doesn't bother me," Dr. Hemingway told me, "because I'm one hundred percent certain you're well now. Dr. Winterman is a notorious skeptic. Time will convince him."

For days I marveled that the Meanings and the Meanings behind Meanings had vanished. Not even a trace of the Meanings returned, leaving me feeling more confident every day that they were gone for good. I could get more work done without the constant distraction of the voices breaking my concentration. Life was so much easier now that I no longer toiled under the constant strain of monitoring all my thoughts every minute of the day to keep objectionable personal thoughts off the TV and radio. This was great! Was this how other people got to live their lives all the time? Incredible—it was so simple.

I waited a few days before phoning my parents with my good news. I wanted to make absolutely certain I didn't raise false hopes.

"I could tell right away, just by the way you sound, that something's different with you," Mom said.

"You sound great!" Dad said.

My mom told me, "This is the greatest gift we could ever receive. I know the Lord had a hand in this. Remember to give Him thanks, will you?"

"Yes, Mom."

Dad asked, "Now that you're better, will you have to continue with the dialysis treatments?"

"Yes," I told him. "I'll have to finish at least the first eight treatments, according to the research protocol. Then, I don't know what. You see, this kind of treatment is so new that the doctors don't know how long my symptoms will stay away, how often they'll need to keep dialyzing me, or even whether I'll relapse. We'll just have to wait and see."

Dr. Roberts never expressed any doubts that my cure was real. He was so excited that he called Dr. Hemingway to ask him more questions. Dr. Roberts especially wanted to know why the dialysis had worked for me when it had failed for other schizophrenics.

"I don't really know," Dr. Hemingway told him. "I can only tell you theories. But my belief is that schizophrenia is a heterogeneous illness, that there are probably several different kinds of schizophrenia, each with its own cause—just as there are many kinds of infections, each with its own bacteria or virus causing it.

"Carol apparently had a toxic substance floating in her blood that is the right size to be filtered out by this particular membrane we're using. Other schizophrenics might have different toxins of different sizes that wouldn't be touched by the membrane."

Dr. Hemingway's first worry was that my cure might not be complete, or that I could have a relapse. There just wasn't enough information from other cases to be able to predict what might happen to me. But he knew that if I did have a recurrence of symptoms in the future, the dialysis would remove them, since it had now been demonstrated that it worked for me.

A few days later I visited Dr. Winterman's office for my weekly psychiatric assessment interview. He noted right away that I no longer walked stiffly like Frankenstein. My gait was normal and my movements fluid. My facial expression had animation in place of my former flat stare. I had taken new interest in my physical appearance.

"Do you ever hear voices?" Dr. Winterman asked me.

"No, not anymore. Not since my second dialysis."

"Can other people read your mind?"

"Not that I know of."

"Can you read other people's minds?"

"No."

"Do you sometimes hear your thoughts as if someone had spoken them aloud?"

"No."

"Do you think someone is controlling your mind or hypnotizing you in any way?"

"No."

"Do you get special messages off the TV or radio, or hear references to yourself on them?"

"Not anymore, thank God—oh, by the way, I've quit receiving messages from God too. I guess I'm not that important. I'm just like everybody else."

Dr. Winterman's mouth was hanging open. "Are you putting me on?"

"No."

He broke into a big smile. I'd never seen him smile before. I hadn't known he could.

After I left, he rushed down to Dr. Hemingway's office, arriving right ahead of me. "I believe it now," Dr. Winterman told Dr. Hemingway. "You're right. This is remarkable, just remarkable! I can't find anything wrong with her. I've never seen anything like this!"

When Dr. Winterman had gone, Dr. Hemingway gave me a big hug. "We did it!" he cried.

"No, you did it!" I corrected him. "I only cooperated."

He hugged me again and twirled me around in a full circle before setting me down. The corners of his eyes were moist. I'd never seen him so emotional.

"Thank you," I told him. I squeezed his arms, hard. "I can never fully repay you for what you've done for me."

"Don't try," he said, "because you already have, twenty times over."

Now I was crying.

I was ready to resume my life. I had a lot of catching up to do.

AFTERWORD

The first thing I wanted to do was finish medical school. Now that I was well, I wanted it more than ever.

"I'm so grateful to Dr. Hemingway, to the medical center, to the university for helping me get better," I told my parents. "Now it's doubly important to me to become a doctor and repay to others the goodness that I have received."

I now had my parents' support one hundred percent.

But it wasn't going to be so easy. To my astonishment, the school officials barred me from returning to classes at the start of the next semester.

I was devastated. "How can they do that to me?" I asked Dr. Hemingway.

Dr. Hemingway was infuriated. He had informed them that I was perfectly well and ready to continue my education. His opinion was effectively ignored.

"But I haven't done anything wrong or flunked anything," I told Dr. Hemingway. "And I've never hurt anyone. Don't they realize I'm better? Don't they want to celebrate our victory over psychiatric illness? I not only got well at this medical center, but now I could double the rewards by becoming a physician here."

"I don't think they understand all that," he told me.

I wasn't going to quit there. I applied to twenty other medical schools for transfer, painfully explaining all the details of my circumstances with total honesty.

Despite heavy odds against my ever getting back into school, it happened. One brave center, a highly respected private medical school, took a chance and admitted me into the sophomore class. Without hesitation, I moved to that city, and resumed my medical studies there. I was ecstatic to have another chance. This was a second miracle, after the dialysis.

"It would be ironic if you went into psychiatry," my mother once said to me.

"Well, I don't want to do something like that just for the novelty of it," I told her. "I'll make my decision on which specialty to choose after I've had a chance to see where my abilities lie, when I can see how I can help people most."

On my psychiatry rotation, I treated several schizophrenic patients. One such patient, Mrs. O'Dell, significantly influenced me.

"Do you hear the voices too?" she asked me in therapy one day.

"What makes you ask that?" I said.

"It's obvious. You seem to understand everything I say—and I can tell you mean it right from your heart. You've helped me more than any doctor I've ever had in the last twenty years."

After that experience I decided to go into psychiatry.

Three years after resuming medical school I successfully graduated with my M.D. degree and two outstanding achievement awards. My entire family and Dr. Hemingway came to the graduation ceremonies.

My graduation gave me the occasion to reflect on the last four and a half years since my emergence from my schizophrenic cocoon. I was conscious of the blissful, ordinary silence I had been enjoying—and I was grateful for it. Always in the back of my mind there remained the tiny but significant fear that my psychosis might return to swallow me up, but I didn't have time to worry about that. The mere fact that the dialysis had initially proved effective in chasing away my symptoms reassured me; if I became sick again, the dialysis would work its magic again.

Dr. Hemingway proceeded to dialyze four other patients, all with only minimal or no success.

"She's one in a million," Dr. Winterman had told him. Dr. Hemingway later related to me a conversation he and Dr. Winterman had had.

"I always told you she was unusual," Dr. Hemingway said. "Back when she was still ill, I never felt she was a typical schizophrenic. She had too much motivation, drive, and goal-directedness—too much spark to look like other burned-out cases. Yet she was chronically psychotic for almost eight years."

"You know," Dr. Winterman said, "one of the great forerunning clinical researchers of modern psychiatry once said that any schizophrenic patient who recovers probably wasn't schizophrenic to begin with."

"Then how do you account for the established figure that one-third of schizophrenics eventually recover spontaneously?" asked Dr. Hemingway. "I think most clinicians would disagree with the opinion that schizophrenics don't recover. And if Carol was not schizophrenic, what do you think she was?"

"I don't know. She sure looked schizophrenic during those eight years. But you do realize, don't you, that we may never understand her case or the reason for her recovery in our lifetimes," Dr. Winterman said. "Just because she recovered with the dialysis doesn't mean that's what made her get better. It could have been coincidental."

Dr. Hemingway chuckled at Dr. Winterman playing his usual role of skeptic. "Yeah, I guess we'll just have to wait for carefully controlled research studies on dialysis to be published."

To date, no careful studies have been published that report dialysis to be conclusively effective as a treatment for schizophrenia, at least so far as I know. Only further research will determine why dialysis works for some schizophrenics and not others.

During my psychiatric internship, I again ran into Mrs. O'Dell on the psychiatric wards.

"Hi, Dr. North!" she yelled. "I want to talk to you!"

Dr. North. It sounded wonderful. I still wasn't used to hearing my name that way. I walked closer to her. "What's on your mind?"

"It's been a long time and you've never answered my question. Do you hear the voices too?"

I smiled and shook my head.

Mrs. O'Dell, when you read this book, you'll know.